The Originality of the Avant-Garde
and Other Modernist Myths

The Originality of the Avant-Garde
and Other Modernist Myths

Rosalind E. Krauss

The MIT Press
Cambridge, Massachusetts
London, England

Printed and bound in the United States of America

Library of Congress Cataloging in Publication Data

Krauss, Rosalind E.
  The originality of the avant-garde and other modernist myths.

  Includes bibliographical references.
  1. Avant-garde (Aesthetics) — History — 20th century.
2. Modernism (Art) — Themes, motives. 3. Creation (Literary,
artistic, etc.) — Psychological aspects. I. Title.
N6490.K727   1984   709'.04   84-11315
ISBN 0-262-11093-8

For Annette Michelson

Contents

Acknowledgments

Several contexts have supported the work that is brought together in this book. The most obvious is the magazine *October*, in which many of these texts were first published. Through its complex relation to the world of current art and critical thought, *October* provided the impetus for these essays. To my co-founder and co-editor, Annette Michelson, I owe my greatest debt for the intellectual adventure we have shared over the last eight years. Douglas Crimp, the magazine's executive editor, has forwarded the project of the analysis of contemporary aesthetic production in immensely important ways; and Joan Copjec, its associate editor, has enlarged this context in the fields of film and psychoanalysis. Without our intense collaboration many of the conceptual opportunities seized by these essays would undoubtedly have slipped away.

Two other contexts have simultaneously provided stimulus and critical distance: the Center for Advanced Study in the Visual Arts, Washington, D.C., where a fellowship in 1980–81 led to the writing of "The Photographic Conditions of Surrealism" and "The Originality of the Avant-Garde"; and the Institute for Advanced Study, Princeton, where membership in 1983–84 permitted me to conceive these essays as a book.

My contact with students at Hunter College and at the Graduate Center of CUNY has consistently provided me a forum within which to try out ideas before an audience that has been as exacting as it is responsive.

One further context has been both challenging and nurturing for texts as involved as these are with the theoretical production of France over the last two decades. This is *Macula*, a critical journal that was produced in Paris from 1976 to 1982 by Yve-Alain Bois and Jean Clay. My discussions with them, as well as with Hubert Damisch, have been of inestimable importance. Other friends and colleagues who have helped with their support as well as their criticism are, Svetlana Alpers, Benjamin Buchloh, Susan Crile, Pierre Fédida, Joel Fineman, Stephen Koch, Richard Howard, Louis Marin, Keith Moxey, Linda Nochlin, Beverly Pepper, John Rajchman, Nan Rosenthal, Margit Rowell, Leo Steinberg, Julia Strand, Mark Strand, and Teri Wehn-Damisch.

The Originality of the Avant-Garde
and Other Modernist Myths

Can it be argued that the interest of critical writing lies almost entirely in its method? Can it be held that the content of any given evaluative statement — "this is good, important," "this is bad, trivial" — is not what serious criticism is, seriously, read for? But rather, that such criticism is understood through the forms of its arguments, through the way that its method, in the process of constituting the object of criticism, exposes to view those choices that precede and predetermine any act of judgment?

When, more than twenty years ago, *Art and Culture* presented the critical work of Clement Greenberg to the generation of artists and writers who were to develop during the 1960s, it presented its readers above all with a system through which to think the field of modernist art. And this system, or method — often referred to, inexactly, as formalist — had far greater effect than the particularities of its author's taste. Greenberg, for example, did not support the work of Frank Stella, but the logic of his system and the privilege it gave to flatness as a pictorial essence or norm provided the conceptual framework within which Stella's first decade of production was understood and, widely, acclaimed. Profoundly historicist, Greenberg's method conceives the field of art as at once timeless and in constant flux. That is to say that certain things, like art itself, or painting or sculpture, or the masterpiece, are universal, trans-historical forms. But in the same breath it is to assert that the life of these forms is dependent upon constant renewal, not unlike that of the living organism. The historical logic of this renewal was what essays like "Collage" or "American-Type Painting" strove to discover, while always insisting as part of that logic that "modernist art develops out of the past without gap or break, and wherever it ends up it will never stop being intelligible in terms of the continuity of art."

It is this declaration of the ontic status of art, of its unbreachable, seamless continuity, that led Greenberg vigorously to deny that it is in the method rather than the content of the judgments that the interest of criticism lies. Art as a universal calls forth and is completed by judgment as another universal capacity of consciousness. There being no way to separate a judgment from its evaluative contents, he would argue that the point of criticism has everything to do with value and almost nothing to do with method.

Practically everything in *The Originality of the Avant-Garde and Other Modernist Myths* stands in contradiction to this position. Written during the decade from 1973 to 1983, these essays chart not only my own critical and intellectual development but that of a generation of American critics, although I must add, not for the most part critics concerned with the visual arts. For, during the years that *Art and Culture*'s impact was felt in a New York-based art world, other sections of American cultural and intellectual life were affected by a discourse coming from abroad and challenging the historicist premises on which almost all the critical thinking of this country had been based. That discourse was, of course, structuralism, with its later poststructuralist modifications, the analytic methods of which produced a radical inversion of the position on which *Art and Culture* depended. On the one hand, structuralism rejected the historicist model as the means to understand the generation of meaning. On the other, within the work of poststructuralism, those timeless, transhistorical forms, which had been seen as the indestructible categories wherein aesthetic development took place, were themselves opened to historical analysis and placement.

To reject the historicist model of the way the work of art comes to mean is to propose several things at once. It is first of all to substitute for the idea of the work of art as an organism (developing out of a past tradition, imbedded in the history of a given medium) the image of it as a structure. To illustrate this notion of structure, Roland Barthes liked to use the story of the Argonauts, ordered by the Gods to complete their long journey in one and the same ship — the *Argo* — against the certainty of the boat's gradual deterioration. Over the course of the voyage the Argonauts slowly replaced each piece of the ship, "so that they ended with an entirely new ship, without having to alter either its name or its form. This ship *Argo* is highly useful," Barthes continues. "It affords the allegory of an eminently structural object, created not by genius, inspiration, determination, evolution, but by two modest actions (which cannot be caught up in any mystique of creation): *substitution* (one part replaces another, as in a paradigm) and *nomination* (the name is in no way linked to the stability of the parts): by dint of combinations made within one and the same name, nothing is left of the origin: Argo is an object with no other cause than its name, with no other identity than its form."

Barthes's depiction of structure is, in a sense, a narrative rendering of Ferdinand de Saussure's definition of language as pure difference, the definition that can be seen as having initiated structuralism. Barthes's *substitution* refers to this system of differences. But his notion of *nomination* calls on that part of the definition of language that Saussure considered even more important. Observing that differences are generally the function of two positive terms that are set in comparison, Saussure insisted that, to the contrary, in the case of language "there are only differences *without positive terms*." With this definitive rejection of "positive terms" Saussure blocked the way for meaning to be understood as the outcome of a correlation between a sound (or word) and an object for which the word is the label. Rather, meaning came to be seen as the result of an entire system by which the use of that word, say, *rock*, can be deployed instead of a large set of possible alternatives or substitutions, say, *stone, boulder, pebble, crag, agate, lump of ore.* . . . The choice one makes within this system of substitutions betrays a whole array of assumptions keyed to vastly different vocabularies: of scale, of technical (geological) mastery, of picturesque emotion, of verbal precision or generality. There is a system of interrelated difference, and in order to enter this system the word *rock* cannot be tied uniquely to this lump of matter at one's feet. Meaning is not the label of a particular thing; nor is it a picture of it. Meaning, for the structuralist, is the result of a system of substitutions.

One of the methodological corollaries of this conception of meaning is that it is a function of the system at a given moment in time — the system synchronically displayed — rather than the outcome of a specific development or history. Rejecting the diachronic, or historical, study of language(s) as a way to arrive at a theory of signification, Saussure's work set a precedent for the attack on the temporal model that structuralist and poststructuralist theories have staged on a variety of fronts. Some of these can be heard in Barthes's way of accounting for the significance of the *Argo*-model, as he dismisses from its field of relevance a concept like "*origin*," with its importance to traditional historical thinking, or concepts like "genius," "inspiration," "determination" and "evolution," by which works of art are imbedded within the conditions of their creation. For the nonstructuralist critic, whole realms of inquiry — aesthetic intention, biographical context, psychological models of creativity, or the possible existence of private worlds of allusion — are raised by these concepts, which not only imply the temporal condition of the work's generation, but call for an interpretive model based on the analogy between the work and its maker: the work's surface thought of as existing in relation to its "depth" much the way that the exterior of the human subject is understood to relate to his internal, or true, self. By contrast, the structuralist model of substitutions and nomination does not call to mind the image of depth — substitution being able, after all, to take place by moving pieces about on a plane surface. Thus if Barthes cherishes the *Argo*-model, it is for its *shallowness*.

There is enormous resistance on the part of the formalist or historicist critic to this conception of the work of art, this refusal, in the name of method, of the idea of it as "profound." We hear this antistructuralist attitude formulated, for example, by Stanley Cavell when, as a professional aesthetician, he insists on the humanist analogy, as follows: "Objects of art not merely interest and absorb, they move us . . . we treat them in special ways, invest them with a value which normal people otherwise reserve only for other people — and with the same kind of scorn and outrage." If the human analogy can be used by the historicist to try to ground the work in the biographical matrix of its author, or to attempt to order and fix its "intentions," it can also serve the critic anxious to understand the work's formal integration. Here it functions as a kind of physicalist model, with the work's putative resemblance to the human body involving not only those conditions of surface and depth, inside and outside, that are supposedly shared by human subject and work of art but also those formal features that preserve and protect the life of the organism, such as unity, coherence, complexity within identity, and so on. Now this call for unity assumes that it is possible to draw boundaries around the aesthetic organism: starting with *this* work within its frame, and the formal decisions it manifests; moving to *this* medium, with the conditions that both unify it and separate it from other media; and continuing to *this* author and the unity or coherence of his oeuvre. The categories of such a discussion — work of art, medium, author, oeuvre — are never, themselves, seriously opened to question.

Having embraced structuralism's rejection of history as a way of getting at the way things (statements, works of art, any cultural production at all) signify, poststructuralism then turns around and submits the vehicles of that production to the test of their own histories. Like the life of the *Argo*, the autonomous or unified nature of concepts like "author," "oeuvre," or "work" tends to dissolve against the background of actual, material history. In his admiration for the *Argo*-model, Barthes called it "luminous and white," undoubtedly thinking of Mallarmé's sail. How many different *Argos*, he went on to wonder, are named by the word *Homer*? And, in further questioning the traditional view of authorship, poststructuralists ask, whose writing is specified by the name Freud? Freud's only? Or that of Abraham, Stekel, Flies? Getting closer to the field of the visual arts, we could extend this question: What does *Picasso* mean for his art — the historical personality who is its "cause," supplying the *meaning* for this or that figure (clown, satyr, minotaur) in his painting? Or were those meanings written long before Picasso selected them? And is not his art a profound meditation on pastiche, for which collage is itself an inspired structural metaphor?

That last group of questions is raised by the essay "In the Name of Picasso," contained in this collection and written in response to the great outpouring of writing stimulated by the massive Picasso retrospective of 1980. If the questions had to be asked, it was for two interrelated reasons, each a reflection of the issues sketched earlier.

The first reason has to do with the model of meaning out of which the various authors of these texts were working, a model (the picture theory of meaning) that demonstrated the degree to which writers about modernist painting and sculpture were unaffected by and, probably, ignorant of the work on signification produced by structuralism. The second has to do with the effects of the relatively recent capture of art-critical writing by art history—an art history that has itself become increasingly historicist in the last several decades and is pursuing questions of origin and authorship as though no critique had ever been advanced about the methodological status of these concepts. But the very concern of Picasso's art with pastiche poses problems—from *within* his work—of "authorship," just as his operations, through collage, on the procedures of signification challenge any simplistic idea of reference.

This, then, is the crux of the contention that method is what criticism is, seriously, read for. Because those questions that could be thought to be statements of value—"the operations of pastiche are what is interesting, here"; "the representation of absence is what is best about Picasso's collage"—are in fact the product of what a given method allows one to ask or even to think of asking.

Each of these essays can be seen as asking one or more of those kinds of questions, having been provoked into doing so by my various, specific encounters with modernist art. Structuralism, for example, in allowing one to think the relationships between heterogeneous integers, permitted release from notions of stylistic coherence or formal consistency that were preventing critics, it seemed to me, from making sense of contemporary production, or historians of modern art from coming to terms with older phenomena. "Notes on the Index," "Sculpture in the Expanded Field," and "The Photographic Conditions of Surrealism" represent the results of that permission.

Poststructuralism, in problematizing all those transhistorical categories out of which most of the work of modernist production is thought, brought certain aspects of that art into focus, and led to considerations of authorship and oeuvre that generated "Photography's Discursive Spaces," and to questions of origin, originality, and the status of the physical original that resulted in the essay on Julio Gonzalez, "The Originality of the Avant-Garde," and "Sincerely Yours."

That last essay, which is extremely polemical in tone, raises the issue of the often combative posture of these texts. Perhaps it is the sweeping nature of the difference in our methodological bases—a difference that makes some of the questions raised by this work flatly incomprehensible to certain of my colleagues—that has encouraged that posture. But it is also a result of my own sense that the art of the last hundred and thirty years, the art of modernism, is not being well served by writing that promotes the myths through which it can be consistently misread.

But of course the very experience of these *as* myths, many of them generated by modernist artists themselves or by the critical writing of their friends and associates, seems to be particularly possible from a certain vantage—that of the present—from which modernist art appears to have come to closure. It is, in fact, from within the perspective of postmodernist production that issues of copy and repetition, the reproducibility of the sign (most obviously in its photographic form), the textual production of the subject, are newly brought to light within modernism itself—revealed as the matter that a euphoric modernism sought both to signal and to repress. Postmodernist art enters this terrain (the theoretical domain of structuralist and poststructuralist analysis) openly. And it is this phenomenon, born of the last two decades, that in turn has opened critical practice, overtly, onto method.

Princeton, 1983

I Modernist Myths

Grids

In the early part of this century there began to appear, first in France and then in Russia and in Holland, a structure that has remained emblematic of the modernist ambition within the visual arts ever since. Surfacing in pre-War cubist painting and subsequently becoming ever more stringent and manifest, the grid announces, among other things, modern art's will to silence, its hostility to literature, to narrative, to discourse. As such, the grid has done its job with striking efficiency. The barrier it has lowered between the arts of vision and those of language has been almost totally successful in walling the visual arts into a realm of exclusive visuality and defending them against the intrusion of speech. The arts, of course, have paid dearly for this success, because the fortress they constructed on the foundation of the grid has increasingly become a ghetto. Fewer and fewer voices from the general critical establishment have been raised in support, appreciation, or analysis of the contemporary plastic arts.

Yet it is safe to say that no form within the whole of modern aesthetic production has sustained itself so relentlessly while at the same time being so impervious to change. It is not just the sheer number of careers that have been devoted to the exploration of the grid that is impressive, but the fact that never could exploration have chosen less fertile ground. As the experience of Mondrian amply demonstrates, development is precisely what the grid resists. But no one seems to'have been deterred by that example, and modernist practice continues to generate ever more instances of grids.

There are two ways in which the grid functions to declare the modernity of modern art. One is spatial; the other is temporal. In the spatial sense, the grid states the autonomy of the realm of art. Flattened, geometricized, ordered, it is antinatural, antimimetic, antireal. It is what art looks like when it turns its back on nature. In the flatness that results from its coordinates, the grid is the means of crowding out the dimensions of the real and replacing them with the lateral spread of a single surface. In the overall regularity of its organization, it is the result not of imitation, but of aesthetic decree. Insofar as its order is that of pure relationship, the grid is a way of abrogating the claims of natural objects to have an order particular to themselves; the relationships in the aesthetic field are shown by the grid to be in a world apart and, with respect to natural objects, to be both prior and final. The grid declares the space of art to be at once autonomous and autotelic.

In the temporal dimension, the grid is an emblem of modernity by being just that: the form that is ubiquitous in the art of *our* century, while appearing nowhere, nowhere at all, in the art of the last one. In that great chain of reactions by which modernism was born out of the efforts of the nineteenth century, one final shift resulted in breaking the chain. By "discovering" the grid, cubism, de Stijl, Mondrian, Malevich . . . landed in a place that was out of reach of everything that went before. Which is to say, they landed in the present, and everything else was declared to be the past.

One has to travel a long way back into the history of art to find previous examples of grids. One has to go to the fifteenth and sixteenth centuries, to treatises on perspective and to those exquisite studies by Uccello or Leonardo or Dürer, where the perspective lattice is inscribed on the depicted world as the armature of its organization. But perspective studies are not really early instances of grids. Perspective was, after all, the science of the real, not the mode of withdrawal from it. Perspective was the demonstration of the way reality and its representation could be mapped onto one another, the way the painted image and its real-world referent did in fact relate to one another—the first being a form of knowledge about the second. Everything about the grid opposes that relationship, cuts it off from the very beginning. Unlike perspective, the grid does not map the space of a room or a landscape or a group of figures onto the surface of a painting. Indeed, if it maps anything, it maps the surface of the painting itself. It is a transfer in which nothing changes place. The physical qualities of the surface, we could say, are mapped onto the aesthetic dimensions of the same surface. And those two planes—the physical and the aesthetic—are demonstrated to be the same plane: coextensive, and, through the abscissas and ordinates of the grid, coordinate. Considered in this way, the bottom line of the grid is a naked and determined materialism.

But if it is materialism that the grid would make us talk about—and there seems no other logical way to discuss it—that is not the way that artists have ever discussed it. If we open any tract—*Plastic Art and Pure Plastic Art* or *The Non-Objective World*, for instance—we will find that Mondrian and Malevich are not discussing canvas or pigment or graphite or any other form of matter. They are talking about Being or Mind or Spirit. From their point of view, the grid is a staircase to the Universal, and they are not interested in what happens below in the Concrete. Or, to take a more up-to-date example, we could think about Ad Reinhardt who, despite his repeated insistence that "Art is art," ended up by painting a series of black nine-square grids in which the motif that inescapably emerges is a Greek cross. There is no painter in the West who can be unaware of the symbolic power of the cruciform shape and the Pandora's box of spiritual reference that is opened once one uses it.

Agnes Martin. Untitled. 1965.

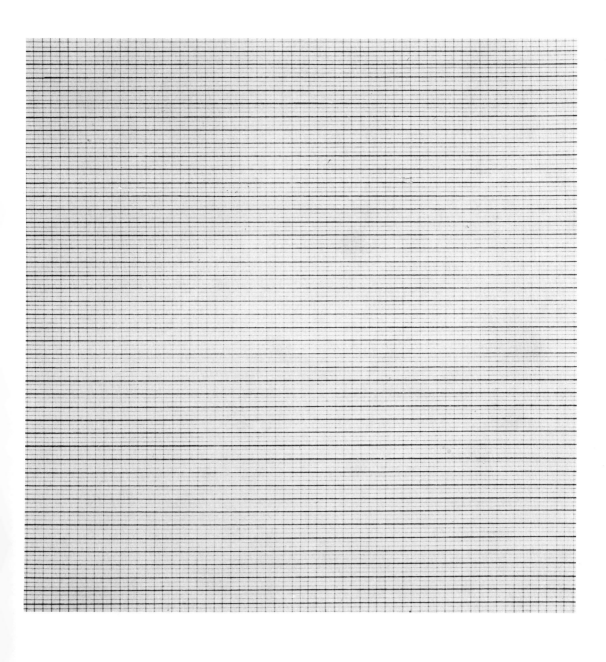

Now it is in this ambivalence about the import of the grid, an indecision about its connection to matter on the one hand or spirit on the other, that its earliest employers can be seen to be participating in a drama that extended well beyond the domain of art. That drama, which took many forms, was staged in many places. One of them was a courtroom, where early in this century, science did battle with God, and, reversing all earlier precedents, won. The result, we were told by the loser's representative, would have the direst of consequences: the result would surely be that we would "inherit the wind." Nietzsche had expressed this earlier and with a somewhat more comic cast when he wrote, "We wished to awaken the feeling of man's sovereignty by showing his divine birth: this path is now forbidden, since a monkey stands at the entrance." Through the Scopes trial, the split between spirit and matter that was presided over by nineteenth-century science became the legitimate heritage of twentieth-century school children. But it was, of course, no less the heritage of twentieth-century art.

Given the absolute rift that had opened between the sacred and the secular, the modern artist was obviously faced with the necessity to choose between one mode of expression and the other. The curious testimony offered by the grid is that at this juncture he tried to decide for both. In the increasingly de-sacralized space of the nineteenth century, art had become the refuge for religious emotion; it became, as it has remained, a secular form of belief. Although this condition could be discussed openly in the late nineteenth century, it is something that is in-admissable in the twentieth, so that by now we find it indescribably embarrassing to mention *art* and *spirit* in the same sentence.

The peculiar power of the grid, its extraordinarily long life in the specialized space of modern art, arises from its potential to preside over this shame: to mask and to reveal it at one and the same time. In the cultist space of modern art, the grid serves not only as emblem but also as myth. For like all myths, it deals with paradox or contradiction not by dissolving the paradox or resolving the contradiction, but by covering them over so that they seem (but only seem) to go away. The grid's mythic power is that it makes us able to think we are dealing with materialism (or sometimes science, or logic) while at the same time it provides us with a release into belief (or illusion, or fiction). The work of Reinhardt or Agnes Martin would be instances of this power. And one of the important sources of this power is the way the grid is, as I said before, so stridently modern to look at, seeming to have left no place of refuge, no room on the face of it, for vestiges of the nineteenth century to hide.

In suggesting that the success[1] of the grid is somehow connected to its structure as myth, I may of course be accused of stretching a point beyond the limits of common sense, since myths are stories, and like all narratives they

---

1.   Success here refers to three things at once: a sheerly quantitative success, involving the number of artists in this century who have used grids; a qualitative success through which the grid has become the medium for some of the greatest works of modernism; and an ideological success, in that the grid is able—in a work of whatever quality—to emblematize the Modern.

unravel through time, whereas grids are not only spatial to start with, they are visual structures that explicitly reject a narrative or sequential reading of any kind. But the notion of myth I am using here depends on a structuralist mode of analysis, by which the sequential features of a story are rearranged to form a spatial organization.[2]

The reason the structuralists do this is that they wish to understand the function of myths; and this function they see as the cultural attempt to deal with contradiction. By spatializing the story—into vertical columns, for example—they are able to display the features of the contradiction and to show how these underlie the attempts of a specific mythical tale to paper over the opposition with narrative. Thus, in analyzing a variety of creation myths, Lévi-Strauss finds the presence of a conflict between earlier notions of man's origins as a process of autochthony (man born from the earth, like plants), and later ones involving the sexual relations between two parents. Because the earlier forms of belief are sacrosanct they must be maintained even though they violate commonsense views about sexuality and birth. The function of the myth is to allow *both* views to be held in some kind of para-logical suspension.

The justification of this violation of the temporal dimension of the myth arises, then, from the results of structural analysis: namely, the sequential progress of the story does not achieve resolution but rather repression. That is, for a given culture, the contradiction is a powerful one, one that will not go away, but will only go, so to speak, underground. So the vertical columns of structuralist analysis are a way of unearthing the unmanageable oppositions that promoted the making of the myth in the first place. We could analogize this procedure to that of psychoanalysis, where the "story" of a life is similarly seen as an attempt to resolve primal contradictions that nevertheless remain in the structure of the unconscious. Because they are there as repressed elements, they function to promote endless repetitions of the same conflict. Thus another rationale for the vertical columns (the spatialization of the "story") emerges from the fact that it is useful to see the way each feature of the story (for structuralist analysis these are called mythemes) burrows down, independently, into the historical past: in the case of psychoanalysis this is the past of the individual; for the analysis of myth, this is the past of the culture or the tribe.

Therefore, although the grid is certainly not a story, it *is* a structure, and one, moreover, that allows a contradiction between the values of science and those of spiritualism to maintain themselves within the consciousness of modernism, or rather its unconscious, as something repressed. In order to continue its analysis— to assess the very success of the grid's capacities to repress—we might follow the lead of the two analytical procedures I have just mentioned. This would mean burrowing along the site of each part of the contradiction down into its historical

2.   See, Claude Lévi-Strauss, *Structural Anthropology*, New York, 1963, particularly "The Structural Analysis of Myth."

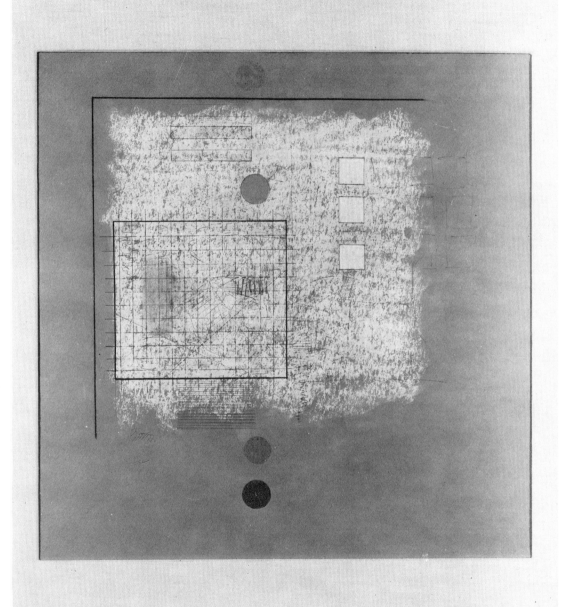

foundations. No matter how absent the grid was in nineteenth-century art, it is precisely into these historical grounds that we must go to find its sources.

Now, although the grid itself is invisible in nineteenth-century painting, it is not entirely absent from a certain kind of accessory literature to which that painting paid an increasing amount of attention. This is the literature of physiological optics. By the nineteenth century the study of optics had split into two parts. One half consisted of the analysis of light and its physical properties: its motion; its refractive features as it was passed through lenses, for example; its capacity to be quantified, or measured. In conducting such studies, scientists presupposed that these were features of light as such, that is, light as it existed independent of human (or animal) perception.

The second branch of optics concentrated on the physiology of the perceiving mechanism; it was concerned with light and color as they are seen. It is this branch of optics that was of immediate concern to artists.

Whatever their sources of information—whether Chevreul, or Charles Blanc, or Rood, Helmholtz, or even Goethe[3]—painters had to confront a particular fact: the physiological screen through which light passes to the human brain is not transparent, like a window pane; it is, like a filter, involved in a set of specific distortions. For us, as human perceivers, there is an unbreachable gulf between "real" color and "seen" color. We may be able to measure the first; but we can only experience the second. And this is because, among other things, color is always involved in interaction—one color reading onto and affecting its neighbor. Even if we are only looking at a single color, there is still interaction, because the retinal excitation of the afterimage will superimpose on the first chromatic stimulus that of a second, which is its complementary. The whole issue of complementary colors, along with the whole edifice of color harmonics that painters constructed on its basis, was thus a matter of physiological optics.

An interesting feature of treatises written on physiological optics is that they were illustrated with grids. Because it was a matter of demonstrating the interaction of specific particles throughout a continuous field, that field was analyzed into the modular and repetitive structure of the grid. So for the artist who wished to enlarge his understanding of vision in the direction of science, the grid was there as a matrix of knowledge. By its very abstraction, the grid conveyed one of the basic laws of knowledge—the separation of the perceptual screen from that of the "real" world. Given all of this, it is not surprising that the grid—as an emblem of the infrastructure of vision—should become an increasingly insistent and visible feature of neo-impressionist painting, as Seurat, Signac, Cross, and Luce applied themselves to the lessons of physiological optics. Just as it is not

3.   Michel-Eugène Chevreul, *De la loi du contraste simultané des couleurs*, Paris, 1839, translated into English in 1872; Charles Blanc, *Grammaire des arts du déssin*, Paris, 1867, translated into English in 1879; Ogden N. Rood, *Modern Chromatics*, New York, 1879, translated into French, 1881; Hermann von Helmholtz, *Handbuch der physiologischen Optik*, Leipzig, 1867; Johann Wolfgang von Goethe, *Farbenlehre*, 1810, translated into English, 1840.

Robert Ryman. Yellow Drawing Number 5. *1963.*

Caspar David Friedrich. View from the Painter's
Studio. *c. 1818.*

surprising that the more they applied these lessons, the more "abstract" their art
became, so that as the critic Félix Fénéon observed of the work of Seurat, science
began to yield its opposite, which is symbolism.

The symbolists themselves stood adamantly opposed to any traffic at all
between art and science, or for that matter, between art and "reality." The object of
symbolism was metaphysical understanding, not the mundane; the movement
supported those aspects of culture that were interpretations rather than imitations
of the real. And so symbolist art would be the last place, we might think, to look
for even an incipient version of grids. But once again we would be wrong.

The grid appears in symbolist art in the form of windows, the material
presence of their panes expressed by the geometical intervention of the window's
mullions. The symbolist interest in windows clearly reaches back into the early
nineteenth century and romanticism.[4] But in the hands of the symbolist painters
and poets, this image is turned in an explicitly modernist direction. For the
window is experienced as simultaneously transparent and opaque.

As a transparent vehicle, the window is that which admits light—or spirit—
into the initial darkness of the room. But if glass transmits, it also reflects. And so
the window is experienced by the symbolist as a mirror as well—something that

4.   See Lorenz Eitner, "The Open Window and the Storm-Tossed Boat: an Essay in the Iconography of Romanticism," *Art Bulletin*, XXXVII (December 1955), 281-90.

Odilon Redon. The Day. *1891.*

freezes and locks the self into the space of its own reduplicated being. Flowing and freezing; *glace* in French means glass, mirror, and ice; transparency, opacity, and water. In the associative system of symbolist thought this liquidity points in two directions. First, towards the flow of birth—the amniotic fluid, the "source"—but then, towards the freezing into stasis or death—the unfecund immobility of the mirror. For Mallarmé, particularly, the window functioned as this complex, polysemic sign by which he could also project the *"crystallization* of reality into art."[5] Mallarmé's *Les Fenêtres* dates from 1863; Redon's most evocative window, *Le Jour,* appeared in 1891 in the volume *Songes.*

If the window is this matrix of ambi- or multivalence, and the bars of the windows—the grid—are what help us to see, to focus on, this matrix, they are themselves the symbol of the symbolist work of art. They function as the multilevel representation through which the work of art can allude, and even reconstitute, the forms of Being.

I do not think it is an exaggeration to say that behind every twentieth-century grid there lies—like a trauma that must be repressed—a symbolist window parading in the guise of a treatise on optics. Once we realize this, we can also understand that in twentieth-century art there are "grids" even where we do not

5.   Robert G. Cohn, "Mallarmé's Windows," *Yale French Studies,* no. 54 (1977), 23-31.

expect to find them: in the art of Matisse, for example (his *Windows*), which only admits openly to the grid in the final stages of the *papiers découpés*.

Because of its bivalent structure (and history) the grid is fully, even cheerfully, schizophrenic. I have witnessed and participated in arguments about whether the grid portends the centrifugal or centripetal existence of the work of art.[6] Logically speaking, the grid extends, in all directions, to infinity. Any boundaries imposed upon it by a given painting or sculpture can only be seen—according to this logic—as arbitrary. By virtue of the grid, the given work of art is presented as a mere fragment, a tiny piece arbitrarily cropped from an infinitely larger fabric. Thus the grid operates from the work of art outward, compelling our acknowledgement of a world beyond the frame. This is the centrifugal reading. The centripetal one works, naturally enough, from the outer limits of the aesthetic object inward. The grid is, in relation to *this* reading a *re*-presentation of

6.   This literature is far too extensive to be cited here; a representative and excellent example of this discussion is, John Elderfield, "Grids," *Artforum*, X (May 1972), 52-9.

AUX CONTES DE FEES.
NOUVEAUX CONTES DE FEES
rouffe fit un plongeon, puis
troisième; enfin on le déta
morceau de pain entre ses quatre
(Page 178.)
es enfants, pour ma fem
de pied lui fut appliqué. (Page 1
efforts inutiles, toujours su
madame la souris; je n'oub
andations. »

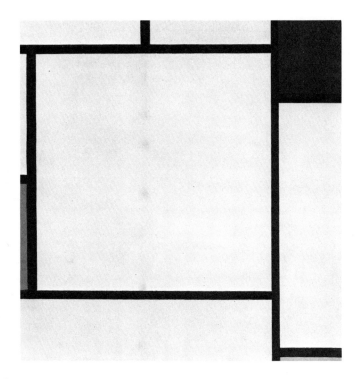

Piet Mondrian. Composition IA. *1930. (facing).*
Composition 2. *1922. (above).*

everything that separates the work of art from the world, from ambient space and from other objects. The grid is an introjection of the boundaries of the world into the interior of the work; it is a mapping of the space inside the frame onto itself. It is a mode of repetition, the content of which is the conventional nature of art itself.

The work of Mondrian, taken together with its various and conflicting readings, is a perfect example of this dispute. Is what we see in a particular painting merely a section of an implied continuity, or is the painting structured as an autonomous, organic whole? Given the visual, or formal, consistency of Mondrian's mature style and the passion of his theoretical pronouncements, we would think that work of this sort would have to hold to one position or the other; and because the chosen position contains a definition about the very nature and goals of art, one would think that an artist would certainly not want to confuse the issue by seeming to imply both. Yet that is exactly what Mondrian does. There are certain paintings that are overwhelmingly centrifugal, particularly the vertical and horizontal grids seen within diamond-shaped canvases—the contrast between frame and grid enforcing the sense of fragmentation, as though we were looking at

a landscape through a window, the frame of the window arbitrarily truncating our view but never shaking our certainty that the landscape continues beyond the limits of what we can, at that moment, see. But other works, even from the same years, are just as explicitly centripetal. In these, the black lines forming the grid are never allowed actually to reach the outer margins of the work, and this cesura between the outer limits of the grid and the outer limits of the painting forces us to read the one as completely contained within the other.

Because the centrifugal argument posits the theoretical continuity of the work of art with the world, it can support many different ways of using the grid— ranging from purely abstract statements of this continuity to projects which order aspects of "reality," that reality itself conceived more or less abstractly. Thus at the more abstract end of this spectrum we find explorations of the perceptual field (an aspect of Agnes Martin's or Larry Poons's use of the grid), or of phonic interactions (the grids of Patrick Ireland), and as we move towards the less abstract we find statements about the infinite expansion of man-made sign systems (the numbers and alphabets of Jasper Johns). Moving further in the direction of the concrete, we find work that organizes "reality" by means of photographic integers (Warhol and, in a different manner, Chuck Close) as well as work that is, in part, a meditation on architectural space (Louise Nevelson, for example). At this point the three-dimensional grid (now, a lattice) is understood as a theoretical model of architectural space in general, some small piece of which can be given material form, and at the opposite pole of this kind of thinking we find the decorative projects of Frank Lloyd Wright and the work of de Stijl practitioners like Rietveld or Vantongerloo. (Sol LeWitt's modules and lattices are a later manifestation of this position.)

And of course, for the centripetal practice, the opposite is true. Concentrating on the surface of the work as something complete and internally organized, the centripetal branch of practice tends not to dematerialize that surface, but to make it itself the object of vision. Here again one finds one of those curious paradoxes by which the use of the grid is marked at every turn. The beyond-the-frame attitude, in addressing the world and its structure, would seem to trace its lineage back to the nineteenth century in relation to the operations of science, and thus to carry the positivist or materialist implications of its heritage. The within-the-frame attitude, on the contrary, involved as it is with the purely conventional and autotelic reading of the work of art, would seem to issue from purely symbolist origins, and thus to carry all those readings which we oppose to "science" or "materialism"—readings which inflect the work as symbolic, cosmological, spiritual, vitalist. Yet we know that by and large this is not true. Through a kind of short-circuiting of this logic, the within-the-frame grids are generally far more materialist in character (take such different examples as Alfred Jensen and Frank Stella); while the beyond-the-frame examples often entail the dematerialization of the surface, the dispersal of matter into perceptual flicker or implied motion. And we also know that this schizophrenia allows for many artists—from

Joseph Cornell, Nouveaux Contes de Fées (Poison Box). *1948.*

Mondrian, to Albers, to Kelly, to LeWitt—to think about the grid in both ways at once.

In discussing the operation and character of the grid within the general field of modern art I have had recourse to words like *repression* or *schizophrenia*. Since these terms are being applied to a cultural phenomenon and not to individuals, they are obviously not intended in their literal, medical sense, but only analogically: to compare the structure of one thing to the structure of another. The terms of this analogy were clear, I hope, from the discussion of the parallel structures and functions of both grids as aesthetic objects and myths.

But one further aspect of this analogy still needs to be brought out, and that is the way in which this psychological terminology functions at some distance from that of *history*. What I mean is that we speak of the etiology of a psychological condition, not the history of it. History, as we normally use it, implies the connection of events through time, a sense of inevitable change as we move from one event to the next, and the cumulative effect of change which is itself qualitative, so that we tend to view history as *developmental*. Etiology is not developmental. It is rather an investigation into the conditions for one specific change—the acquisition of disease—to take place. In that sense etiology is more like looking into the background of a chemical experiment, asking when and how a given group of elements came together to effect a new compound or to precipitate something out of a liquid. For the etiology of neuroses, we may take a "history" of the individual, to explore what went into the formation of the neurotic structure; but once the neurosis is formed, we are specifically enjoined from thinking in terms of "development," and instead we speak of repetition.

With regard to the advent of the grid in twentieth-century art, there is the need to think etiologically rather than historically. Certain conditions combined to precipitate the grid into a position of aesthetic preeminence. We can speak of what those things are and how they came together throughout the nineteenth century and then spot the moment of chemical combination, as it were, in the early decades of the twentieth. But once the grid appears it seems quite resistant to change. The mature careers of Mondrian or Albers are examples of this. No one would characterize the course of decade after decade of their later work as *developmental*. But by depriving their world of development, one is obviously not depriving it of quality. There is no necessary connection between good art and change, no matter how conditioned we may be to think that there is. Indeed, as we have a more and more extended experience of the grid, we have discovered that one of the most modernist things about it is its capacity to serve as a paradigm or model for the antidevelopmental, the antinarrative, the antihistorical.

This has occurred in the temporal as well as the visual arts: in music, for example, and in dance. It is no surprise then, that as we contemplate this subject, there should have been announced for next season a performance project based on the combined efforts of Phil Glass, Lucinda Childs, and Sol LeWitt: music, dance, and sculpture, projected as the mutually accessible space of the grid.

New York, 1978

In the Name of Picasso

Exhibit A: Picasso's *Seated Bather*, 1930. Against an azure wall of water, fragments of bone and bleached carapace assemble the monumental image of isolated, predatory woman. Woman-as-insect, with great mandibles in place of mouth evoking more effectively than any Masson or Miró the threat of the *vagina dentata*, this painting has functioned for years as a major emblem of Picasso's affinities with surrealism, as it has also established his preoccupation with an especially surrealizing notion of metamorphosis. The Museum of Modern Art showed the picture in 1939, and then again in 1946, at both major Picasso exhibitions. Thereafter it entered the collection to be placed on permanent view and to be installed—permanently it had seemed—within a particular "view" of the 1930s Picasso. This was a notion of a metamorphic "style" concerned with the body as a loose assembly or construction of parts often suggestive of found objects. This style was fundamental to the early sculpture of David Smith, as it was to the early painting of Gorky and de Kooning. They understood it as a mode or manner having a rather general application: that of biomorphic construction to create an image of transmutation. Not only artists, but generations of students imbibed this conception of the Picasso of the '30s and this particular style.

Exhibit B: Picasso's *Bather with Beach Ball*, 1932. Against a pale cobalt sea and sky, the monumental form of female adolescence is assembled from a collection of pneumatic parts: bulbous bones so pumped with air that the figure appears to float. As a pendant to the *Seated Bather*, this work displays a contrary mood, a lugubrious sense of play instead of the earlier image's desicated wrath. But in all those conditions that we would call style the paintings are nearly twins. Both exploit a simple backdrop to force a sculptural experience of their theatrically isolated forms. Both conceive the figure as constructed out of parts whose provisional coherence effects a transformation from one thing (bone, balloon) to another (pelvis, breast).

Exhibit C: At a lecture this fall at the Baltimore Museum of Art, William Rubin, one of the leading Picasso scholars, showed both paintings.[1] With these

---

1. The lecture was presented on October 12, 1980, at a symposium on the cubist legacy in twentieth-century sculpture.

Pablo Picasso. Seated Bather. *1930. (Left.)* Bather with
Beach Ball. *1932. (Right.)*

two works, he said, we find ourselves looking at two different universes—and by
this he meant different formal as well as symbolic worlds. This is hard to
understand; as difficult as if someone pointed first to a Hals portrait of a Dutch
militia officer and then to his rendering of the *Malle Babbe* and maintained that
they were products of different styles. But Rubin was insisting on this difference, a
difference become incontrovertible by the very fact that behind each picture there
lay a real-world model, each model with a different name: Olga Picasso; Marie-
Thérèse Walter.

    We are by now familiar with the sordid conditions of Picasso's marriage in
the late '20s, as we are with his passion for the somnolent blond he met when she
was seventeen and who was to reign, a sleepy Venus, over a half-dozen years of his
art. But in Rubin's suggestion that Olga and Marie-Thérèse provide not merely
antithetical moods and subjects for the pictorial contemplation of the same artist,
but that they actually function as determinants in a change in style, we run full tilt
into the Autobiographical Picasso. And in this instance Rubin himself was the
first to invoke it. The changes in Picasso's art, he went on to say, are a direct

function of the turns and twists of the master's private life. With the exception of his cubism, Picasso's style is inextricable from his biography.

With the Museum of Modern Art's huge Picasso retrospective has come a flood of critical and scholarly essays on Picasso, almost all of them dedicated to "Art as Autobiography." That latter phrase is the title of a just-published book on Picasso by an author who sees everything in his work as a pictorial response to some specific stimulus in his personal life, including the *Demoiselles d'Avignon*, which she claims was made in an effort to exorcise "his private female demons."[2] This same author, who proudly pounces on a mish-mash of latter-day accounts to "prove" that Picasso's turn-of-the-century decision to go to Paris to pursue his art was due to his need to "exile himself from Spain in order to escape his tyrannical mother," provides us with a delicious, if unintended parody of the Autobiographical Picasso.[3]

But prone to parody or not, this argument is upheld by many respected scholars and is attracting many others. John Richardson, of course, took the opportunity of reviewing the Museum of Modern Art exhibition to forward the case for the Autobiographical Picasso. Agreeing with Dora Maar that Picasso's art is at any one time a function of the changes in five private forces—his mistress, his house, his poet, his set of admirers, his dog (yes, dog!)—Richardson exhorts art-historical workers to fan out among the survivors of Picasso's acquaintance, to record the last scraps of personal information still outstanding before death prevents the remaining witnesses from appearing in court.[4] Richardson's trumpet has been sounding this theme for over twenty years, so on this occasion his call was not surprising. But the Autobiographical Picasso is new to William Rubin and that this view of matters should now hold him convert is all the more impressive in that it had to overcome the resistance of decades of Rubin's training. Rubin's earlier practice of art history was rich in a host of ways of understanding art in transpersonal terms: ways that involve questions of period style, of shared formal and iconographic symbols that seem to be the function of larger units of history than the restricted profile of a merely private life. So the Rubin case is particularly instructive, all the more because in his account the personal, the private, the biographical, is given in a series of proper names: Olga, Marie-Thérèse, Dora, Françoise, Jacqueline. And an art history turned militantly away from all that is transpersonal in history—style, social and economic context, archive, structure—is interestingly and significantly symbolized by an art-history as a history of the proper name.

2.   Mary Mathews Gedo, "Art as Exorcism: Picasso's 'Demoiselles d'Avignon.'" *Arts*, LV (October 1980), 70–81.
3.   *Ibid.*, p. 72; see also *Art as Autobiography*, Chicago, University of Chicago Press, 1980.
4.   John Richardson, "Your Show of Shows," *The New York Review*, July 17, 1980. Eugene Thaw uses Richardson's essay as an occasion for his own attack on art as autobiography. See, "Lust for Life," *The New York Review*, October 23, 1980.

> *I can call nothing by name if that is not*
> *its name. I call a cat a cat, and Rolet a*
> *rogue.*
>
> —Boileau

A proper name, we could say, is a token without a type. Not transferable and not reusable, it applies only to me. And I am its complete significance. The proper name completes, exhausts itself in an act of reference. Aside from labeling the object that is its bearer, it has no further meaning, and thus no "sense" such as other words have. Those words, like the common nouns *horse* or *house* have definitions: a set of predicates by which we grasp the concept that can be said to be their sense, or meaning. But a proper name has no such definition—only an individual who bears the name and to whom it refers. That is not only common sense, but it is the view that philosophy held until the end of the last century.[5] But then this traditional no-sense view was attacked first by Frege and then by Russell.[6] Proper names, Frege argued, must not only have a sense, but in cases where one is naming a nonexistent character (like Santa Claus), they may even have a sense but no referent. Russell went on to enlarge this view by claiming that ordinary proper names are, in fact, disguised definite descriptions and thus we learn how correctly to apply a proper name by recourse to sets of characteristics. (Thus the "sense" of the name Aristotle is supplied by some or all of a set of descriptions, such as: a Greek philosopher; the tutor of Alexander the Great; the author of the *Nicomachean Ethics.* . . .) We could call this the intensional or sense view of the proper name; and it has been variously argued by the later Wittgenstein and by Searle,[7] to be itself more recently challenged by a causal theory of nominal reference.[8]

In an extraordinary essay Joel Fineman has recently indicated the importance of the philosophical debate on proper names to literary theory and criticism:

> The progressive and increasingly dogmatic subordination by philoso-
> phy of nominal reference, first to extension, then to expression, then to

5.   John Searle writes: "Perhaps the most famous formulation of this no-sense theory of proper names is Mill's statement that proper names have denotation but not connotation. For Mill a common noun like "horse" has both a connotation and a denotation; it connotes those properties which would be specified in a definition of the word "horse," and it denotes all horses. But a proper name only denotes its bearer. See, Searle, "Proper Names and Descriptions," *The Encyclopedia of Philosophy*, Paul Edwards, ed., New York, Macmillan, 1967, vol. 6, p. 487.
6.   Gottlob Frege, "On Sense and Reference," in *Translations from the Philosophical Writings of Gottlob Frege*, Peter Geach, Max Black, eds., Oxford, Basil Blackwell, 1960. This essay was first published in 1892. Bertrand Russell, "Descriptions," in *Readings in the Philosophy of Language*, Jay Rosenberg, Charles Travis, eds., Englewood, Prentice-Hall, 1971. Reprinted from Russell, *Introduction to Mathematical Philosophy*, London, 1919.
7.   Thus Wittgenstein in the *Philosophical Investigations*, Para. 40: "When Mr. N. N. dies one says that the bearer of the name dies, not that the meaning dies." See also Para. 79. John Searle, "Proper Names," *Mind*, LXVII (April 1958), 166–173.
8.   This literature is anthologized in *Naming, Necessity, and Natural Kinds*, Stephen P. Schwartz, ed., Ithaca, Cornell University Press, 1977.

intention, and finally to a historicity that postpones its own temporality, in many ways parallels the development and eventual demise of an aesthetics of representation. That is to say, the perennial awkwardness philosophy discloses in the collation of word and thing is closely related to the uneasy relation our literary tradition regularly discovers when it connects literal to figurative literary meaning.[9]

Whatever its status within current considerations of literary representation, it is clear that the proper name has a definite role to play within current art-historical and critical notions of the relation between image and meaning.

Classical theories of mimesis would, like the classical theory of proper names, limit meaning to reference. A visual representation of something "means" that thing in the world of which it is a picture. "Hence," Aristotle writes, "the pleasure [all men] receive from a picture: in viewing it they learn, they infer, they discover what every object is, that this, for instance, is such a particular man, etc."[10] A picture is thus a label—only a visual rather than a verbal one—which picks out something in the world and refers to it. And its meaning is used up in this act of reference. It is in this sense that the mimetic image (or representation) is like the traditionally understood proper name. Both are types of labels, modes of reference; in both cases the meaning is conducted through, limited to, just this referential channel. In this view both names and pictures would constitute representations that, in the philosophical sense, have extension but no intension. The meaning of the label extends over the object to which it refers, but comes to an end at its boundaries. It denotes the object. But it is without connotation or intension, without, that is, a conceptual status that would allow it to be applied over a plurality of instances, without, finally, general conditions of signification. In the classical sense of the proper name, it has a referent but no sense.

It is too obvious to need restating that art history was launched through a sense of, among other things, the inadequacy of classical mimetic theories to explain the multiplicity of visual representation over the course of world art. In a search for reasons for a particular culture's maintenance of nearness or distance between its art's images and their referents, art historians turned to a notion (or rather a whole host of notions) of signification. Thus we have Riegl insisting that late Roman sculpture is unnaturalistic because it intends a meaning that cannot be netted by, or completed within, the confines of that material object the sculpture could be said to represent. From its very beginning art history called upon a theory of representation that would not stop with mere extension (or denotation) but would allow for intension (or connotation). Iconology, as Panofsky presents it, would be unthinkable without such a theory. However, those

9.   Joel Fineman, "The Significance of Literature: *The Importance of Being Earnest,*" *October,* no. 15 (Winter 1980), fn. 7, p. 89.
10.   Aristotle, *Poetics,* Part I, Section V.

early generations of art historians almost never, themselves, theorized their own assumptions about representation. They simply took it as a given that it was in the connotative richness and density—that is, the intension—of the aesthetic sign, that it lay claim to being art at all. Its intension we could say, was taken as a record or index of the multiplicity of human meaning or intention; and they equated this capacity for multivalent content with the very capacity to conceive aesthetic signs.

No technical field is monolithic, and of course art historical practice has been divided about method, purview, and almost everything else one could name. But it is probably the case that, with very few exceptions, the unspoken assumptions about the intensive powers of visual representation were shared by most practitioners in the first part of this century.

Thus the revision in the theory of representation that is currently underway, in its overturning of those older beliefs, is all the more striking. The revision involves a return to a notion of pictorial representation as constituted by signs with referents but no sense: to the limiting of the aesthetic sign to extension, to the dependent condition of the classically conceived proper name. Although the epidemic of extension is widespread in art-historical practice, nowhere is it more virulent and obvious than in Picasso studies. And as I shall go on to demonstrate, nowhere should its spread evoke more irony.

> *I have said everything when I have*
> *named the man.*
> —Pliny the Younger

What I have been calling an aesthetics of extension or an art history of the proper name can be likened to the detective story or the *roman à clef*, where the meaning of the tale reduces to just this question of identity. In the name of the one "who did it" we find not only the solution, but the ultimate sense of the murder mystery; and in discovering the actual people who lie behind a set of fictional characters, we fulfill the goal of the narrative: those characters' *real* names *are* its sense. Unlike allegory, in which a linked and burgeoning series of names establishes an open-ended set of analogies—Jonah/Lazarus/Christ—there is in this aesthetics of the proper name a contraction of sense to the simple task of pointing, or labeling, to the act of unequivocal reference. It is as though the shifting, changing sands of visual polysemy, of multiple meanings and regroupings, have made us intolerably nervous, so that we wish to find the bedrock of sense. We wish to achieve a type of signification beyond which there can be no further reading or interpretation. Interpretation, we insist, must be made to stop somewhere. And where more absolutely and appropriately than in an act of what the police call "positive identification"? For the individual who can be shown to be the "key" to the image, and thus the "meaning" of the image, has the kind of singularity one is looking for. Like his name, his meaning stops within the boundaries of identity.

The instance of "positive identification" that led off the last dozen years' march of Picasso studies into the terrain of biography was the discovery that the major painting of the Blue Period—*La Vie*, 1904—contained a portrait of the Spanish painter and friend of Picasso, Casagemas, who had committed suicide in 1902.[11] Until 1967, when this connection with Casagemas was made, *La Vie* had been interpreted within the general context of fin-de-siècle allegory, with works like Gauguin's *D'Où Venons Nous?* and Munch's *Dance of Life* providing the relevant comparisons.[12] But once a real person could be placed as the model for the standing male figure—moreover a person whose life involved the lurid details of impotence and failed homicide but achieved suicide—the earlier interpretations of *La Vie* as an allegory of maturation and development could be put aside for a more local and specific reading. Henceforth the picture could be seen as a *tableau vivant* containing the dead man torn between two women, one old and one young, the meaning of which "is" sexual dread. And because early studies for the painting show that the male figure had originally been conceived as Picasso's self-portrait, one could now hypothesize the artist's identification with his friend and read the work as "expressing . . . that sense of himself as having been thrust by women into an untenable and ultimately tragic position. . . ."[13]

The problem with this reading is not that the identification is wrong, but that its ultimate aesthetic relevance is yet to be proved or even, given current art-historical fashion, argued. And the problem of its aesthetic relevance is that this reading dissociates the work from all those other aspects, equally present, which have nothing to do with Casagemas and a sexually provoked suicide. What is most particularly left out of this account is the fact that the work is located in·a highly fluctuating and ambiguous space of multiple planes of representation due to the fact that its setting is an artist's studio and its figures are related, at least on one level, to an allegory of painting.[14] Whatever its view of "life," the work echoes such distinguished nineteenth-century forebears as Courbet and Manet in insisting that, for a painter, life and art allegorize each other, both caught up equally in the problem of representation. The name Casagemas does not extend far enough to signify either this relationship or this problem. Yet current art-historical

11.   Pierre Daix, "La Période Bleue de Picasso et le suicide de Carlos Casagemas," *Gazette des Beaux-Arts*, LXIX (April 1967), 245.
12.   Anthony Blunt and Phoebe Pool, *Picasso, The Formative Years*, New York Graphic Society, 1962, pp. 18-21.
13.   Theodore Reff, "Themes of Love and Death in Picasso's Early Work," in *Picasso in Retrospect*, Roland Penrose, John Golding, eds., New York, Praeger, 1973, p. 28.
14.   At the beginning of his discussion of *La Vie*, Reff has no trouble locating the work: "the setting, an artist's studio with two of his canvases in the background" (p. 24). But after "reading" it through the proper name of Casagemas, his account of the location changes and, curiously, "the setting is no longer necessarily an artist's studio" (p. 28). This is a niggling detail, but I bring it to the attention of the reader who feels that there is nothing inherently objectionable to a history of proper names, since that merely adds another dimension to the interpretation of a given work. In practical fact, what we find in most cases is not addition, but restriction.

wisdom uses "Casagemas" to explain the picture—to provide the work's ultimate meaning or sense. When we have named Casagemas, we have (or so we think) cracked the code of the painting and it has no more secrets to withhold.

La Vie is after all a narrative painting and this close examination of its dramatis personae is an understandable (though insufficient) response to the work. The methodology of the proper name becomes more astonishing, however, when practiced on the body of work inaugurated by cubism.

Two examples will serve. A recent study by Linda Nochlin takes up the question of Picasso's color, an issue almost completely ignored by earlier scholar-

Pablo Picasso. The Scallop Shell (Notre avenir est dans l'air). *1912.*

ship.[15] Within modernist art, color would seem to be a subject set at the furthest possible remove from a reading by proper names. This turns out not to be true, as Nochlin analyzes a 1912 cubist painting that is mostly *grisaille,* broken by the intrusion of a flat plane broadly striped in red, white, and blue, and carrying the written words, *"Notre avenir est dans l'air."* Conceived at about the same time as the famous first collage, *Still Life with Chair Caning,* the work in question echoes many other canvases from early 1912, in which the introduction of some kind of

15.   Linda Nochlin, "Picasso's Color: Schemes and Gambits," *Art in America,* vol. 68, no. 10 (December 1980), 105–123; 177–183.

large plane which, like the chair-caning or the pamphlet *"Notre avenir . . . ,"* is a wholly different color and texture from the monochrome faceting of analytic cubism, and inaugurates both the invention of collage and the opening of cubism to color.

This, however, is not Nochlin's point. The actual red-white-and-blue *tricolore* pamphlet that Picasso depicted in this cubist still life had been issued originally to promote the development of aviation for military use. Thus the pamphlet "means" French nationalism; its colors bear the name of Picasso's adopted country. Behind the *tricolore* we read not only "France" but the name of the artist's assumed identity: "Picasso/Frenchman." Color's meaning contracts to the coding of a proper name. (Later in the same essay Nochlin reveals that behind Picasso's use of violet in his work of the early '30s there lies yet another name, which is its meaning: once again, Marie-Thérèse.)

Thus the significance of color reduces to a name, but then, in the following example, so does the significance of names. In his essay "Picasso and the Typography of Cubism," Robert Rosenblum proposes to read the names printed on the labels introduced into cubist collage, and thus to identify the objects so labeled.[16] In Picasso's collages many newspapers are named: *L'Indépendant, Excelsior, Le Moniteur, L'Intransigeant, Le Quotidien du Midi, Le Figaro*; but none with such frequency as *Le Journal*. Rosenblum describes at length the way this name is fractured—most characteristically into JOU, JOUR, and URNAL— and the puns that are thereby released. But that the word-fragments perform these jokes while serving to label the object—the newspaper—with its name, is very much Rosenblum's point. For he concludes his argument by declaring the realism of Picasso's cubist collages, a realism that secures, through printed labels, the presence of the actual objects that constitute "the new imagery of the modern world."[17]

This assumption that the fragmented word has the ultimate function of a proper name leads Rosenblum to the following kind of discussion:

> Such Cubist conundrums are quite as common in the labelling of the bottles of Picasso's compatriot, Juan Gris. On his café table tops, even humble bottles of Beaujolais can suddenly be transformed into verbal jokes. Often, the word BEAUJOLAIS is fragmented to a simple BEAU . . . in another example . . . he permits only the letters EAU to show on the label (originally B*eau*jolais, B*eau*ne, or Bord*eaux*), and thereby performs his own Cubist version of The Miracle at Cana.[18]

We are to expand the word-fragment to grasp the name (we have our choice

16. Robert Rosenblum, "Picasso and the Typography of Cubism," in *Picasso in Retrospect*, pp. 49–75.
17. *Ibid.*, p. 75.
18. *Ibid.*, p. 56.

of three reds) and thereby to secure the original object. In this certainty about word-world connection there is realism indeed.

But are the labels EAU and JOU a set of transparent signifiers, the nick-names of a group of objects (the newspaper, the winebottle) whose real names (*Journal, Beaujolais*) form the basis for this labor of the cubist pun? Is the structure of cubist collage itself supportive of the semantic positivism that will allow it to be thus assimilated to the art history of the proper name? Or are the word-fragments that gather on the surfaces of Picasso's collages instead a function of a rather more exacting notion of reference, representation, and signifi-cation?

> *This is a portrait of Iris Clert if I say so.*
> —Robert Rauschenberg

The most recent major addition to the scholarly inquiry on cubism is Pierre Daix's catalogue raisonné, *Picasso: 1907–1916*. Daix's suggestive text expands the somewhat limited art-historical vocabulary for describing what transpires with the advent of collage, for Daix insists on characterizing collage-elements as signs—not simply in the loose way that had occurred earlier on in the Picasso literature—but in a way that announces its connection to structural linguistics.[19]

Daix is careful to subdivide the sign into signifier and signified—the first being the affixed collage-bit or element of schematic drawing itself; the second being the referent of this signifier: newspaper, bottle, violin.[20] Though this is rare in his discussion, Daix does occasionally indicate that the signified may not be an object at all but rather a free-floating property, like a texture—for example, wood, signified by a bit of wood-grained wallpaper—or a formal element such as verticality or roundness—although this element is usually shown to function as the property of an object: of the round, vertical winebottle, for example.[21] Again and again Daix hammers away at the lesson that cubist collage exchanges the natural visual world of things for the artificial, codified language of signs.

But there is, nowhere in Daix's exposition, a rigorous presentation of the concept of the sign. Because of this, and the manner in which much of Daix's own discussion proceeds, it is extremely easy to convert the issue of the collage-sign into a question of semantics, that is, the sign's transparent connection to a given

19.   Daix's relation to structuralism and an analysis of the sign is documented as being through Lévi-Strauss, to whom he refers at points throughout his text.
20.   Because Daix seems, indeed, to equate the *signified* with the *referent*, he deviates in the most crucial way from Saussure's characterization of the signified as the *concept* or *idea* or *meaning* of the sign. Saussure is careful to distinguish between the concept evoked by the sign and any real-world, physical object to which the signifier could be attached as a label. It is to the former that the designation *signified* belongs. Daix, who never mentions Saussure's name, seems likewise unaware of the major import of Saussure's analysis.
21.   See Pierre Daix, *Picasso: The Cubist Years 1907–1916*, New York, New York Graphic Society/ Little, Brown, 1980, p. 123.

referent, thereby assimilating collage itself to a theater of the proper name: "EAU is really Beaujolais, and JOU is in fact Journal."

If we are really going to turn to structural linguistics for instruction about the operation of the sign we must bear in mind the two absolute conditions posited by Saussure for the functioning of the linguistic sign. The first is the analysis of signs into a relationship between signifier and signified ($\frac{s}{S}$) in which the signifier is a *material* constituent (written trace, phonic element) and the signified, an immaterial idea or concept. This opposition between the registers of the two halves of the sign stresses that status of the sign as substitute, proxy, stand-in, for an absent referent. It insists, that is, on the literal meaning of the prefix /re/ in the word *representation*, drawing attention to the way the sign works away from, or in the aftermath of, the thing to which it refers.

This grounding of the terms of representation on absence—the making of absence the very condition of the representability of the sign—alerts us to the way the notion of the sign-as-label is a perversion of the operations of the sign. For the label merely doubles an already material presence by giving it its name. But the sign, as a function of absence rather than presence, is a coupling of signifier and immaterial concept in relation to which (as in the Frege/Russell/Wittgenstein notion of the proper name) there may be no referent at all (and thus no *thing* on which to affix the label).

This structural condition of absence is essential to the operations of the sign within Picasso's collage. As just one from among the myriad possible examples, we can think of the appearance of the two *f*-shaped violin soundholes that are inscribed on the surface of work after work from 1912–14. The semantic interpretation of these *f*s is that they simply signify the presence of the musical instrument; that is, they label a given plane of the collage-assembly with the term "violin." But there is almost no case from among these collages in which the two *f*s mirror each other across the plane surface. Time and again their inscription involves a vast disparity between the two letters, one being bigger and often thicker than the other. With this simple, but very emphatic, size difference, Picasso composes the sign, not of violin, but of foreshortening: of the differential size within a single surface due to its rotation into depth. And because the inscription of the *f*s takes place within the collage assembly and thus on the most rigidly flattened and frontalized of planes, "depth" is thus written on the very place from which it is— within the presence of the collage—most absent. It is *this* experience of inscription that guarantees these forms the status of signs.

What Picasso does with these *f*s to compose a sign of space as the condition of physical rotation, he does with the application of newsprint to construct the sign of space as penetrable or transparent. It is the perceptual disintegration of the fine-type of the printed page into a sign for the broken color with which painting (from Rembrandt to Seurat) represents atmosphere, that Picasso continually exploits. In so doing, he inscribes transparency on the very element of the collage's fabric that is most reified and opaque: its planes of newspaper.

Pablo Picasso. Glass and Violin. *1912.*

If one of the formal strategies that develops from collage, first into synthetic and then into late cubism, is the insistence of figure/ground reversal and the continual transposition between negative and positive form, this formal resource derives from collage's command of the structure of signification: no positive sign without the eclipse or negation of its material referent. The extraordinary contribution of collage is that it is the first instance within the pictorial arts of anything like a systematic exploration of the conditions of representability entailed by the sign.

From this notion of absence as one of the preconditions of the sign, one can begin to see the objections to the kind of game that literalizes the labels of cubist collages, giving us the "real" name of the wine marked by EAU or the newspaper by JOUR. Because the use of word-fragments is not the sprinkling of nicknames on the surfaces of these works, but rather the marking of the name itself with that condition of incompleteness or absence which secures for the sign its status as *re*presentation.

The second of Saussure's conditions for the operation of the sign turns not so much on absence as on difference. *"In language there are only differences,"*

Pablo Picasso. Violin. *1912. (Daix cat. no. 524.) (Left.)*
Violin Hung on a Wall. *1913? (Daix cat. no. 573.)*
(Right.)

Saussure lectured. "Even more important: a difference generally implies positive terms between which the difference is set up; but in language there are only differences *without positive terms*."[22] This declaration of the diacritical nature of the sign establishes it as a term whose meaning is never an absolute, but rather a choice from a set of possibilities, with meaning determined by the very terms *not* chosen. As a very simple illustration of meaning as this function of difference (rather than "positive identification") we might think of the traffic-light system where red means "stop" only in relation to an alternative of green as "go."

In analyzing the collage elements as a system of signs, we find not only the operations of absence but also the systematic play of difference. A single collage element can function simultaneously to compose the sign of atmosphere or luminosity and of closure or edge. In the 1913 *Violin and Fruit*, for example, a piece of newsprint, its fine type yielding the experience of tone, reads as "transparency" or "luminosity." In the same work the single patch of wood-grained paper

22.   Ferdinand de Saussure, *Course in General Linguistics*, trans. Wade Baskin, New York, McGraw-Hill, p. 120.

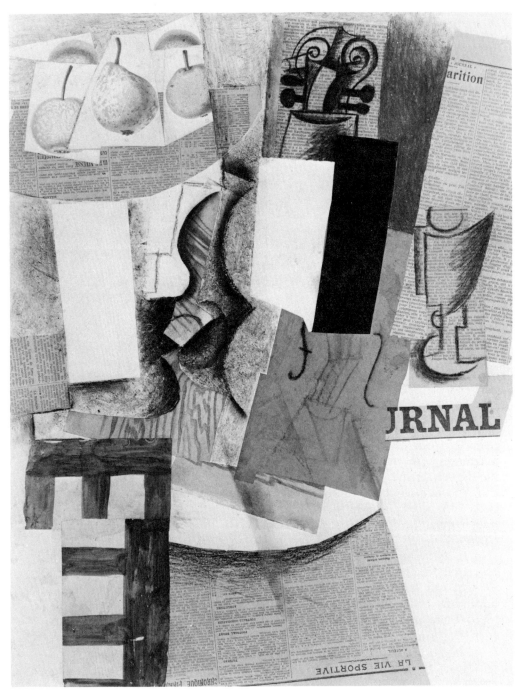

Pablo Picasso. Compote Dish with Fruit, Violin, and Glass. *1912. (Daix cat. no. 530.)*

ambiguously allocated to table and/or musical instrument composes the sign for open, as opposed to closed form. Yet the piece of wood graining terminates in a complex contour that produces the closed silhouette of a neighboring form. And the transparent colorism of the newsprint hardens into opaque line at the definitiveness of its edges. In the great, complex cubist collages, each element is fully diacritical, instantiating both line and color, closure and openness, plane and recession. Each signifier thus yields a matched pair of formal signifieds. Thus if the elements of cubist collage do establish sets of predicates, these are not limited to the properties of objects. They extend to the differential calculus at the very heart of the formal code of painting. What is systematized in collage is not so much the forms of a set of studio paraphernalia, but the very system of form.[23]

That form cannot be separated from Picasso's meditation on the inner workings of the sign—at least as it operates within the pictorial field—is a function of the combined formal/significatory status of the most basic element of collage. For it is the affixing of the collage piece, one plane set down on another, that is the center of collage as a signifying system. That plane, glued to its support, enters the work as the literalization of depth, actually resting "in front of" or "on top of" the field or element it now partially obscures. But this very act of literalization opens up the field of collage to the play of representation. For the supporting ground that is obscured by the affixed plane resurfaces in a miniaturized facsimile in the collage element itself. The collage element obscures the master plane only to represent that plane in the form of a depiction. If the element is the literalization of figure against field, it is so as a figure of the field it must literally occlude.

The collage element as a discrete plane is a bounded figure; but as such it is a figure of a bounded field—a figure of the very bounded field which it enters the ensemble only to obscure. The field is thus constituted inside itself as a figure of its own absence, an index of a material presence now rendered literally invisible. The collage element performs the occultation of one field in order to introject the figure of a new field, but to introject it *as* figure—a surface that is the image of eradicated surface. It is this eradication of the original surface and the reconstitution of it through the figure of its own absence that is the master term of the entire condition of collage as a system of signifiers.

The various resources for the visual illusion of spatial presence becomes the ostentatious subject of the collage-signs. But in "writing" this presence, they guarantee its absence. Collage thus effects the representation of representation. This goes well beyond the analytic cubist dismemberment of illusion into its constituent elements. Because collage no longer retains these elements; it signifies or represents them.

What collage achieves, then, is a metalanguage of the visual. It can talk

23. This and the next six paragraphs are adopted from my "Re-Presenting Picasso," *Art in America*, vol. 68, no. 10 (December 1980), 91–96.

about space without employing it; it can figure the figure through the constant superimposition of grounds; it can speak in turn of light and shade through the subterfuge of a written text. This capacity of "speaking about" depends on the ability of each collage element to function as the material signifier for a signified that is its opposite: a presence whose referent is an absent meaning, meaningful only in its absence. As a system, collage inaugurates a play of differences which is both about and sustained by an absent origin: the forced absence of the original plane by the superimposition of another plane, effacing the first in order to represent it. Collage's very fullness of form is grounded in this forced impoverishment of the ground—a ground both supplemented and supplanted.

It is often said that the genius of collage, its modernist genius, is that it heightens—not diminishes—the viewer's experience of the ground, the picture surface, the material support of the image; as never before, the ground—we are told—forces itself on our perception. But in collage, in fact, the ground is literally masked and riven. It enters our experience not as an object of perception, but as an object of discourse, of *re*presentation. Within the collage system all of the other perceptual données are transmuted into the absent objects of a group of signs.

It is here that we can see the opening of the rift between collage as system and modernism proper. For collage operates in direct opposition to modernism's search for perceptual plenitude and unimpeachable self-presence. Modernism's goal is to objectify the formal constituents of a given medium, making these, beginning with the very ground that is the origin of their existence, the objects of vision. Collage problematizes that goal, by setting up discourse in place of presence, a discourse founded on a buried origin, a discourse fueled by that absence. The nature of this discourse is that it leads ceaselessly through the maze of the polar alternatives of painting displayed as system. And this system is inaugurated through the loss of an origin that can never be objectified, but only represented.

> *The power of tradition can preserve no art in life that no longer is the expression of its time. One may also speak of a formal decay in art, that is, a death of the feeling for form. The significance of individual parts is no longer understood—likewise, the feeling for relationships.*
>
> —Heinrich Wölfflin

We are standing now on the threshold of a postmodernist art, an art of a fully problematized view of representation, in which to name (represent) an object may not necessarily be to call it forth, for there may be no (original) object. For this postmodernist notion of the originless play of the signifier we could use the term *simulacrum.*[24] But the whole structure of postmodernism has its proto-history in those investigations of the representational system of absence that we can only now recognize as the contemporaneous alternative to modernism. Picasso's collage was an extraordinary example of this proto-history, along with Klee's pedagogical art of the 1920s in which representation is deliberately characterized as absence.

At the very same moment when Picasso's collage becomes especially pertinent to the general terms and conditions of postmodernism, we are witnessing the outbreak of an aesthetics of autobiography, what I have earlier called an art history of the proper name. That this maneuver of finding an exact (historical) referent for every pictorial sign, thereby fixing and limiting the play of meaning, should be questionable with regard to art in general is obvious. But that it should be applied to Picasso in particular is highly objectionable, and to collage—the very system inaugurated on the indeterminacy of the referent, and on absence—is grotesque. For it is collage that raises the investigation of the impersonal workings of pictorial form, begun in analytical cubism, onto another level: the *impersonal* operations of language that are the subject of collage.

In his discussion of classic collage, Daix repeatedly stresses the depersonalization of Picasso's drawing in these works, his use of preexistent, industrialized elements (which Daix goes so far as to call *readymade*), and his mechanization of the pictorial surfaces—in order to insist on the objective status of this art of language, this play of signs.[25] Language (in the Saussurian sense of *langue*) is what is at stake in Daix's reference to the readymade and the impersonal: that is, language as a synchronic repertory of terms into which each individual must assimilate himself, so that from the point of view of structure, a speaker does not so much speak, as he is spoken by, language. The linguistic structure of signs "speaks" Picasso's collages, and in the signs' burgeoning and transmuting play *sense* may transpire even in the absence of *reference*.

The aesthetics of the proper name involves more than a failure to come to terms with the structure of representation, although that failure at this particular juncture of history is an extremely serious one. The aesthetics of the proper name is erected specifically on the grave of form.[26]

One of the pleasures of form—held at least for a moment at some distance from reference—is its openness to multiple imbrication in the work, and thus its hospitableness to polysemy. It was the new critics—that group of determined "formalists"—who gloried in the ambiguity and multiplicity of reference made available by the play of poetic form.

24. *Simulacrum* is a term used by both Jean Baudrillard and Guy de Bord.
25. Daix, *Picasso: The Cubist Years*, pp. 132-137.
26. The passage from Heinrich Wölfflin, cited at the beginning of this section, which faces the possibility of the "death of the feeling for form," is taken from Wölfflin's unpublished journals. For that passage, as for its translation, I am indebted to Joan Hart and her PhD dissertation *Heinrich Wölfflin*, University of California, Berkeley, 1981.

For the art historians of the proper name, form has become so devalued as a term (and suspect as an experience), that it simply cannot be a resource for meaning. Each of the studies on Picasso-via-the-proper-name begins by announcing the insufficiencies of an art history of style, of form. Because Rosenblum's essay on cubist typography was written a decade ago, it therefore opens by paying lip-service to the importance of a formal reading of cubism, modestly describing its own area of investigation as "a secondary aspect," a matter of "additional interpretations that would enrich, rather than deny, the formal ones."[27] But Rosenblum's simple semantics of the proper name does not enrich the forms of cubist collage; it depletes and impoverishes them. By giving everything a name, it strips each sign of its special modality of meaning: its capacity to represent the conditions of representation. The deprecation of the formal, the systematic, is now much more open in what Rosenblum has to say about method. "Certainly the formalist approach to the 19th century seems to me to have been exhausted a long time ago," he recently told two graduate-student interviewers. "It's just too boring . . . it's so stale that I can't mouth those words anymore."[28]

This petulant "boredom" with form is emblematic of a dismissal that is widespread among historians as well as critics of art. With it has come a massive misreading of the processes of signification and a reduction of the visual sign to an insistent mouthing of proper names.

Washington, D.C., 1980

27.   Rosenblum, p. 49.
28.   In *The Rutgers Art Review*, I (January 1980), p. 73.

To describe Giacometti's *Invisible Object* as "a young girl with knees half-bent as though offering herself to the beholder (a pose suggested to the sculptor by the attitude once assumed by a little girl in his native land)" is to participate in the work of rewriting his beginnings that Giacometti himself started in the 1940s. But this cooperation on the part of Michel Leiris, as he constructed the text for the sculptor's 1951 exhibition catalogue, placing *Invisible Object* in the service of a simple transparency to the observable world, is an expression of the ruptures and realignments that were transforming postwar Paris.[1] For this description is a slap in the face of André Breton.

Who can forget the magisterial example through which Breton opens the world of *L'amour fou* onto the strange but impressive workings of objective chance? Giacometti and Breton go to the flea market where each one is "claimed" by a seemingly useless object that each is impelled, as though against his will, to buy. Giacometti's purchase was a sharply angled, warriorlike mask, for which neither he nor Breton could determine the exact, original use.[2] However, the point of the example was not the object's initial but its ultimate destination. This, according to Breton's account, was in the service of resolving the conflicts paralyzing Giacometti as he attempted to bring parts of *Invisible Object* into focus. The head, particularly, had resisted integration with the rest of the work, and it was to this problem that the mask seemed to address itself. "The purpose of the mask's intervention," wrote Breton, "seemed to be to help Giacometti overcome his indecision in this regard. We should note that here the finding of the object strictly serves the same function as that of a dream, in that it frees the individual from paralyzing emotional scruples, comforts him, and makes him understand that the obstacle he thought was insurmountable has been cleared."[3] In Breton's account, then, the world of real objects has

1.   Michel Leiris, "Pierres pour un Alberto Giacometti," *Brisées*, Paris, Mercure de France, 1966, p. 149.
2.   André Breton, *L'Amour fou*, Paris, Gallimard, 1937, pp. 40-57. This was originally published as "L'équation de l'objet," *Documents 34*, no. 1 (June 1934), 17-24.
3.   Breton, *Documents 34*, 20.

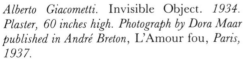

Alberto Giacometti. Invisible Object. *1934. Plaster, 60 inches high. Photograph by Dora Maar published in André Breton,* L'Amour fou, *Paris, 1937.*

Iron Mask. *Photograph by Man Ray published in André Breton,* L'Amour fou, *Paris, 1937.*

Figure. Bougainville, Solomon Islands. Painted wood, 69 inches high. Museum für Völkerkunde, Basel.

nothing to do with an art of mimesis; the objects are in no sense models for the sculptor's work. The world is instead a great reserve against which to trace the workings of the unconscious, the litmus paper that makes it possible to read the corrosiveness of desire. Without the mask, the dream, Giacometti could no more have finished *Invisible Object* than Breton, without his own *trouvaille* from the market, could have entered the written world of *L'amour fou*.

But the little Swiss girl of Giacometti's later recollection (and Leiris's account) has nothing to do with this key example of the marvelous and objective chance. By serving as a direct, real-world model for a work of art, the little Swiss girl withdraws *Invisible Object* from the orbit of surrealism and places it in the postwar realm of Giacometti's studio, as he notoriously strained, month after month, through trial and retrial, to catch the likeness of the model posed in front of him.[4] Recontextualizing the work, setting it in relation to a new group of friends and allies, like Sartre and Genet, Leiris's account draws it closer to the problematic of *The Phenomenology of Perception* and further from that of *Les vases communicants*.[5]

This a-chronicity is, of course, unacceptable to the historian, and thus Reinhold Hohl, the leading scholar of Giacometti's work, does not even mention the memory of the Swiss child in discussing this masterpiece of the sculptor's prewar career. But then Breton's story is, for Hohl, equally suspect. "Contrary to Breton's account," he begins, "that a mysterious object found at the flea market (it was, in fact, the prototype for an iron protection mask designed by the French Medical Corps in the First World War) had helped the artist to find his forms, Giacometti had borrowed the stylized human shapes from a Solomon Islands *Seated Statue of a Deceased Woman* which he had seen at the Ethnological Museum in Basel, and had combined them with other elements of Oceanic art, such as the bird-like demon of death."[6]

Despite the certainty of his tone, Hohl's evidence for this connection is both scant and indirect. In 1963 Giacometti had spoken to an interviewer of a reconstructed Oceanic house installed in the Basel Museum.[7] Since the Solomon Islands figure had been displayed in the same gallery early in the 1930s, when it was brought back to Switzerland from the expedition that had plucked it from the South Seas, Hohl could at least assume Giacometti's knowledge of the

---

4.   One of these sitters wrote a detailed account of this process, observing that "inasmuch as it was then expressed in the particular acts of painting and posing, there were elements of the sado-masochistic in our relationship . . . [although] it would have been difficult to determine exactly what acts were sadistic and/or masochistic on whose side and why." James Lord, *A Giacometti Portrait*, New York, The Museum of Modern Art, 1965, p. 36.
5.   See, Simone de Beauvoir, *La Force de l'Age*, Paris, Gallimard, 1960, pp. 409–503.
6.   Reinhold Hohl, *Alberto Giacometti*, New York, The Solomon Guggenheim Museum, 1974, p. 22. See also Hohl, *Alberto Giacometti*, London, Thames and Hudson, 1972, p. 298, fn. 15.
7.   Jean Clay, *Visages de l'Art moderne*, Paris, Editions Rencontre, 1969, p. 160.

Alberto Giacometti. The Couple. *1926. Bronze,
25 inches high. The Alberto Giacometti Foundation, Kunsthaus, Zürich.*

object.[8] The detail that lends the greatest credence to Hohl's claim is the schematic, railinglike support for the half-seated figure, a construction that is entirely characteristic of this type of statue and is not commonly found elsewhere.[9] Since part of the power of the pose of Giacometti's sculpture comes from the enigmatic relation between the half-kneeling posture and the structural elements that seem to contain it — a flat plate against the shins in front of the figure and the peculiar scaffolding behind it — and since this construction is not "natural" to a model posed in a studio, the probability was always that its source was in another work of art. Because of the railing, because of the posture, because of the forward jut of the head and the articulation of the breasts, the Solomon Islands statue of Hohl's nomination seems a logical candidate.[10]

Behind Hohl's assertion of this statue as the source for *Invisible Object* there is a whole reservoir of knowledge about the role of primitive art in the sculptor's work in the years leading up to 1934. Primitivism had been central to Giacometti's success in freeing himself not only from the classical sculptural tradition but also from the cubist constructions that had appeared in the early 1920s as the only logical alternative. Quite precisely, Giacometti's work matured as a function of its ability to invent in very close relation to primitive sources. Just two years after leaving Bourdelle's studio he was able to execute a figure on a major scale that was "his own" by virtue of belonging, quite profoundly, to African tribal art.

8.   The statue came to the museum from the 1929–30 expedition of Felix Speiser and was published in 1933 in *Führer durch das Museum für Völkerkunde Basel, Salomonen*, as figure 11 (*Totenstatue, Bougainville*), p. 21. In 1930 the art of the Solomon Islands was the focus of an essay in *Documents* that dealt with the visual and religious significance of its production. See Louis Clarke, "L'Art des Iles Salomon," *Documents* II, no. 5 (1930).
9.   See, for example, the *duka* figure in the British Museum, 1944, Oc.2.1177.
10.   Hohl publishes the Solomon Islands figure in his monograph (p. 291, figure 30) without the "railing," although this structural support appeared in the 1933 publication of the Basel Ethnological Museum. (Subsequent to this publication of the figure, the support bars were lost.) Instead Hohl postulates the influence of Egyptian statuary for the architectural elements of *Invisible Object* (Hohl, 1972, p. 300, fn. 34). William Rubin has suggested Sepik River spirit figures as another possible source for the structure behind the woman's body in Giacometti's sculpture. One of these, now in the Rietberg Museum (RMe 104), was in that part of the van der Heydt collection deposited in the Musée de l'Homme in 1933 and placed on display, where Giacometti may have seen it. (I owe this information to Philippe Peltier, who has generously shared with me his knowledge of the disposition of the great collections of Oceanic art of this period.) However, a vertical structure that either flanks the body or appears to contain it is also found in New Ireland *mallanggan*, an Oceanic type admired and collected by the surrealists. But neither the Sepik River nor the New Ireland sculptures relate morphologically to the smooth-surfaced, generalized anatomical style of *Invisible Object*. Evan Maurer suggests the presence of the Caroline Islands figural type on the basis of stylistic similarity and because one of Giacometti's drawings after Oceanic objects represents such a figure. See Maurer, "In Quest of the Myth: An Investigation of the Relationships between Surrealism and Primitivism," unpublished Ph.D. dissertation, University of Pennsylvania, 1974, p. 318. The Caroline Islands figural type, however, does not assume the bent-knee position that is so forceful in *Invisible Object*, nor is it supported by any structural adjunct.

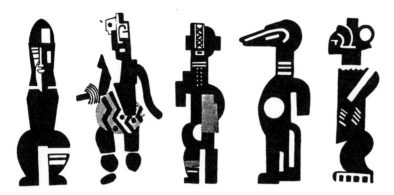

Fernand Léger. Sketch for Création du Monde.
Published in L'Esprit nouveau, *no. 18 (1924).*

The 1927 *Spoon Woman* goes beyond the applied use of the modish *style nègre* that was influencing everything from Art Deco furniture to Léger's theatrical curtains in the mid-1920s and which Giacometti had employed in his *The Couple* the year before.[11] The decorative application of tribalizing detail to a stylized, planar background is the formal strategy of what might be called Black Deco; it is this one finds in *The Couple*, giving the work its generalized character of the Africo-primitive in the absence of any specific sculptural source.[12] But moving toward a much deeper level of structural assimilation of African carved objects, *Spoon Woman* acknowledges the metaphor frequently put in place by Dan grain scoops, in which the bowl of the implement is likened to the lower part of the female seen as a receptacle, or pouch, or cavity.[13] Giacometti may have seen these spoons in the years before 1927. Six spoons from Paul Guillaume's collection were included in the massive exhibition of African and Oceanic art at the Musée des Arts Décoratifs in the winter of 1923–24.[14] By taking the metaphor and inverting it, so that "a spoon is like a woman" becomes "a woman is like a spoon," Giacometti was able to intensify the idea, and to universalize it by

11.   *Spoon Woman* is conventionally assigned to 1926 except in Hohl's monograph where, for reasons not argued, it is dated 1927. In following Hohl's dating, I am proposing the greater stylistic maturity, accomplishment, and thus later date of *Spoon Woman*, precisely on the basis of Giacometti's developing relationship to primitive sources. *The Couple*, on the other hand, seems to me to participate in the stylizations *à la nègre* that were widespread by the early 1920s. The sketches published, for example, by Léger in *L'Esprit Nouveau*, no. 18 (1924) as "personnages" for *La Création du monde*, manifest the same generalized overall shapes (trapezoidal, oval) for the body-as-a-whole, and use the same types of ornamental detail for the indications of anatomy. Sculptors like Miklos and Lambert-Rucki, within the context of Art Deco, were producing stylized "African" masks and figurative sculptures by 1925. The designer Pierre Legrain was producing elegant furniture for clients such as Jacques Doucet, modeled directly on seats and stools from tribal Africa. These were widely published during the period, cf; *Art et Décoration* I (1924), 182. It is this stylizing attitude toward the primitive source that *The Couple* participates in but *Spoon Woman* renounces.

generalizing the forms of the sometimes naturalistic African carvings toward a more prismatic abstraction. In forcing on the Dan model the image of the woman who is almost nothing but womb, Giacometti assimilated the formal elegance of the African object to the more brutish conception of stone-age fertility Venuses.[15]

With this celebration of the primal function of woman seen through a primitivized formal logic, Giacometti had assumed the most vanguard of positions. He found himself in concert with the agressive anti-Western stance of the visual avant-garde, given verbal form by, for example, Georges Henri Rivière, soon to be the assistant director of the Trocadéro, when he published a panegyric to archeology — "parricidal daughter of humanism" — in the initial volume of *Cahiers d'art*.[16] Opening with the bald statement that the miracle of Greek art had run its course, Rivière went on to say that if Louis Aragon and Jean Lurçat were now to go to Spain, unlike their fathers, their most urgent

12.   Previous attempts to assign a tribal, sculptural source for the female half of *The Couple* seem unconvincing on the basis of conceptual and morphological comparison. Maurer suggests a Mahongwe reliquary figure, Cowling proposes Makonde body shields (see Maurer, p. 316, and Elizabeth Nesbitt Cowling, "The Primitive Sources of Surrealism," unpublished M. A. thesis, London, the Courthault Institute, 1970, p. 46). But however unpersuasive the specific "source" might be, the suggestions put forward by these authors attest to their experience of the Africanizing character of the figures in *The Couple*. This quality makes suggestions of a Neolithic source for the work, put forward by other scholars, somewhat dubious. There is a strong compositional (but not conceptual) resemblance between the female figure of *The Couple* and one of the menhir figures from St. Sernan sur Rance, a work that figures in the illustrations of the Carnac Museum catalogue of 1927. This connection was first suggested by Stephanie Poley ("Alberto Giacomettis Umsetzung Archaischer Gestaltungsformen in Seinem Werk Zwischen 1925 und 1935," *Jahrbuch der Hamburger Kunstsammlungen* 22 [1977], 177) and later by Alan Wilkenson (*Gauguin to Moore, Primitivism in Modern Sculpture*, Art Gallery of Toronto, 1981, p. 222). There are other examples of the effect of prehistoric images and objects on Giacometti's work, most obviously in the 1931 sculpture *The Caress* in which the splayed hand etched onto the surface mimics the "stencilled" palm prints of the caves. Interest in this detail from prehistoric painting is to be found everywhere in the 1920s, one famous example of which is the cover of Ozenfant's *Foundations of Modern Art* (1931). But in *The Couple* the prehistoric image, if it indeed functioned as a suggestion for the composition, has been converted into an evident *style nègre*.
13.   The Dan source was first suggested by Jean Laude, *La Peinture française (1905–1914) et l'art nègre*, Paris Klincksieck, 1968, p. 13.
14.   The *Exposition de l'art indigène des colonies d'Afrique et d'Océanie*, Musée des Arts Décoratifs (November 1923–January 27, 1924) was organized by André Level. Among the collections drawn upon for the exhibition were those of Félix Fénéon, André Lhote, Patrick-Henry Bruce, Paul Guillaume, and of course the Trocadéro. Guillaume contributed 79 objects, of which six were spoons listed as "Côte d'Ivoire." Jean-Louis Paudrat believes that these must have included Dan objects. Two other spoon/women that Giacometti could have seen were: the Lega spoon in Carl Einstein, *La Sculpture africaine*, Paris, Editions Crès, 1922, plate 42; and the utensil illustrated in plate 3 of Paul Guillaume and Thomas Munro, *Primitive Negro Sculpture*, New York, Harcourt, Brace, 1926. The French edition of this book appeared in 1929.
15.   See the copy Giacometti made of the Venus von Laussel, published in Luigi Carluccio, *A Sketchbook of Interpretive Drawings*, New York, Harry N. Abrams, 1968, plate 2. It is difficult to date these drawings, but this page also contains the sketch-idea for Giacometti's *Trois personnages dehors* of 1929.

Jean Lambert-Rucki. Two Masks, *1924.*
Wood.

Alberto Giacometti. Spoon Woman. *1926.*
Bronze, 56 inches high. The Solomon Guggenheim
Museum, New York.

Spoon. Wobe. Ivory Coast. Wood. Musée de l'Homme, Paris.

Spoon. Dan. Liberia or Ivory Coast. Wood. Musée de l'Homme, Paris.

goal would not be the Prado, but the caves of Altamira. *Spoon Woman*, contemporary with this statement, is also its confirmation.

But *Spoon Woman* is something else as well. It is what another wing of the intellectual vanguard would view as "soft" primitivism, a primitivism gone formal and therefore gutless. Indeed, to associate *Spoon Woman* with *Cahiers d'art* is to place it within the context of a formalizing conception of the primitive that we hear, for example, behind the praise Christian Zervos bestowed on Brancusi as the most successful sculptor of the postwar period. Since the great influx of black culture, Zervos wrote in 1929. "Brancusi has explored all the vistas that the Negros have opened up to him, and which . . . permitted him to achieve pure form. . . ."[17] *Spoon Woman* participates in both the sense of scale and the quality of formal reduction that Giacometti achieved, doubtless through knowledge of Brancusi's work.

One year before Giacometti made this sculpture, Paul Guillaume published a book that represented the extreme of the movement to aestheticize primitive art.[18] *Primitive Negro Sculpture*, conceived under the aegis of Albert Barnes, written at the Barnes Foundation, and published in English, acknowledges as its only real precedent an analysis of the formal structure of African art

16.   Georges Henri Rivière, "Archéologismes," *Cahiers d'art*, no. 7 (1926), 177.
17.   Christian Zervos, "Notes sur la sculpture contemporaine," *Cahiers d'art*, no. 10 (1929), 465.
18.   Guillaume and Munro, *Primitive Negro Sculpture*.

by Roger Fry.[19] Because of Guillaume's prominence in the art world the book would undoubtedly have been well known in Paris even before its translation into French, and indeed, one of its illustrations may have reinforced Giacometti's conception of the woman/spoon.

Maintaining that every work of African art can be understood as the solution to a formal problem, *Primitive Negro Sculpture* presents each of its objects as "a rhythmic, varied sequence of some theme in mass, line, or surface," describing the way the geometrically conceived elements are first articulated and then unified by the plastic genius of the primitive sculptor. But what is insisted upon throughout the text is the continuous presence of a will to art, an aesthetic drive that is understood to be originary, or primal. Preceding all ideas, religious or otherwise, this instinct is the joint possession of children of all races as well as those "children" of the human race: primitive men and women. It is thus the Western child's creative play with paints, clay, and crayons that gives us access to the processes that drive primitive art. In concluding with the certainty that "it is not hard to imagine, then, the continuous development of negro art out of the free, naïve play of the aesthetic impulse," Guillaume joins the aestheticizing interests of the art world to the most euphoric position of developmental psychology as that was being enunciated in the late 1920s.[20] He places himself in accord with the psychologist G. H. Luquet.

Luquet's conviction that the art of children and the art of primitive man form a single category, one which contests the values of "civilized" art, was undoubtedly what interested Georges Bataille and drew him to review Luquet's book in the magazine *Documents*.[21] At the point, however, where Bataille sharply diverges from Luquet's benign view of the forces at work behind the development of primitive figuration, we can start to take the measure of the attack launched by this wing of the radical avant-garde on the art-for-art's-sake view of primitivism. Since, as I will argue, Bataille's attitude had a great deal to do with shaping Giacometti's ultimate conception and use of primitive material, it is worth attending to his criticism of Luquet.

Luquet presents the child as having *no* initial figurative intentions but rather as taking pure pleasure in manifesting his own presence by dragging his dirty fingers along walls or covering white sheets of paper with scrawls. Having made these marks, the child later begins to invest parts of them with representational value. With this "reading" of the lines he has made, the child is even-

19.   Roger Fry, "Negro Sculpture," *Vision and Design*, New York, Brentano's, 1920.

20.   As one of many examples of the aestheticizing discourse that analyzed primitive art as just one moment of the collective representation of Art-in-general, and thus of the aesthetic impulse common to all humanity, see A. Ozenfant, *Foundations of Modern Art: The Ice Age to 1931*, London, 1931 (French publication, 1928).

21.   G. H. Luquet, *L'Art primitif*, Paris, Gaston Doin, 1930. For Bataille's review, see "L'Art primitif," *Documents*, II, no. 7 (1930), 389–97. Collected in Georges Bataille, *Oeuvres Complètes*, Paris, Gallimard, 1970, vol. I, pp. 247–254.

tually able to repeat the images voluntarily. Since the basis of the interpretation is enormously schematic, what is involved is the connection of a mark with the idea of an object, a process that has to do with conception and not with resemblance. For this reason Luquet calls primitive figuration *intellectual realism*, reserving the term *visual realism* for the Western adult's preoccupation with mimesis.

Luquet's presentation of the development of prehistoric cave painting follows the same schema as that of the present-day child: random marking changes gradually to intentional patterning, which in turn gives rise to a figurative reading. Resemblance to external objects having been first "recognized" within the nonfigurative patterns, it can be elaborated and perfected over time.

In Luquet's program, then, an absolute freedom and pleasure initiates the impulse to draw; it is this instinct, not the desire to render reality, that is primal. On top of this foundation a procedure is gradually built for adjusting the mark to the conditions of representation, and within this a "system" of figuration develops with consistent characteristics over the entire domain of primitive art, whether that be the drawings of children, graffittists, aborigines, or peasants. Characteristics like the profiles of faces endowed with two eyes and two ears, or the rendering of houses and bodies as transparent in order to display their contents, or the free combination of plan and elevation, are what remain unchanged through the practice of "intellectual realism." In Luquet's scheme, knowledge is thus generously added to pleasure.

Of course, the chronology of prehistoric art does not support Luquet's cheerful progressivism. The caves of Lascaux, with their astonishing naturalism, precede the much cruder renderings of later periods. Yet if Bataille draws his reader's attention to this obvious flaw in Luquet's scheme, it is not for reasons of historical accuracy but in order to assert something that had already become a staple of his thinking throughout his editorship of *Documents*, and was to continue beyond. What Bataille points to is the unequal mode of representation, within the same period, of animals and men. "The reindeer, the bison, or the horses," Bataille attests, "are represented with such perfect detail, that if we were able to see as scrupulously faithful images of the men themselves, the strangest period of the avatars of humanity would immediately cease being the most inaccessible. But the drawings and sculptures that are charged with representing the Aurignacians themselves are almost all *informe* and much less human than those that represent the animals; others like the Hottentot Venus are ignoble caricatures of the human form. This opposition is the same in the Magdalenian period."[22]

---

22.   *Oeuvres Complètes*, Vol. I, p. 251. *Informe* translates as "unformed," although Bataille intends the word to undo the Aristotelian distinction between form and matter.

It is because "this crude and distorting art has been reserved for the human figure," that Bataille insists on its willfulness, on its status as a kind of primal vandalism wrought on the images of men. Indeed, Bataille wishes to substitute destructiveness for Luquet's serene view of the pleasure principle at work at the origin of the impulse to draw. The child's marking on walls, his scrawls on paper, all proceed from a wish to destroy or mutilate the support. In each subsequent stage of the development charted by Luquet, Bataille sees the enactment of new desire to alter and deform what is there before the subject: "Art, since it is incontestably art, proceeds in this way by successive destructions. Thus insofar as it liberates instincts, these are sadistic."[23]

The term that Bataille finds to generalize the phenomenon of sadism in both children's art and that of the caves is *alteration*, and this word, in the precision of its ambivalence, is characteristic of Bataille. Alteration derives from the Latin *alter*, which by opening equally onto a change of state and a change (or advancement) of time, contains the divergent significations of *devolution* and *evolution*. Bataille points out that alteration describes the decomposition of cadavers as well as "the passage to a perfectly heterogeneous state corresponding to . . . the *tout autre*, that is, the sacred, realized for example by a ghost."[24] Alteration — which Bataille uses to discribe the primal impulse of man's self-representation — thus becomes a concept that simultaneously leads downward and upward: like *altus* and *sacer*, the double-directed, primal concepts that interested Freud. The primal, or originary, is therefore irresolvably diffuse — fractured by an irremediable doubleness at the root of things that was, in his closeness to Nietzsche's thought, dear to Bataille. In its confounding of the logic that maintains terms like high and low, or base and sacred as polar opposites, it is this play of the contradictory that allows one to think the truth that Bataille never tired of demonstrating: that violence has historically been lodged at the heart of the sacred; that to be genuine, the very thought of the creative must simultaneously be an experience of death; and that it is impossible for any moment of true intensity to exist apart from a cruelty that is equally extreme.[25]

Bataille is well aware that the civilized Westerner might wish to maintain himself in a state of ignorance about the presence of violence within ancient religious practice, so that he either does not notice or does not reflect upon the

23.   *Oeuvres Complètes*, vol. I, p. 253.
24.   *Ibid.*, p. 251. This notion of the double sense of the root word of a given concept takes into account Freud's interest in this kind of etymological study in which precisely *altus* and *sacer* are used as examples. See Freud's "Antithetical Sense of Primal Words," published in 1910 in the *Jahrbuch für psychoa- und psychopath. Forschungen*, vol. I, as a review of Karl Abel's *Gegensinn der Urworte*. For Bataille's knowledge of this text, see Denis Hollier, *La Prise de la Concorde,* Paris, Gallimard, 1974, p. 240.
25.   Obviously Bataille was dependent upon the ethnological data available to him at the time, from which he made his own particular selection in order to support his critique of philosophy. For a discussion of Bataille's connection to ethnography in the 1920s and '30s see Alfred Métraux, "Rencontre avec les ethnologues," *Critique,* no. 195–196 (1963), 677–684.

significance of the deformed anthropoids that appear in the caves, or so that he aestheticizes the whole of African art. In the first essay that he wrote on primitive civilization Bataille remarked this resistance on the part of scholars to acknowledge what is hideous and cruel in the depiction of the gods of certain peoples. The text, included in a collection of ethnological essays occasioned by the first major exhibition of pre-Columbian art in Paris (1928), was called "L'Amérique disparue," and in it Bataille tried to understand the reality behind the representation of the Aztec gods, depicted as caricatural, monstrous, and deformed.[26] Although his knowledge of pre-Columbian culture was still rather superficial, his analysis proved to be extremely prescient, according to the ethnologist Alfred Métraux as he looked back on this early performance of Bataille's.[27] For what Bataille could read into these images was the presence of malign and dissembling gods, trickster gods to whom was dedicated a religious fervor in which pitiless cruelty combined with black humor to create a culture of delirium: "Doubtless, a bloodier eccentricity was never conceived by human madness: crimes continually committed in broad sunlight for the sole satisfaction of god-ridden nightmares, of terrifying ghosts! The priests' cannibalistic repasts, the ceremonies with cadavers and rivers of blood—more than one historical happening evokes the stunning debaucheries described by the illustrious Marquis de Sade."[28] Broadening the reference from Mexico to de Sade was characteristic of the intellectual field common to 1920s ethnological thinking (particularly in the circle around Marcel Mauss), with its focus on the violent performance of the sacred in Africa, Oceania, and the Americas.

But in speaking of the Aztecs' insatiable thirst for blood, of their sacrificial practices in which the living victim's heart was cut out of his body and held up, still palpitating, by the priest at the altar, Bataille stresses the "astonishingly joyous character of these horrors." As in the case of the concept of alteration, the practice of sacrifice by the Aztecs allows the double condition of the sacred

26.　In Jean Babelon, *L'Art précolumbien*, Paris, Editions Beaux-Arts, 1930. This collection of essays was to accompany the 1928 *Exposition de l'art de l'amérique*, in the Pavillon de Marsan and included texts by Alfred Métraux and Paul Rivet, among others. Pre-Columbian art was seen at the time as occupying a continuous field with that of Africa and Oceania; for example, in the text "L'Art nègre" that Zervos wrote to introduce a special issue of *Cahiers d'art* (no. 7–8, 1927), he speaks of "the attachment of our generation for *art nègre*" specifying, "That is what was produced twenty years ago with Negro sculpture, it is what is produced right now with Melanesian and pre-Columbian art" (p. 230). On this same subject Breton wrote: "The very particular interest that painters at the beginning of the 20th century had for African art, today it is American art from before the conquest that, along with Oceanic art, exercises an elective influence on artists" (Breton, *Mexique*, Paris, Renous and Colle, 1939, preface). The Breton and Eluard collections auctioned in 1931 were given over to pre-Columbian art to almost as great an extent as to Oceanic objects. The 1936 exhibition of surrealist objects at the Charles Ratton Gallery included American objects along with those of Oceania; the catalogue specifies these American works as Eskimo, Peruvian, and pre-Columbian.
27.　Métraux, "Rencontre avec les ethnologues."
28.　Bataille, *Oeuvres Complètes*, vol. I, p. 152.

to be experienced. "Mexico was not only the most streaming of the human slaughterhouses," Bataille writes in comparing Aztec culture with that of the Incas, which he found bureaucratic and dour, "it was also a rich city, a veritable Venice of canals and bridges, of decorated temples and beautiful flower gardens over all."[29] It was a culture of blood that bred both flowers and flies.

If Giacometti had begun in 1926 and 1927 with a conception of primitive art inscribed on the Luquet side of the ledger, he had moved by 1930, the year "L'Amérique disparue" was published, to that of Bataille's. For in the intervening years, Giacometti had been assimilated into the group that made up *Documents*.

In 1928, the year after he finished *Spoon Woman*, Giacometti showed his work for the first time. What he exhibited were two of the plaquelike heads and figures he had made that year, objects that carried the blank frontality of *Spoon Woman* to a new simplicity and elegance. In accordance with the direction implied in the aestheticized view of primitivism, preclassical objects now became his models for abstracting and reducing his form. The presence of these models within his practice was immediately apparent to the viewers of this work. In one of the earliest commentaries on Giacometti's sculpture, Zervos spoke of its connection to Cycladic art.[30]

On the basis of these two exhibited objects, André Masson asked to meet Giacometti. Immediately thereafter began the sculptor's initiation into the group that included Masson, Desnos, Artaud, Queneau, Leiris, and Bataille, the group that was known as the dissident surrealists, for whom the intellectual center was *Documents*. Since three of the editors of *Documents* were Bataille, who was deeply committed to the development of ethnographic theory as that was being formulated at the Ecole des Hautes Etudes in the seminars of Marcel Mauss,[31] Michel Leiris, who had become an ethnologist by 1931, and Carl Einstein, who had published his study of primitive sculpture by 1915, the commitment of the magazine to this subject is obvious. Giacometti's close and lasting friendship with Leiris, which began at this moment, brought with it a relation to the details and theories not only of ethnography but of the uses to which it was being put by the *Documents* group.[32] In 1930, at the end of his initiation into

29.   *Ibid.*, p. 157.
30.   Zervos, "Notes sur la sculpture contemporaine," p. 472.
31.   For an account of the way Bataille's thought was shaped by Mauss, see Métraux, "Rencontre avec les ethnologues." Another discussion of this relationship is James Clifford's "On Ethnographic Surrealism," *Comparative Studies in Society and History*, XXIII (October 1981), 543–564.
32.   Hohl insists on Giacometti's knowledge and employment of the kind of precise ethnographic information about the contexts of tribal art that would have come to him easily through his connection with Leiris (Hohl, 1972, p. 79.). In an interview with the author (February 24, 1983), Leiris supplied no detailed information but agreed that Giacometti was present at discussions concerning ethnography held by the *Documents* group.

Alberto Giacometti. Suspended Ball.   Suspended Ball *(detail).*
1930–31. Plaster and metal, 24 by 14¼ by
13½ inches. The Alberto Giacometti
Foundation, Kunstmuseum, Basel.

Documents, Giacometti made *Suspended Ball*. A sculpture that was to cause a sensation among the orthodox surrealists, giving Giacometti instant access to Breton and Dali, a sculpture that set off the whole surrealist vogue for creating erotically charged objects, it was nonetheless a work that had much less to do with surrealism than it did with Bataille.[33]

Maurice Nadeau remembers the reactions originally triggered by *Suspended Ball*: "Everyone who saw this object functioning experienced a strong but indefinable sexual emotion relating to unconscious desires. This emotion was in no sense one of satisfaction, but one of disturbance, like that imparted by the irritating awareness of failure."[34] An erotic machine, *Suspended Ball* is, then, like

33.   Along with Miró and Arp, Giacometti exhibited in the autumn of 1930 at the Galerie Pierre. Georges Sadoul recalls, "At the end of 1930 I met Alberto Giacometti. He had just been admitted into the Surrealist group . . . In 1930 he introduced a new mode into Surrealism with his sculptures that were mobile objects. This launched the vogue of Surrealist objects with a symbolic or erotic function, the making of which became practically obligatory" (Cited in Hohl, 1972, p. 249). The date of Dali's "Objets à fonctionnement symbolique" (*Le Surréalisme au service de la révolution*, no. 3 [1931], 16–17), demonstrates this later attempt to absorb Giacometti's innovative work into the heart of the surrealist movement.
34.   Maurice Nadeau, *Histoire du Surréalisme*, Paris, Seuil, 1945, p. 176.

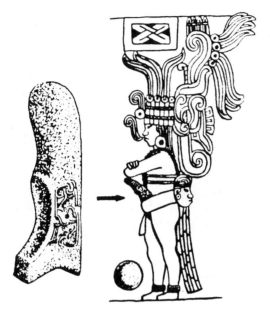

Ball-game player. Vega de Aparicio, Veracruz, Mexico. (Drawing adapted from a stone sculpture in the Museo Nacional de Antropologia, Mexico City.)

Duchamp's *Large Glass*, an apparatus for the disconnection of the sexes, the nonfulfillment of desire. But *Suspended Ball* is more explicitly sadistic than *The Bride Stripped Bare*. For the sliding action that visibly relates the sculpture's grooved sphere to its wedge-shaped partner suggests not only the act of caressing but that of cutting: recapitulating, for example, the stunning gesture from the opening of *Chien Andalou*, as a razor slices through an opened eye.[35]

In this double gesture incarnating love and violence simultaneously one can locate a fundamental ambiguity with regard to the sexual identity of the elements of Giacometti's sculpture. The wedge, acted upon by the ball, is in one reading its feminine partner, in another, distended and sharp, it is the phallic instrument of agression against the ball's vulnerable roundness: it is not only the razor from *Chien Andalou* but the bull's horn from Bataille's *l'Historie de l'OEil*, which penetrates the matador, killing him by ripping out his eye.[36]

35.   Bataille's article "l'OEil," *Documents*, no. 4 (1929) — the same issue that carried the first essay on Giacometti's work (Michel Leiris, "Alberto Giacometti," 209–210) — opens with a discussion of this image and lists the various screenings of *Chien Andalou* as the places where the image had been reproduced. Not only does Bataille's concentration on the theme of the eye carry forward his own preoccupations from *L'Histoire de L'OEil*, but through Marcel Griaule's article on the evil eye and its significance in primitive belief systems, published in this number as well, the link is once again forged between ethnographic analysis and modern thematic interests.
36.   In his article "La pointe à l'oeil d'Alberto Giacometti," *Cahiers du Musée National d'Art Moderne*, no. 11 (1983), 64–100), Jean Clair argues for the direct connection between Bataille's eroticized, phallic conception of the eye, as found in both *L'Histoire de l'Oeil* and the *Documents* material, and Giacometti's sculpture *Point to the Eye*. His discussion of this work turns, in part, on Bataille's notion of vision objectified at the limiting condition of the exorbited eye.

Alberto Giacometti. Circuit. *1931. Wood, 1⅞
by 18½ by 18½ inches. Collection
Henriette Gomès, Paris.*

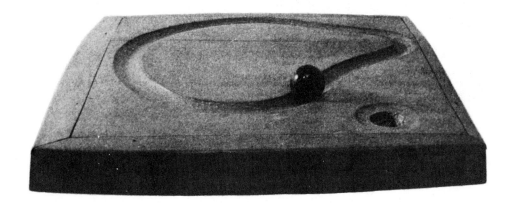

And the wedge is possibly a third substitute for the phallus, joined in yet
another way to the universe of sacred violence that had, by 1930, become the
shared interest of Giacometti and Bataille. The wedge is shaped like the palmette
stones of the ancient Mexican ballgame—wedge-shaped elements that were
thought to have been worn for protection by the nearly naked participants in a
game in which the ball could only be kept in play by being hit with the knees
and buttocks and in which the very names used for the game stressed the in-
strumentality of the buttocks (for example, from Molina's 1571 Nahua dictionary one finds, *ollama*: to play ball with the buttocks; and *olli*: certain gum of
medicinal trees of which they make balls with which they play with their buttocks).[37] Like everything else in the Mexico Bataille admired, the Toltec
ballgame was a combination of exuberance and cruelty, with accounts of
bloody wounds caused by the ball and deaths of the players on the courts. With
its use of the buttocks as a principle instrument of play, the game had a further
homoerotic overtone. If, as I am suggesting, the Mexican ballgame was a component in the formation of *Suspended Ball*—opening as the work does onto
Giacometti's immediately subsequent investigation of sculpture itself as a ball
court, or playing field, or gameboard, as in *Point to the Eye*, *Circuit*, and "*On ne*

37.   See Frans Blom, "The Maya Ball-Game Pok-Ta-Pok," *Middle American Papers*, Tulane
University, 1932. This essay published in the 1930s represents the level of ethnographic knowledge of the ballgame at the time we are here considering.

Alberto Giacometti. Point to the Eye. *1932.*
Wood and metal, 4 ¾ by 24 by 14 inches.
Musée National d'Art Moderne, Centre Georges
Pompidou, Paris.

Alberto Giacometti. Head. *1925. Plaster,*
12 ¼ inches high. Musée National d'Art
Moderne, Centre Georges Pompidou, Paris.

joue plus" (*No More Play*) — then a "third sex" must be added to the cycle of indeterminacy of the work's sexual signifiers.

    Giacometti's early sculpture had already demonstrated an interest in pre-
Columbian art, along with that of Africa and the Cyclades. Jacques Dupin,
whose study was completed during the sculptor's lifetime, reports that
Giacometti's early "exotic" sources were Africa, Oceania, and Mexico.[38] Two
works that bear obvious witness to this early Mexican connection are the
Crouching Man of 1926 and a possibly even earlier plaster *Head*; and third
sculpture, *Hour of the Traces* of 1930, permits a reading of more than an
aesthetic relationship to Mexico but rather a Bataille-like experience of the
ethos of Aztec culture. It is the imagery of "l'Amérique disparue" and the other
reports of Aztec culture published in *Documents* — the full series of which
Giacometti carefully guarded his entire lifetime[39] — that provides a possible
reading of *Hour of the Traces* as the ecstatic image of human sacrifice. For the
figure at the top of the work, whose rictus is either that of extreme ecstasy or
pain (or as Bataille would have it, both), appears posed on an altar below
which swings the form of a disembodied heart.[40]

38.   Jacques Dupin, *Alberto Giacometti*, Paris, Maeght, 1962, p. 88.
39.   Jacques Dupin told me that when he began work on his monograph on Giacometti, the
sculptor lent him his own carefully protected, full set of *Documents* to work from. For one of the
Documents articles on this subject, illustrated by codex representations of the victims and the places
of sacrifice, see Roger Hervé, "Sacrifices humains du Centre-Amérique," *Documents*, II, no. 4
(1930).
40.   *Cahiers d'Art*, no. 10 (1929), 456, reproduces a photograph of an Aztec pyramid topped by
an altar whose structure is suggestive for that of *l'Heure des traces*.

Hour of the Traces immediately preceded *Suspended Ball*. The two sculptures are structurally connected by virtue of their shared play with a pendant element swung from a cagelike support. Within the universe of ideas associated at that moment to Aztec culture, the sculptures may be thematically connected as well. But without any doubt they are both assimilable to Giacometti's fully elaborated accounts of his own thoughts of sadism and violence. Although first published in Breton's magazine, a text like "Hier, sables mouvants," with its fantasy of rape ("the whole forest rang with their cries and groans") and slaughter, has little to do with the notions of convulsive beauty authorized by surrealism.[41] Its relationship is to Georges Bataille, whose own writing and preoccupations seem to have given Giacometti permission to express these fantasies of brutality. Like his lifetime attachment to Bataille's magazine, Giacometti's writing about violence—as in his essay on Jacques Callot or his text "Le rêve, le Sphinx et la mort de T."—continued well beyond the 1930s

41 Alberto Giacometti, "Hier, sables mouvants," *Le Surréalisme au service de la révolution*, no. 5 (1933).

Alberto Giacometti. The Hour of the Traces. *1930. Whereabouts unknown.*

Aztec pyramid. (Published in Cahiers d'art, *no. 10 (1929).)*

and his repudiation of surrealism. In both their structure and imagery these texts often call Bataille to mind.[42]

I said before that *alteration* functions as a Bataillian concept because of the primal contradiction that operates its relation to meaning, such that the signifier oscillates constantly between two poles. This same kind of oscillation of meaning (for the complexity involved the more accurate term might be *migration*) is what is put into play by *Suspended Ball*. For though the work is structured as a binary opposition, with the two sexes, male and female, juxtaposed and contrasted, the value of each of these terms does not remain fixed. Each element can be read as the symbol of either the masculine or feminine sex (and for the ball, in addition to an interpretation as testicles, there are the additional, possible semantic values of buttocks and eye, neither of these determined by gender). The identification of either form within any given reading of the work is possible only in opposition to its mate; and these readings circulate through a constantly shifting theater of relationships, cycling through the metaphoric statement of heterosexual connection into the domains of transgressive sexuality—masturbatory, homosexual, sadistic—and back again. The transgression contained in the sculpture's signifying gesture, we should note, sets it apart simultaneously from Breton's adamant rejection of the sexually perverse, and the rather anodine, formal *jeux d'esprit* of Picasso's transformations of the human body in the late '20s, with which *Suspended Ball* is often compared.[43] In its continual movement, its constant "alteration," this play of meaning is thus the enactment in the symbolic realm of the literal motion of the work's pendular action.

Although the alter(n)ation of *Suspended Ball* is constant, it is nonetheless regulated in a way that is entirely structued by the possibilities of metaphorical expansion of its two elements—wedge and sphere—and the oscillations of their sexual values. In this erotic play within a structurally closed system, the sculpture participates in the daemonic logic of Bataille's *l'Historie de l'OEil*. In Bataille's work, which as Roland Barthes points out is literally the story of an object—the eye—and what happens to it (and not to the novel's characters), a

42.   Alberto Giacometti, "A propos de Jacques Callot," *Labyrinthe*, no. 7 (April 15, 1945), 3. This essay relates the fascination with horror and destruction on the part of Callot, Goya, and Gericault: "For these artists there is a frenetic desire for destruction in every realm, up to that of human consciousness itself." In a thought that is obviously close to Bataille, Giacometti concludes that in order to understand this one would have to speak, "on the one hand of the pleasure in destruction that one finds in children, of their cruelty . . . and on the other hand of the subject-matter of art." "Le rêve, le Sphinx et la mort de T.," *Labyrinthe*, no. 22/23 (December 15, 1946), 12–13. Not only does the story of the spider, in the dream recounted in this text, recall Bataille's theme of the *informe*, but the description of T.'s head, rendered hideously objective by death, is pure Bataille. Become "an object, a little, measurable, insignificant box," the head is seen as a rotting cadaver, "miserable debris to be thrown away," into the mouth of which, to Giacometti's horror, a fly enters.
43.   Hohl declares, for example, "It is certain that the club and sphere forms that Picasso elaborated in his *Projet pour un monument* informed the structure of *Suspended Ball* (Hohl, 1972, p. 81).

condition of migration is established in which the object is, as it were, "declined" through various verbal states. As a globular element the eye is transformed through a series of metaphors by means of which, at any given point in the narrative, other globular objects are substituted for it: eggs, testicles, the sun. As an object containing fluid, the eye simultaneously gives rise to a secondary series related to the first: yolk, tears, urine, sperm. The two metaphoric series thus establish a system of combination by means of which terms can interact to produce a near infinity of images. The sun, metaphorized as eye and yolk, can be described as "flaccid luminosity," and can give rise to the phrase "the urinary liquifaction of the sky." Yet it is more correct to characterize the two metaphorical series as two chains of signifiers, "because for each one it is obvious that any term is never anything but the signifier of a neighboring term."[44] And if, as one part of one chain connects to that of the other, this *combinatoire* is a machine for the production of images, it is essential to note that because of the logical constraints regulating the chains, there is nothing surrealist in these "encounters"; they are not meetings by chance.

The structure of these metaphoric substitutions thus produces not only the course of the erotic action of the narrative, but the verbal fabric through which the *récit* is woven. And this aspect of *l'Histoire de l'OEil* is also important to compare to the action of *Suspended Ball*. For, conceived as the action of metaphor, the story of the eye is not the story of a literal eye. Deprived of a point of origin in the real world, a moment that would be anterior to the metaphorical transformations, conferring on them both their point of departure and their sense, the story has no privileged term. As Barthes says of the work's structure, "the paradigm has no beginning anywhere." Because the eye's sexual identity remains perfectly ambiguous (a round phallicism), the narrative does not have a single sexual fantasy hidden within its depths that would provide its ultimate meaning. "We are left no other possibility than to reflect on a perfectly spherical metaphor within *l'Histoire de l'OEil*: each of its terms is always the signifier of another term (and no term is ever a simple signified), without the relay ever being able to be halted."[45]

This round phallicism, this collapse of distinction between what is properly masculine and what is properly feminine, this obliteration of difference, is for logic what the perversions are for eroticism: it is transgressive. As Bataille explains in his "Dictionary entry" in *Documents* for the word *informe*, philosophy's task is to make sure that everything *has* its proper form, its defined boundaries, its limits. But certain words, and *informe* is one of them, have a contrary mission. Their task is to declassify, to strip away the "mathematical frockcoats" that philosophy drapes over everything. Because by opening onto formlessness,

---

44.   Roland Barthes, "La métaphore de l'oeil," *Critique*, no. 195–96 (1963), 722. My discussion of the structure of metaphor in Bataille's novel follows that of Barthes.
45.   *Ibid.*, p. 773.

to the collapse of difference, *informe* "comes down to saying that the world is something like a spider or a piece of spit [crachat]."[46] *Informe* denotes what alteration produces, the reduction of meaning or value, not by contradiction — which would be dialectical — but by putrefaction: the puncturing of the limits around the term, the reduction to the sameness of the cadaver — which is transgressive. Round phallicism is a destruction of meaning/being. This is not to say that the objects and images of *l'Histoire de l'OEil* or *Suspended Ball* literally have no form by resembling spittle, but rather that the work they do is to collapse difference. They are machines for doing this.

Bataille's "Dictionary" was dedicated to revealing the jobs that words do.[47] His magazine *Documents*, within which it was housed, also had a "job," and part of this was to use ethnographic data to transgress the neat boundaries of the art world with its categories based on *form*. This is the "hard" use of primitivism, as opposed to what I referred to as the "soft" or aestheticized view of it. It certainly cannot limit itself to borrowing this or that shape from the repertory of primitive objects the way even art-school students (particularly within the decorative arts) were being encouraged to do during the 1920s.[48] Instead it uses the "primitive" in an expanded sense (although with close attention to ethnographic detail), to embed art in a network that, in its philosophical dimension, is violently anti-idealist and antihumanist. Bataille ends his article "Primitive Art" by invoking the modern art that he respects, art that "rather quickly presented a process of decomposition and destruction, which has been no less painful to most people than would have been the sight of the decomposition and destruction of a cadaver."[49] Intellectual realism" — Luquet's aestheticizing, cognitively constructive category, which itself owes much to the early defense of cubist painting[50] — will no more address the conditions of this "rotting painting," Bataille insists, than it can address the whole of sculpture in general. When it comes Bataille's turn in *Documents* to think about Picasso's work, he does so under the rubric "Soleil Pourri."[51]

Only through this expanded conception of the "job" that *primitivism* performed for the dissident surrealists can we think about the brilliance of a sculpture like *Suspended Ball* or adjudicate among the claims about the "source"

46.   "Informe" was Bataille's entry in the "Dictionnaire" of *Documents*, I, no. 7 (1929).
47.   For a discussion of Bataille's "Dictionary" within the context of the various avant-garde dictionaries, see Denis Hollier, *La Prise de la Concorde*, pp. 59–65.
48.   For example, a four-volume series of photographic reproductions was published specifically for the instruction of arts and design students under the title *La décoration primitive*, Calavas Editeur, Paris, 1922. The volumes were equally devoted to African, Oceanic, and pre-Columbian objects, both sculptures and textiles.
49.   Bataille, *OEuvres Complètes*, vol. I, p. 253.
50.   For example, Apollinaire insists in *Les Peintres cubistes* (Paris, 1913) that cubism "is not an art of imitation, but an art of conception." Or, in Léger's essay "Les Origines de la peinture et sa valeur représentative" (*Montjoie!*, no. 8 [May 1913], 7), he concentrates on the difference between "visual realism" and a "realism of conception."
51.   This appeared in the special issue on Picasso, *Documents*, II, no. 3 (1930).

Alberto Giacometti. Head. *1934. Plaster. Whereabouts unknown.*

of *Invisible Object*. For the elaborate network of the primitive that had been developed by the early '30s tends to provide a sculpture like *Invisible Object* with many interconnected references, thus supporting not only Hohl's assertions about the work but Breton's and Leiris's as well, and opening onto still further conditions that grenerated the work.

If we start with Leiris's report about the little Swiss girl, which in the context of this moment of Giacometti's art is certainly the most questionable of referents, we see that in fact it fits into the circumstances surrounding the development of the work. Breton reports that the first stage of the head, the one ultimately replaced by the mask from the flea market, was flat and undefined, although the conception of the eyes as large wheels—the right one intact, the left one broken—continued through the first and second versions.[52] Just prior to making *Invisible Object*, in 1934, Giacometti made a plaster that fits Breton's description and was undoubtedly the sketch for the initial idea of the figure's head. Where the final version is crystalline and defined, the plaster sketch is flabby and almost formless, but what connects the two conceptions (beyond the wheel-like eyes) is the condition of being a mask.[53] For the plaster head is clearly

52.   Breton, *Documents 34*, 20.
53.   The year before making the plaster mask/sketch for *Invisible Object*, Giacometti executed another "mask" in plaster: the deformed head of *Flower in Danger* (1933). This sculpture, with its images of incipient decapitation of the flower/head, is like a little machine for the production of the *acéphale*. It is possible that a plaster head by Arp, published in the special issue on surrealism in *Variétés* (June 1929), contributed to the notion of the head as a mask in the process of decomposition.

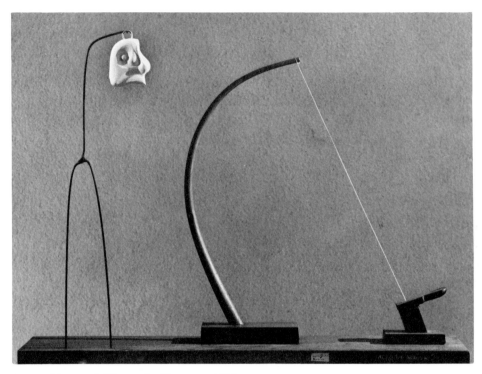

Alberto Giacometti. Flower in Danger. *1933.*
Wood, metal, plaster, 21⅛ by 30¾ by 7⅛
inches. The Alberto Giacometti Foundation,
Kunsthaus, Zürich.

copied from one of the carnival masks photographed by Jacques-André Boiffard
and reproduced in *Documents* to accompany Georges Limbour's text "Eschyle, le
Carnaval et les Civilisés."[54]

The setting for Limbour's meditation on this subject is a chaotic general
store in which the author watches a little girl shyly pick up a carnival mask of a
bearded man and, trying it on, transform herself into a kind of Lolita by lasciv-
iously running her tongue along the lips of the papier-mâché face. The vivid
description of this "Salomé of the streets" may well be the vehicle of association
with the little Swiss girl.

The rest of Limbour's article also rewards attention. Speaking first of the
conception of death into which the grimacing masks of Greek tragedy froze
the mobility of the human face, Limbour then turns to primitive masks. For the
Documents group as well as for the orthodox surrealists, the preferred domain of

54.   *Documents*, II, no. 2 (1930), 97–102.

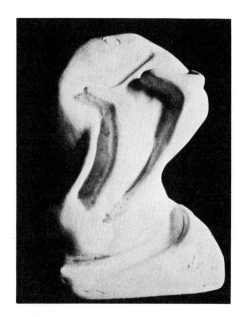 

Jean Arp. Head. *1929. Published in* Variétés
June 1929), *special issue:* Surrealism in 1929.

primitive art was no longer that of Africa (which was considered too rational, too formalist) but that of Oceania, and it is to this that Limbour refers.[55] In a passage representative of the angrily anticolonialist feeling of both groups, Limbour castigates the violation of these territories by the white man, who substitutes his "missionaries of Lent, his paper-maché Jesuits" for the incredible force of the Melanesian conception of the mask.[56] And in an image that is right out of Bataille's conception of the *soleil pourri*, he speaks of the faces carved onto the great poles stuck into the earth, "staring straight into the sun."[57] Having raped the South Seas to send its sacred objects back to the art markets and

55.   For example, the surrealist map of the world in 1929 places Oceania at the very center (*Variétés* [June 1929]: Surrealism in 1929).
56.   In 1931 Louis Aragon organized an anticolonialist exhibition in a meeting hall in the rue de la Grange-Batelière, to protest the official *Exposition Coloniale*. Giacometti's contribution consisted of political cartoon drawings. Two photographs of the room set up by Aragon, Eluard, and Tanguy for the exhibition *La Vérité sur les colonies* appear in *Le Surréalisme su service de la révolution*, no. 4 (December 1931).
57.   "Soleil pourri" concentrates on the Mithriac cult and the spasmodic practices incited by looking into the sun. This theme was elaborated in the series of texts entitled "L'oeil pinéal."

Jacques-André Boiffard. Photograph. Published in Documents, *II, no. 2 (1930).*

"La Protection des hommes," from Variétés, *II, no. 9 (January 1930).*

Trocadéros of "civilization," the West has also developed its own masks, ones, Limbour writes, that are worthy of Aeschylus. These, of course, are the gas masks that alone are authentic to our times. "Because if religion, the cult of the dead, and the festivals of Dionysos turned the mask into a sacred, ritual orna- ment among the various ancient peoples, we too have our own religion, our own societal games, and consequently our own masks. Only the general stan- darization of our age requires that we all wear the same one."

The thought of the gas mask, which substitutes for the "humanity" of the face a horrific image of the brutality of industrialized war, had become ex- tremely widespread among the 1920s avant-garde. A suite of photographs in *Variétés* showing wearers of gas masks and other kinds of mechanical devices displays this fascination for what modern imagination has dreamed to replace the head of man.[58] As with all the mechanical candidates, but with extraor- dinary force in the case of the gas mask, this substitute calls to mind not higher stages in the evolution of the species but much, much lower ones. Because the wearer of the gas mask looks like nothing so much as an insect.

The man with the insect head is *informe*, altered. What should be the sign of his highest faculties, his mind, his spirit, has become lowly, like the crushed spider, or the earthworm. The man with the insect head is, like the deformed

58.   "Aboutissements de la méchanique," *Variétés* II, no. 9 (January 1930).

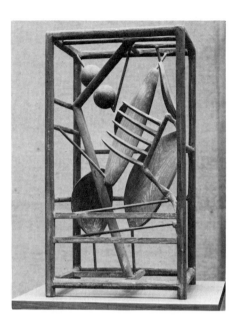

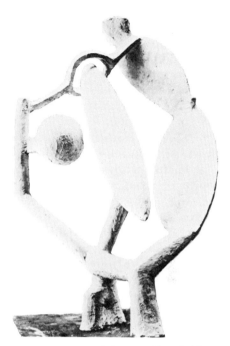

Alberto Giacometti. Cage. *1931. Wood, 19¼ inches high. Moderna Museet, Stockholm.*

Alberto Giacometti. Woman, Head, Tree. *1930. Plaster.*

anthropoids of the caves, *acéphale*: a transgressive thought of the human.[59] The term is, of course, Bataille's, and in his work it functioned as a kind of password by which to enter the conceptual theater where humanity displays the richness of its contradictory condition. For *acéphale* opens onto the experience of man's verticality — his elevation in both its biological and moral significance — as a negation: a development toward the primitive, an ascendance downward. As we shall see, this conceptual inversion also played a structural role in the redefinition of sculpture that Giacometti explored in these years. But for Giacometti, as well as for many of his fellow artists, its most obvious impact was thematic.

Within the imaginative circuit of the period we are considering, the man with the insect head is also the *woman* with the insect head: the praying mantis. The symbol of a collapse of the distinction between life — or procreativity — and death, the praying mantis fascinated the vanguard of *Variétés*, *Documents*, and *Minotaure* on the basis of a single detail: the female of the species was known to

59.   Bataille's concentration on the *acéphale* led, in 1936, to the creation of a journal of that name for which Masson designed the cover. One of his early treatments of the representation of man in ancient culture as *acéphale* was his text "Le bas matérialisme et la gnose," *Documents*, II, no. 1 (1930), 1–8. Leo Frobenius deals with this theme in "Bêtes hommes ou dieux," *Cahiers d'art*, no. 10 (1929).

eat its partner after, or even during, copulation. Because of the strongly an-
thropomorphic character of this insect, its mating habits seemed extremely
portentous to the surrealists. Roger Caillois's essay on the mantis, published in
Minotaure in 1934, which became the basis of his later studies of the function of
myth and the ambiguity of the sacred, reported that Breton, Eluard, and Dali
all kept large collections of these insects, in cages.[60]

Caillois's essay released a swarm of praying mantises onto the surfaces of
surrealist painting.[61] But even before 1934 the insect had appeared in
Giacometti's work as well as Ernst's. Giacometti's 1930 *Woman, Head, Tree*
depicts the woman as a mantis and seems to have introduced the production of
the two *Cages* of the following year. In both of these an abstracted image of the
mantis is at work within the nightmarish confines of the sculpture, attacking its
masculine partner emblematically represented by a simple sphere, or cranium.[62]
With these *Cages*, the mantis appears as well as to have been thought through
the medium of extreme formal disjunction that was considered to be the major
visual characteristic of Oceanic art, giving it its power and its savage poetry.
One of the several *mallanggan* from New Ireland that could have been known to
Giacometti at this time is extremely suggestive as a possible source for the idea
of a disjoint, caged figure.[63] And in the analysis of Melanesian motifs that Carl
Einstein published in the 1920s, the *mallanggan's* structure, conceived as a
cranium contained within a scaffolding of bones that is the primitive reconcep-
tion of the skeleton, is even more suggestive for an iconological reading of the
Cage.[64]

After this it was Ernst who took up the theme of the mantis and in his production of *Une Semaine de Bonté*, executed in 1933, one finds the image imbedded
within a whole oeuvre dedicated to the conditions of the *acéphale*.[65] In one
chapter of this collage novel in which the human (male) head is replaced by
everything from worms to birds to lions, the actors are depicted with the heads
of the great Easter Island statues, and juxtaposed to one such figure regarding
(it)self in a mirror is a mantis in the act of consuming her mate.[66]

The rapport between Giacometti and Ernst during the early 1930s
resulted in Ernst's visit to the Giacometti family's summer house at Maloja in
1934, where with Giacometti's help Ernst made a series of sculptures by slightly

60.   Roger Caillois, "La mante réligieuse," *Minotaure*, I, no. 5 (May 1934), 25. See also, "La
Nature et l'amour," *Variétés*, II, no. 2 (June 1929).
61.   William Pressly, "The Praying Mantis in Surrealist Art," *Art Bulletin*, LV (December
1973), 600–615.
62.   Hohl traces the use of the sphere as the metonymic representation of the male, in the works
of these years (Hohl, 1972, pp. 81–82).
63.   This is D 62.2.10 of the Musée des Arts africains et Océaniens, formerly in the collection
of M. Girardin.
64.   Carl Einstein, "Sculptures mélanésiennes," *L'Amour de l'art*, no. 8 (1926), 256.
65.   Ernst's *Femme 100 Têtes* (1929) was nominally dedicated to this theme even though it does
not directly illustrate it.
66.   *Une Semaine de Bonté*, p. 168.

Max Ernst. Collage from Une Semaine de
Bonté. *1934. Fifth book. Element: Darkness.
Example: Easter Island.*

*Mallanggen. New Ireland. Painted Wood.
Musée des Arts Africains et Océaniens, Paris.*

reworking and etching large stones that the two men dragged from the glacial moraine. The figures Ernst chose to represent on these sculptures were both the birds from the Easter Island cults and the Papuan bird from New Guinea, with which Ernst identified and which he used as his alter ego Loplop.[67] Much of the sculpture that Ernst went on to make in the following years shows the effects of this visit on his art. His *Lunar Asparagus* (1935), for example, is obviously indebted to *Trois personnages dans un près*, a work resonant with primitive associations, which Giacometti had set up in 1930 in the Swiss countryside.[68] But the interest obviously ran both ways as Giacometti's *Project for a Passageway* (1930–31) indicates, with its closeness to images like Ernst's *Anatomy of a Bride* or *La Belle Jardinière*.

Thus Ernst's association in *La Semaine de Bonté* of the mantis with the context of Oceania and the site of the Papuan spirit bird provides yet one more aspect of the many factors that determined the conception of *Invisible Object*, with its own inclusion of a bird's head reminiscent of Loplop's. It establishes a conceptual site within which to see how the logic of *Invisible Object* works to combine the Solomon Islands spirit of the dead with the mythic/biological purveyor of death supplied by the form of the mantis. In Breton's story of the substitution of one version of the work's head by another, what we can now read as the constant factor is the idea of the head as a mask, and the figure, therefore, as *acéphale*. As the mask itself becomes increasingly cruel of aspect, it more and more closely resembles the pointed shape of the mantis's face, with its huge staring eyes.[69] Giacometti's attraction to the flea-market mask was indeed, as Freud would have said, overdetermined.

One wing of Giacometti scholarship is extremely focused on the psycho-biographical underpinnings of his art.[70] To what has been said about the factors contributing to *Invisible Object*, this interpretive strategy would undoubtedly add a hallucinatory maternal presence hovering behind the Solomon Islands spirit of the dead. Dressed in black, the woman whom Giacometti rapes and slaughters in his adolescent fantasies is the same woman who enters the *Palace at 4 a.m.* to disrupt its erotic idyll. The great proscriber of his sexuality, she is

67.   Although Ernst's extensive collection of Oceanic art contained other things as well, he largely specialized in objects of the Papuan Gulf (New Guinea), according to the research of Philippe Peltier. (See Peltier in *Primitivism in 20th Century Art*, The Museum of Modern Art, New York, 1984.)

68.   Now destroyed, the work was published in *Minotaure*, no. 3/4 (1933), 40. There is an obvious resemblance between these stakelike personages driven directly into the ground and the tribal wooden posts totemically carved and set into the earth at the entrance to villages or houses, to protect a given area, that were widely known at this time.

69.   Giacometti spoke of his attraction to Oceanic sculpture in terms of the exaggeration of the eyes: "New Hebrides sculpture is true, and more than true, because it has a gaze. It's not the imitation of an eye, it's purely and simply a gaze. All the rest is a prop for the gaze." Georges Charbonnier, *Le monologue du peintre*, Paris, René Juilliard, 1959, p. 166.

70.   This is true not only of Hohl's monograph, but also of the approach taken by Yves Bonnefoy, who is preparing a major study of the artist. See "Etudes comparées de la Fonction poétique," *Annuaire du Collège de France*, 1982, pp. 643–653.

Annetta Stampa Giacometti.[71] It is possible to trace the way this maternal force was simultaneously associated with the ideas of death that haunt his work and its equally strong focus on pregnancy and birth. Giacometti was obsessed with the idea of the rock that bears fruit, or, as Arp had written, "The stones are full of entrails. Bravo. Bravo."[72] Interesting as that territory might be to explore, it lies at a tangent to the subject of this study, although in what follows, with its concern with death and the monument, the additional testimony of this personal, biographic motivation is certainly not unwelcome.

Any artist's work can be seen from the vantage of either of two, possibly conflicting, perspectives. One of these looks at the oeuvre from within the totality of the individual. The other regards it, far more impersonally, within a historical dimension, which is to say, comparatively, in relation to the work of others and the collective development of a given medium. Often these two perspectives overlap. The shape of Mondrian's career, for example, in its search for the neoplastic elements of painting, coincides with his position at the forefront of the general development of abstraction within twentieth-century art.

In Giacometti's case this is not so. For Giacometti's sculpture viewed from the perspective of his individual oeuvre is overwhelmingly that of the monument: the single, vertical figure, raised commemoratively in space, hieratic, immobile, tall. From the *Spoon Woman*, to *Invisible Object*, to any of the 1950s standing figures, we can follow the trajectory of this concern, using it to bestow a conceptual unity on Giacometti's art. But from the point of view of the history of sculpture—an impersonal and far less sympathetic measure—Giacometti's entire production of the vertical monument is less interesting, which is to say, less totally innovatory, than the work he made in the years from 1930 to 1933. For that intervening work is horizontal.

The formal innovation of those sculptures, almost wholly unprepared for by anything else in the history of the medium, was their ninety-degree turn of the axis of the monument to fold its vertical dimension onto the horizontality of the earth. In objects like *Project for a Passageway*, *Head /Landscape*, and the extraordinary gameboard sculptures like *Circuit* and "*On ne joue plus*," the work itself is simply and directly conceived of as a base. We could challenge the innovatory character of this invention by saying that already, in the teens, Brancusi had cancelled the distinction between sculpture and base, but we would then be missing the point of the profound originality of Giacometti's move. For Brancusi's base/sculptures remain vertical. They continue to house the object within the domain created by the primal opposition between what is not artistically determined—the ground—and what is—the sculpture. The very axis

71.   Giacometti, "Le palais de quatre heures," *Minotaure*, no. 3/4 (1933), 46.
72.   This is the epigraph for the chapter of *Une Semaine de Bonté* that contains the Easter Island section. Giacometti's text, "Hier, sables mouvants," begins with his account of the large rock into which he would crawl when he was a child, remaining there for hours.

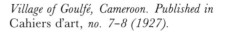

Village of Goulfé, Cameroon. Published in
Cahiers d'art, *no. 7–8 (1927).*

of verticality declares the apartness of sculpture's representational field from
the world of actuality, and this dimension is traditionally introduced by the
uprightness of a pedestal, with its initiation of the lift of the work above the
ground, its removal from the space of the real. Like a picture frame, the pedestal closes off the virtual field of representation from the actual space around it.

But if the picture is somehow *only* its frame, then this distinction is not so
easy, and the representation begins to fuse with its literal surroundings. This
was the transformation of the sculptural that Giacometti put in place between
1930 and 1933. For the rotation of the axis onto the horizontal plane was further specified by the contents of the work as the "lowering" of the object,
thereby joining it simultaneously to the ground and to the real — to the actuality
of space and the literalness of motion in realtime. From the perspective of the
history of modern sculpture, this is the inaugural act of Giacometti's art, with
implications for much of what was to take place in the rethinking of sculpture
after World War II. And it is precisely within this theater of operations that we
once again encounter Giacometti's relationship to tribal art and the primitive.

The earliest of these sculptures is *Project for a Passageway* (1930–31), an object both close to Ernst's "anatomies" and determined by the ethnographic
metaphor of the body as a cluster of African clay huts.[73] Giacometti's alternate
name for this work — *The Labyrinth* — reinforces the relationship of its conception
to the world of the primitive.[74] For in the thinking of the early 1930s, with its
obsession with the Minotaur, the labyrinth was set in primal opposition to
classical architecture's connotations of lucidity and the domination of space. In
the grip of the labyrinth, it is man who is dominated, disoriented, lost.[75]

With the second of these horizontal sculptures the issue of *rotation* of the
axis becomes more prespicuous. *Head/Landscape* (1930–31) was initially called

73.   See André Gide, "Architecture nègres," *Cahiers d'art*, no. 7/8 (1927), particularly the image
on p. 265.
74.   *Die Sammlung der Alberto Giacometti-Stiftung*, Kunsthaus, Zurich, 1971, p. 94.
75.   It was Bataille who contributed the name for the review *Minotaure*, in 1933.

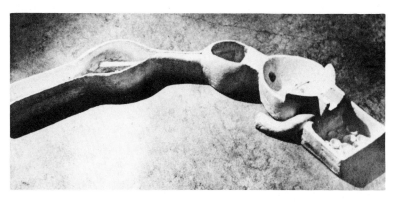

Alberto Giacometti. Project for a Passageway.
*1930–31. Plaster, 6 by 50 by 17 inches. The
Alberto Giacometti Foundation, Kunsthaus,
Zürich.*

Fall of a Body onto a Diagram, and it is this notion of the body's fall that verbally acknowledges what the sculpture visually performs.[76] The structural principle of *Head/Landscape* depends on the metaphorical relation between the two things operated through the spatial device of anamorphosis: rotated onto the horizontal plane, the face resembles a landscape. This precise relationship was spelled out in a display of "paranoid critical" thinking by Salvador Dali when he "read" a photograph of African natives sitting in front of their huts as a Picasso head, a (mis)reading that resulted, he explained, by his disorientation with regard to the photograph. In Dali's presentation the image is then, like *Head/Landscape*, rotated ninety degrees.[77] But Giacometti's sculpture is less like a head in rotation than it is like a mask or flat covering of some sort. And the landscape that is its alternate reading does not seem like the neutral terrain of Dali's example but rather resembles a necropolis, its rectangular openings suggesting a tomb.[78] (This combination of tomb and necropole would be made more precise by the coffins sunk into the ground of "*On ne joue plus*" of the following year.)

76. In Zervos's "Quelques notes sur les sculptures de Giacometti," (*Cahiers d'art* [1932], 337–342), the work, which bore the written inscription "la vie continue," was published with the title *Chute d'un corps sur un graphique*. Later, in picturing his art of these years, Giacometti labeled this now-lost sculpture *Paysage — Tête couchée*. See "Lettre à Pierre Matisse," *Alberto Giacometti*, New York, Pierre Matisse Gallery, 1948. Carola Giedion-Welcher, who knew Giacometti, published an Etruscan votive bronze from the museum in Piacenza as the possible inspiration for *Project for a Square* (in Giedion-Welcher, *Contemporary Sculpture*, New York, Wittenborn, 1960). Hohl suggests that this ancient object was more likely related to *Chute d'un corps sur un graphique* and is the source of this name, since the Etruscan work is covered with runes. Hohl, 1972, p. 299, fn. 29.
77. Salvador Dali; "Communication:visage paranoïaque," *Le Surréalisme au service de la révolution*, no. 3 (December 1931), 40.
78. See Hohl, 1972, p. 82.

Child's coffin. Nouméa, New Caledonia. Wood, fiber, 15¾ inches. Musée de l'Homme, Paris.

Fish. Easter Island. Wood, 6¾ inches long. Formerly Museum für Völkerkunde, Berlin. Whereabouts unknown.

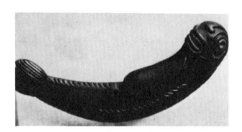

Various African masks, photographed and published lying down, may have played a role in suggesting the morphology of *Head/Landscape*.[79] But the object that weaves together most of the threads of association suggested by the work's metaphorical play, and which for that reason could well have been a source, is the lid of a child's coffin from New Caledonia, in the Musée de l'Homme. This object figured in the copious illustrations of the 1929 *Cahiers d'art* special issue on Oceania, an issue that Giacometti possessed and from which he made many copy-drawings. Giacometti had constantly insisted that his frequent drawing after other works of art was most often done from illustrations rather than in front of the things themselves.[80] The example of his pre-1945 drawings of Oceanic objects bears this out, for they are practically all taken from the same published source.[81] This resource, at the time the largest easily accessible repertory of Oceanic images (containing, moreover, many representatives of the surrealists' collections: Breton, Aragon, Tzara), may have suggested other types of relationship to Giacometti besides the head/landscape of the coffin lid (figure 122). The Easter Islands bird/fish of figure 180 could have operated behind the development of the phallically conceived *Disagreeable Objects* (1931), and the tusklike earring owned by Tzara, figure 169, is strongly related to the same series' *Disagreeable Object to Be Disposed Of*.[82] Fur-

79.   For example, the special issue on *art nègre* of *La Nervie*, no. 9–10 (1926), figure 9.
80.   Alberto Giacometti, "Notes sur les copies," *L'Ephémère*, no. 1 (1966), 104–108. Diego Giacometti confirmed to me that the drawings of Oceanic objects reproduced in Carluccio, *A Sketchbook of Interpretive Drawings*, were copied from 1929 issue of *Cahiers d'art*.
81.   Carluccio plate 5 shows three sculptures from the Basel Museum: figures 104, 105, and 114 in the 1929 *Cahiers d'art*. Plate 6 represents Easter Islands statues, figure 188 and 187 in *Cahiers d'art*. Carluccio plate 8 shows two New Guinea objects copied from figures 43 and 41 respectively. Plate 9 displays copies of figures 2, 153, and 157 from the *Cahiers d'art*.
82.   There is also the probable influence of the extremely phallic *casses-têtes* from New Caledonia and Fiji, many examples of which had been in the Musée de l'Homme since the end of the nineteenth century.

Alberto Giacometti. Head/Landscape. *1930–31.*
Plaster, 9½ by 27½ inches. Whereabouts
unknown.

Alberto Giacometti. Disagreeable Object.
1931. Wood, 19 inches long. Private collection,
New York.

Ear Ornament. Marquesas Islands. Ivory, 3½
inches high. Formerly collection Tristan Tzara.
Private collection.

Alberto Giacometti. Disagreeable Object to
Be Disposed Of. *1931. Wood, 8½ inches*
long. Private collection, London.

ther, the bird/woman statue of figure 46 resembles one of the two personages
that inhabit the necropolis of "*On ne joue plus*"; and as has been suggested above
with regard to the object owned by Max Ernst, the various *mallanggan*, particularly the one belonging to Louis Aragon (figure 65), contain the idea of
sculptural scaffolding that one finds in Giacometti's repeated use of the cage.

Given the almost exclusive identification of the surrealists with Oceania,
the upsurge of these sources among the range of primitive images that were
fueling his imagination at this time might be used to reinforce the general characterization of this period of Giacometti's work (1930–32) as his "surrealist
epoch."[83] However, Giacometti's connection to the orthodox surrealists did not
really begin in 1930. *Suspended Ball*, the object that excited their attention, was
not exhibited until the end of that year. It is not to the surrealist conceptual domain, to its fascination with the aleatory, with games of chance and the *objet
trouvé*, that we should look for the matrix of ideas that operate Giacometti's conception of sculpture's rotated axis: the horizontal gameboard, movement in real
time, the sculpture as base, the base as necropolis. The year this all began was
1930, and at that period Giacometti was still connected to *Documents*. The
preoccupation with real time that enters his work with *Suspended Ball* and *Hour*

83.   Hohl, 1972, p. 81.

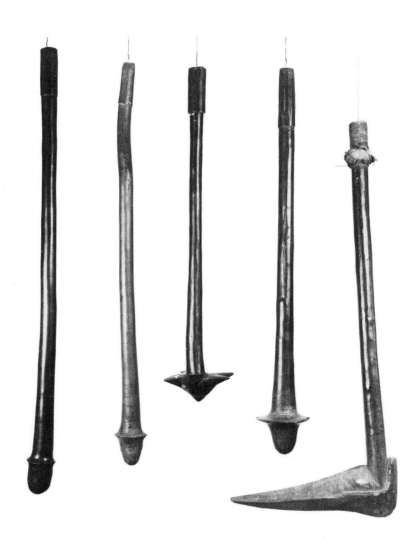

Casses-Têtes. New Caledonia. Wood. Musée de l'Homme, Paris.

of the Traces opens onto a consideration of real space; and real space is defined
by sculpture that has become nothing but its base, a vertical that is rotated into
"baseness." This very operation was made continually by Bataille as he
developed the concept of *"basesse"* — a low or base materialism — in *Documents*.[84]

In the anatomical geography of Bataille's thought the vertical axis
emblematizes man's pretensions toward the elevated, the spiritual, the ideal:
his claim that the uprightness separating him biologically from the bestial
distinguishes him ethically as well. Bataille, of course, does not believe this
distinction, and insists on the presence — behind the repressive assumptions of
verticality — of lowness as the real source of libidinal energy. Lowness here is
both an axis and a direction, the horizontality of the mud of the real. If feet are
highly charged objects, Bataille insists in "Le gros orteil," it is because,
simultaneously the focus of disgust and eros, they are the part of the body that
is mired in the ground. "A return to reality implies no new acceptance whatever, but it means that we are basely seduced, without symbolic substitutions
and up to the point of crying out, in staring, eyes wide open: staring thus in
front of a big toe."[85]

In the "Dictionary" entry *Bouche* this opposition between the vertical and
horizontal axes is thought specifically through the operation of rotation. The
mental axis is the one connecting eyes and mouth, issuing in language, the expressive function that heralds the human. The biological axis on the other hand
connects mouth to anus — locating the alimentary functions of ingestion and ex-
cretion. To lower the mental, or spiritual, axis onto the biological one is to
think about the real transformation of articulate sounds into bestial ones at the
moments of man's greatest pain or pleasure, and to see these in their true
operation as excretory. The summit of the body is thus given an opening that
has nothing to do with the ideational, but is rather a hole resembling the anus.
In *Documents* this text was illustrated by a full-page photograph by Boiffard of a
mouth, wide open, wet with saliva.[86]

This idea of a hole at the top of man's head — one that functions to de-
idealize, de-rationnate, dis-equilibrate — led Bataille to try to construct the
mythoanatomical legend of the pineal eye. Bataille conceived of this gland at
the summit of the human structure as a blind spot. The very opposite of
Descartes' belief that the pineal eye was the organ connecting the soul to the
body, Bataille's notion of the gland's function is that it propels man upward, attracting him toward the empyrion — representative of all that is lofty — impelling
him however to stare straight into the sun, becoming as a result, crazed and

84.   Bataille,"Le bas matérialisme et la gnose."
85.   "Le gros orteil," *Documents*, no. 6 (1929), 302.
86.   In a 1926 drawing of a nude, Giacometti depicts this axial rotation by conflating the mouth
and genitals. This relationship is the formal idea as well behind the female figure in *The Couple* of
the same year, and is a common motif in African art.

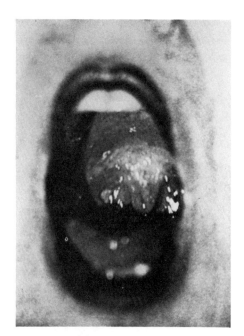

Jacques-André Boiffard. Photograph. Published in Documents, *II, no. 5 (1930).*

Jacques-André Boiffard. Photograph. c. 1930.

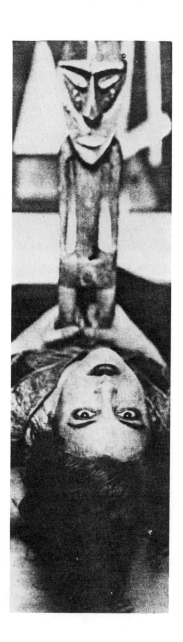

Alberto Giacometti. Woman. *1926. Ink on paper, 7 by 5 inches.*

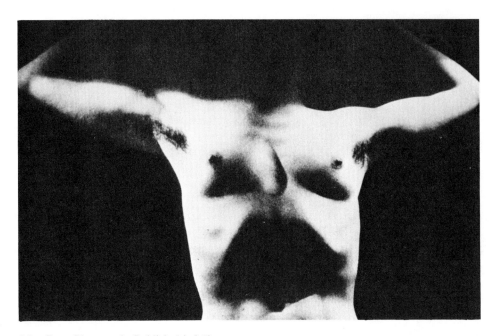

Man Ray. Photograph. Published in Minotaure,
no. 7 (1935).

blind.[87] The obsession with the sun promoted by the pineal (blind) eye is, then,
another instance of the collapse of the vertical into the horizontal, as man in his
disorientation literally and symbolically loses his head.[88] The image of the man
with the hole at the top of his cranium — another form of the *acéphale* — connects
in this way to the experience of the labyrinth, the space of implosion, as the distinction is blurred between inside and outside, between beginning and end.

   The blinding, crazing sun is the *soleil pourri* at which the Easter Island
idols stare and to which Bataille consecrated his essay on Picasso's "rotting art."
But then, for Bataille, the entire problematic of modern painting subtends his
conception of the beginnings of art as the representation of sacrifice, the symbolic correlative of the mutilation of the human body. The space of this mutilation is initially the cave or grotto of the prehistoric painters, the first occupiers
of the labyrinth. There art begins, but not with an act of self-duplication — as
the relationship of painting's origins with the myth of Narcissus would have it.

87.   The five texts on the pineal eye were written between 1927 and 1930. Never published,
they are collected in the *Oeuvres Complètes*, vol. II, pp. 13–50.
88.   See, "Soleil pourri," where Bataille speaks of "un être anthropomorphe *dépourvu de tête*" (p.
174). Hollier in *La Prise de la Concorde*, discusses this notion of the change of axis, pp. 137–154.

Painting is born with man's refusal to reproduce himself, and out of an act of self-mutilation.[89]

This set of connections between painting, a fascination with the sun, and the mutilation of the body in an act of sacrificial madness, is spelled out in Bataille's essay "La mutilation sacrificielle et l'oreille coupée de Vincent Van Gogh." For Bataille, Van Gogh's is not an aberrant gesture but is entirely representative of art's essential, archaic function. As one scholar of Bataille's work explains, "Self-mutilation demands to be thought of as an act, in fact, *the* pictorial act *par excellence*. Because painting is nothing if it doesn't strike at the architecture of the human body; this architecture which, precisely, is not simple because it implies self-mutilation."[90] The Minotaur, not Narcissus, presides over the birth of an art in which representation represents alteration.

One after another, Giacometti's gameboard, horizontal sculptures enact the marriage of the field of representation with the condition of the base, the ground, the earth. This rotation of the axis into the dimension of the physical is the shift of direction of the *acéphale*. But these rotated works share another aspect with the themes of the headless man and the labyrinth. For, with one exception, all of them carry the further signification of death. "*On ne joue plus*" conceives of the "sculpture" as a game, its board cratered with semicircular hollows modeled on the African pebble game *i*;[91] but into its center are sunk two tiny coffins, their lids askew. The literal space of the board on which pieces can be moved in real time fuses with the image of the necropolis.

The *Littré Dictionary* lists the sheet that covers an empty coffin as one of the primal meanings of *representation*. Representation, a stand-in for the dead, is thus conceptually suspended between the symbolic and the real decay of matter — the precise condition of alteration. Bataille's notion of a "base materialism" operates in this very middle ground between the literal and the symbolic, for it conceives the entire field of social relationships as wholly structured by the conditions of representation, which is to say, language. But language is thought of as a directionless maze in which, for example, the sacred is the function of the very conditions of the word itself: *sacer*, like *altus*, pointing in two directions, toward the blessed and the damned. Classical philosophy wishes to repress this

89.   In "La mutilation sacrificielle et l'oreille coupée de Vincent Van Gogh," *Documents*, II, no. 8 (1930), Bataille attacks, for example, Luquet's acceptance of the "folded-finger" hypothesis to explain the cave paintings in which stenciled hands are recorded with missing fingers (*Oeuvres Complètes*, vol. I, p. 267). A motif of great fascination, the stenciled hand is used in *La Caresse* (1930).
90.   Hollier, *La Prise de la Concorde*, p. 148.
91.   Hohl mentions wooden Benin gameboards that Giacometti might have seen at the Charles Ratton Gallery, which could have served as a model for this work (Hohl, 1972, p. 299, fn. 27). M. Ratton, however, says that no Benin objects of this type exist. Instead, one has only to turn to the wooden gameboards for *i*, which are still being produced today. The surfaces for this game were often improvised, hollowed out of the earth or in stone. Marcel Griaule's dissertation shows such a board in stone (Griaule, "Jeux Dogons," Paris, 1938, figure 95).

doubleness and reconstruct a language in which each element has a specific value, and only one. It wants to build vertical monuments to cover over the necropolis where meaning burrows into the dirt of decay, contamination, death. The space of this linguistic necropolis, in which language both forms and represents the real desires of the *acéphale*, is the labyrinth.

The gameboard of "*On ne joue plus*" is not a readymade, its horizontality is not the unmodulated topple of the snowshovel of Duchamp's *In Advance of a Broken Arm*. The gameboard, with its little pieces, is a representation in which the symbolic is made a function of the base, the base in Bataille's sense (*basesse*), a concept far from surrealist poetics, forged instead out of a vision of the primitive.

In 1935 Giacometti's art changed abruptly. He began to work from life, with models who posed in the studio, instead of making sculptures—as he later said of his work of the early 1930s—that "used to come to me complete in my mind."[92] The break this precipitated with the surrealists left Giacometti violently hostile. He declared that "everything he had made up to that time had been masturbation and that he had no other goal but to render a human head."[93] As part of this repudiation he is also reported to have denied his connection to

92.   James Lord, *A Giacometti Portrait*, p. 48. See Giacometti's account in "Le palais de quatres heures."
93.   Marcel Jean, *Histoire de la Peinture surréaliste*, Paris, Seuil, 1959, p. 227.

Alberto Giacometti. "On ne joue plus" (No More Play). *1933. Marble, wood, and bronze, 15¾ by 11¾ by 2 inches. Private collection.*

primitive art, saying that if he had taken anything from objects of this type it was simply because *art nègre* was modish during his early career.[94]

What Giacometti was rejecting was not simply surrealism or a related connection to tribal art. At a deeper, structural level, he renounced the horizontal and everything it meant: both a dimension within which to rethink the formal concerns of sculpture, and a matrix through which human anatomy was "altered." From 1935 on, he devoted himself to vertical sculpture. Having made this decision, he left behind those two concerns that had worked together to generate the brilliance of his work of the early '30s: the base and the primitive.

Paris, 1983

94.   In the late 1930s Giacometti is reported to have said this to Greta Knutson, then the wife of Tristan Tzara, for whom he sat for a portrait (as told to me by Knutson's daughter-in-law, Madame Tzara).

The game of i. *Dogon. Mali. Published in Marcel Griaule*, Jeux dogons, *Paris, 1938*

The Photographic Conditions of Surrealism

I open my subject with a comparison. On the one hand, there is Man Ray's *Monument to de Sade*, a photograph made in 1933 for the magazine *Le Surréalisme au service de la révolution*. On the other, there is a self-portrait by Florence Henri, given wide exposure by its appearance in the 1929 *Foto-Auge*, a publication that catalogued the European avant-garde's position with regard to photography.[1] This comparison involves, then, a slight adulteration of my subject—surrealism—by introducing an image deeply associated with the Bauhaus. For Florence Henri had been a student of Moholy-Nagy, although at the time of *Foto-Auge* she had returned to Paris. Of course the purity of *Foto-Auge*'s statement had already been adulterated by the presence within its covers of certain surrealist associates, like Man Ray, Maurice Tabard, and E. T. L. Mesens. But by and large *Foto-Auge* is dominated by German material and can be conceived of as organizing a Bauhaus view of photography, a view that we now think of as structured by the Vorkors's obsession with form.

Indeed, one way of eavesdropping on a Bauhaus-derived experience of this photograph is to read its analysis from the introduction to a recent reprint portfolio of Henri's work. Remarking that she is known almost exclusively through this self-portrait, the writer continues,

> Its concentration and structure are so perfect that its quintessence is at once apparent. The forceful impression it produces derives principally from the subject's intense gaze at her own reflection. . . . Her gaze passes

Florence Henri. Self-Portrait. *1928.*

dispassionately through the mirror and is returned—parallel to the lines made by the joints in the table. . . . The balls—normally symbols of movement—here strengthen the impression of stillness and undisturbed contemplation. . . . They have been assigned a position at the vertex of the picture . . . their exact position at the same time lends stability to the structure and provides the dominant element of the human reflection with the necessary contrast.[2]

In light of the writer's determination to straightjacket this image within the limits of an abstracting, mechanically formalist discourse, the strategy behind a

2.   *Florence Henri Portfolio*, Cologne, Galerie Wilde, 1974, introduction by Klaus-Jürgen Senbach.

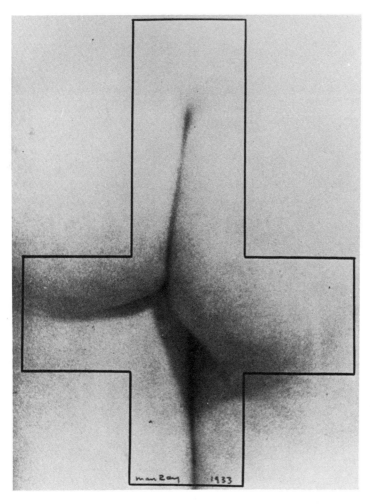

Man. Ray. Monument to de Sade. *1933. Published in*
Le Surréalisme au service de la révolution, *May 1933.*

juxtaposition of Man Ray's photograph with Florence Henri's becomes apparent.
Because the comparison forces attention away from the contents of the Henri—
whether those contents are conceived of as psychological (the "intense gaze" and
its dispassionate stare) or as formal (the establishment of stillness through
structural stability, etc.). And being turned from the photograph's contents, one's
attention is relocated on the container—on what could be called the character of
the frame as sign or emblem. For the Henri and the Man Ray share the same
recourse to the definition of a photographic subject through the act of framing it,
even as they share the same enframing shape.

   In both cases one is treated to the capture of the photographic subject by the
frame, and in both, this capture has a sexual import. In the Man Ray the act of
rotation, which transmutes the sign of the cross into the figure of the phallus,
juxtaposes an emblem of the Sadean act of sacrilege with an image of the object

of its sexual pleasure. And two further aspects of this image bespeak the structural reciprocity between frame and image, container and contained. The lighting of the buttocks and thighs of the subject is such that physical density drains off the body as it moves from the center of the image, so that by the time one's gaze approaches the margins, flesh has become so generalized and flattened as to be assimilated to printed page. Given this threat of dissipation of physical substance, the frame is experienced as shoring up the collapsing structure of corporeality and guaranteeing its density by the rather conceptual gesture of drawing limits. This sense of the structural intervention of frame inside contents is further deepened by the morphological consonance—what we could call the visual rhyming—between shape of frame and shape of figure: for the linear intersections set up by the clefts and folds in the photographed anatomy mimic the master shape of the frame. Never could the object of violation have been depicted as more willing.

In Florence Henri's self-portrait there is a similar play between flatness and fullness, as there is a parallel sense of the phallic frame as both maker and captor of the sitter's image. Within the spell of this comparison, the chromed balls function to project the experience of phallicism into the center of the image, setting up (as in the Man Ray) a system of reiteration and echo; and this seems far more imperatively their role than that of promoting the formal values of stillness and balance.

It can, of course, be objected that this comparison is tendentious. That it is a false analogy. That it suggests some kind of relationship between these two artists that cannot be there since they operate from across the rift that separates two aesthetic positions: Man Ray being a surrealist and Florence Henri being committed to an ideology of formal rigor and abstraction received initially from Léger and then from the Bauhaus. It can be argued that if there is a kind of phallicism in Henri's portrait, it is there inadvertently; she could not really have intended it.

As art history becomes increasingly positivist, it holds more and more to the view that "intention is some internal, prior mental event causally connected with outward effects, which remain the evidence for its having occurred," and thus, to say that works of art are intentional objects is to say that each bit of them is separately intended.[3] But, sharing neither this positivism nor this view of consciousness, I have no scruples in using the comparative method to wrest this image from the protective hold of Miss Henri's "intention" and to open it, by analogy, to a whole range of production that was taking place at the same time and in the same locale.

Yet with these two images I do not mean to introduce an exercise in comparative iconography. As I said, the area of interest is far less in the contents of these photographs than it is in their frame. Which is to say that if there is any question of phallicism here, it is to be found within the whole photographic

---

3.   Stanley Cavell, *Must We Mean What We Say?*, New York, Scribners, 1969, pp. 226, 236.

enterprise of framing and thereby capturing a subject. Its conditions can be generalized way beyond the specifics of sexual imagery to a structural logic that subsumes this particular image and accounts for a wide number of decisions made by photographers of this time, both with regard to subject and to form. The name that an entirely different field of critical theory gives to this structural logic is "the economy of the supplement."[4] And what I intend to reveal in the relatedness of photographic practice in France and Germany in the 1920s and '30s is a shared conception of photography as defined by the supplement.

But I am getting ahead of my argument. My reason at the outset for introducing my subject by means of comparison is that I wish to invoke the comparative method *as such*, the comparative method as it was introduced into art-historical practice in order to focus on a wholly different object than that of intention. The comparative method was fashioned to net the illusive historical beast called style, a prey which, because it was transpersonal, was understood as being quite beyond the claims of either individual authorship or intention. This is why Wölfflin believed the lair of style to be the decorative arts rather than the domain of masterpieces, why he looked for it—Morelli-fashion—in those areas that would be the product of inattention, a lack of specific "design"—going so far as to claim that the "whole development of world views" was to be found in the history of the relationship of gables.

Now it is precisely *style* that continues to be a vexing problem for anyone dealing with surrealist art. Commenting on the formal heterogeneity of a movement that could encompass the abstract liquifaction of Miró on the one hand, and the dry realism of Magritte or Dali on the other, William Rubin addresses this problem of style, declaring that "we cannot formulate a definition of Surrealist painting comparable in clarity with the meanings of Impressionism and Cubism."[5] Yet as a scholar who has to think his way into and around the mass of material that is said to be surrealist, Rubin feels in need of what he calls an *"intrinsic* definition of Surrealist painting." And so he produces what he claims to be "the first such definition ever proposed." His definition is that there are two poles of surrealist endeavor—the automatist/abstract and the academic/illusionist—the two poles corresponding to "the Freudian twin props of Surrealist theory, namely automatism [or free association] and dreams." Although these two pictorial modes look very unlike indeed, Rubin continues, they can be united around the concept of the irrationally conceived metaphoric image.

Now, in 1925 André Breton began to examine the subject surrealism and

4.   The seminal text is Jacques Derrida, *Of Grammatology*, trans. Gayatri Chakravorty Spivak, Baltimore, Johns Hopkins, 1974.
5.   The references throughout this paragraph are to Rubin's attempt, at the time of the Museum of Modern Art exhibition *Dada, Surrealism, and Their Heritage*, of which he was curator, to produce a concise synthetic statement which would serve as a theory of surrealist style. See William Rubin, "Toward a Critical Framework," *Artforum*, vol. V, no. 1 (September 1966), 36.

painting, and from the outset he characterized his material in terms of the very twin poles—automatism and dream—and the subject matter of Rubin's later definition.[6] If forty years afterward Rubin was so unhappy with Breton's attempt at a synthetic statement that he had to claim to have produced *the first such definition ever*, it is undoubtedly because Rubin, like everyone else, has been unconvinced that Breton's *was* a definition in the first place. If one wishes to produce a synthesis between A and B, it is not enough simply to say, "A plus B." A synthesis is rather different from a list. And it has long been apparent that a catalogue of subject matter held in common is neither necessary nor sufficient to produce the kind of coherence one is referring to by the notion of style.

If Rubin's nondefinition is a mirror-image of Breton's earlier one, this relationship is important, because it locates Breton's own theory as a source for the problem confronting all subsequent discussions. But Breton, as the most central

6.   André Breton, "Le Surréalisme et la peinture," *La Révolution surréaliste*, vol. 1 (July 1925), 26–30. The complete series of essays was collected in Breton, *Surrealism and Painting*, trans. Simon Watson Taylor, New York, Harper & Row, Icon edition, 1972. Further references are to this translation.

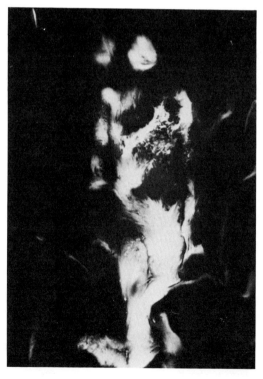

Maurice Tabard. Hand and Woman. *1929.*   *Raoul Ubac.* La Nébuleuse. *1939.*

spokesman for surrealism, is an obstacle one must surmount; one cannot avoid him, if the issue is to deal with the movement comprehensively—as one must if a synthetic notion like style is involved.

The same failure to *think* the formal heterogeneity of Miró and Magritte into something like stylistic unity plagues every effort of Breton as theoretician of the movement. Attempting to define surrealism, Breton produces instead a series of contradictions which, like the one between the linearity of Magritte and the colorism of Miró, strike one as being irreducible.

Thus, Breton introduces "Surrealism and Painting" with a declaration of the absolute value of vision among the sensory modes. Rejecting the late nineteenth-century dictum that all art should aspire to the condition of music, an idea very much alive among twentieth-century abstract artists, Breton insists that "visual images attain what music never can," and he bids this great medium farewell with the words, "so may night continue to descend upon the orchestra." His hymn of praise to vision had begun, "The eye exists in its savage state. The marvels of the earth . . . have as their sole witness the wild eye that traces all its colors back to the rainbow." And by this statement he is contrasting the immedi-

Brassaï. Temptation of St. Anthony. *1935.*

acy of vision—its perceptual automatism, as it were—to the premeditated, reflective gait of thought. The savageness of vision is good, pure, uncontaminated by ratiocination; the calculations of reason (which Breton never fails to call "bourgeois reason") are controlling, degenerate, bad.

Besides being untainted by reason, vision's primacy results from the way its objects are present to it, through an immediacy and transparency that compels belief. Indeed, Breton often presents surrealism-as-a-whole as defined by visuality. In the *First Manifesto* he locates the very invention of psychic automatism within the experience of hypnogogic images—that is, of half-waking, half-dreaming, visual experience.

But as we know, the privileged place of vision in surrealism is immediately challenged by a medium given a greater privilege: namely, writing. Psychic automatism is itself a written form, a "scribbling on paper," a textual production. And when it is transferred to the domain of visual practice, as in the work of André Masson, automatism is no less understood as a kind of writing. Breton describes Masson's automatic drawings as being essentially cursive, scriptorial, the result of "this hand, enamoured of its own movement and of that alone." "Indeed," Breton writes, "the essential discovery of surrealism is that, without preconceived intention, the pen that flows in order to write and the pencil that runs in order to draw *spin* an infinitely precious substance."[7] So, in the very essay that had begun by extolling the visual and insisting on the impossibility of imagining a "picture as being other than a window," Breton proceeds definitively to choose writing over vision, expressing his distaste for the "other road available to Surrealism," namely, "the stabilizing of dream images in the kind of still-life deception known as trompe l'oeil (and the very word 'deception' betrays the weakness of the process)."[8]

Now this distinction between writing and vision is one of the many antinomies that Breton speaks of wanting surrealism to dissolve in the higher synthesis of a surreality which will, in this case, "resolve the dualism of perception and representation."[9] It is an old antinomy within Western culture, and one which does not simply hold these two things to be opposite forms of experience, but places one higher than the other. Perception is better, truer, because it is immediate to experience, while representation must always remain suspect because it is never anything but a copy, a re-creation in another form, a set of signs for experience. Perception gives directly onto the real, while representation is set at an unbridgeable distance from it, making reality present only in the form of substitutes, that is, through the proxies of signs. Because of its distance from the real, representation can thus be suspected of fraud.

In preferring the products of a cursive automatism to those of visual,

7.   Breton, *Surrealism and Painting*, p. 68.
8.   *Ibid.*, p. 70.
9.   André Breton, "Océanie" (1948), reprinted in Breton, *La Clé des champs*, Paris, Sagittaire, 1953, 1973 edition, p. 278.

imagistic depiction, Breton appears to be reversing the classical preference of vision to writing, of immediacy to dissociation. For in Breton's definition, it is the pictorial image that is suspect, a "deception," while the cursive one is true.[10]

Yet in some ways this apparent reversal does not really overthrow the traditional Platonic dislike of representation, because the visual imagery Breton suspects is a picture and thus the representation of a dream rather than the dream itself. Breton, therefore, continues Western culture's fear of representation as an invitation to deceit. And the truth of the cursive flow of automatist writing or drawing is less a representation of something than it is a manifestation or recording: like the lines traced on paper by the seismograph or the cardiograph. What this cursive web makes present by making visible is a direct experience of what Breton calls "rhythmic unity," which he goes on to characterize as "the absence of contradiction, the relaxation of emotional tensions due to repression, a lack of the sense of time, and the replacement of external reality by a psychic reality obeying the pleasure principle alone."[11] Thus the unity produced by the web of automatic drawing is akin to what Freud called the oceanic feeling—the infantile, libidinal domain of pleasure not yet constrained by civilization and its discontents. "Automatism," Breton declares, "leads us in a straight line to this

10.   Thus, Breton insists that "any form of expression in which automatism does not at least advance undercover runs a grave risk of moving out of the surrealist orbit" (*Surrealism and Painting*, p. 68).
11.   *Ibid.*

Roger Parry. Illustration for Léon-Paul Fargue,
Banalité, *1928.*

J.-A. Boiffard. Illustration for André Breton,
Nadja, *1928.*

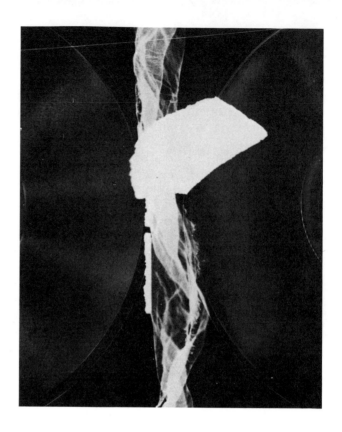

region," and the region he has in mind is the unconscious.[12] With this directness, automatism makes the unconscious, the oceanic feeling, present. Automatism may be writing, but it is not, like the rest of the written signs of Western culture, representation. It is a kind of presence, the direct presence of the artist's inner self.[13] This sense of automatism as a manifestation of the innermost self, and thus not representation at all, is also contained within Breton's description of automatic writing as "spoken thought." Thought is not a representation but is that which is utterly transparent to the mind, immediate to experience, untainted by the distance and exteriority of signs.

But this commitment to automatism and writing as a special modality of presence, and a consequent dislike of representation as a cheat, is not consistent in Breton, who contradicts himself on this matter as he contradicts himself on almost every point in surrealist theory. In many places we find Breton declaring, "It makes no difference whether there remains a perceptible difference between beings which are evoked and beings which are present, since I dismiss such differences out of hand at every moment of my life."[14] And as we will see, the welcome Breton

12. *Ibid.*
13. In Breton's words, "The emotional intensity stored up within the poet or painter at a given moment...." (*Surrealism and Painting*, p. 68).
14. *Ibid.*, p. 2.

le chien qui chie le chien bien coiffé malgré les difficultés du terrain causées par

ine neige abondante la femme à belle gorge la chanson de la chair / max ernst

Right: Max Ernst. 1922.

accords to representation, to signs, is very great indeed, for representation is the very core of his definition of Convulsive Beauty, and Convulsive Beauty is another term for the Marvelous, which is the great talismanic concept at the heart of surrealism itself.

The contradictions about the priorities of vision and representation, presence and sign, are typical of the confusions within surrealist theory. And these contradictions are focused all the more clearly if one reflects on Breton's position on photography. Given his aversion to "the real forms of real objects," and his insistence on another order of experience, we would expect Breton to despise photography. As the quintessentially realist medium, photography would have to be rejected by the poet who insisted that "for a total revision of real values, the plastic work of art will either refer to a *purely internal model* or will cease to exist."[15]

But in fact Breton has a curious tolerance for photography. Of the first two artists that he claimed for surrealism proper—Max Ernst and Man Ray—one of them was a photographer. And if we imagine that he accepted Man Ray on the

---

15.   *Ibid.,* p. 4. Breton goes on to express his distaste for what he calls photography's positivist values, asserting that "in the final analysis it is not the *faithful* image that we aim to retain of something" (p. 32).

Brassaï. Illustration for André Breton, L'Amour fou,
1937.

basis of the presumed anti-realism of the rayographs, this is in fact not so. Breton protested against characterizing the rayographs as abstract or making any distinction between Man Ray's cameraless photography and that produced with a normal lens.[16] But even more than his support for specific photographers, Breton's placement of photography at the very heart of surrealist publication is startling. In 1925 he had asked, "and when will all the books that are worth anything stop being illustrated with drawings and appear only with photographs?"[17]

This was not an idle question, for Breton's next three major works were indeed "illustrated" with photographs. *Nadja* (1928) bore images almost exclusively by Boiffard; *Les Vases communicants* (1932) has a few film stills and photographic documents; and the illustrative material for *L'Amour fou* (1937) was divided for the most part between Man Ray and Brassaï. Within the high oneiric atmosphere of these books, the presence of the photographs strikes one as extremely eccentric—an appendage to the text that is as mysterious in its motivation as the images themselves are banal. In writing about surrealism Walter Benjamin focuses on the curious presence of these "illustrations."

> In such passages photography intervenes in a very strange way. It makes the streets, gates, squares of the city into illustrations of a trashy novel, draws off the banal obviousness of this ancient architecture to inject it with the most pristine intensity towards the events described, to which, as in old chambermaids' books, word-for-word quotations with page numbers refer.[18]

But photography's presumed eccentricity to surrealist thought and practice must itself be reconsidered. For it was not injected into the very heart of the surrealist text only in the work of Breton; it was the major visual resource of the surrealist periodicals. The founding publication of the movement, *La Révolution surréaliste*, bore no visual relation to the vanguardist typographic extravaganzas of the Dada broadsheets. Rather, at the instigation of Pierre Naville, it was modeled specifically on the scientific magazine *La Nature*. Conceived almost exclusively as the publication of documents, the first issues of *La Révolution surréaliste* carried two types of verbal testimony: specimens of automatic writing and records of dreams. Sober columns of test carrying this data are juxtaposed

16.   The protest was against attitudes like that of Ribemont-Dessaignes, who, in introducing a 1924 Man Ray exhibition, honored "these abstract photographs . . . that put us in contact with a new universe."
17.   This question had begun, "The photographic print . . . is permeated with an emotive value that makes it a supremely precious article of exchange" (*Surrealism and Painting,* p. 32).
18.   Walter Benjamin, "Surrealism: The Last Snapshot of the European Intelligentsia," in *Reflections,* trans. Edmund Jephcott, New York, Harcourt Brace Jovanovich, 1978, p. 183.

(*Photo Brassaï*)

11. A PARIS LA TOUR SAINT-JACQUES
CHANCELANTE... (p. 55)

with visual material, most of it Man Ray's photographs, all of it having the documentary impact of illustrative evidence.

Naville's hostility to the traditional fine arts was well known, and the third issue of the journal carried his declaration: "I have no tastes except distaste. Masters, master-crooks, smear your canvases. Everyone knows there is no *surrealist painting*. Neither the marks of a pencil abandoned to the accident of gesture, nor the image retracing the forms of the dream. . . . " But spectacles, he insists, are acceptable. "Memory and the pleasure of the eyes," Naville writes, "that is the whole aesthetic." The list of things conducive to this visual pleasure includes streets, kiosks, automobiles, cinema, and photographs.[19]

One of the effects of the extraordinary 1978 Hayward Gallery exhibition, *Dada and Surrealism Reviewed*, was to begin to force attention away from the pictorial and sculptural production that surrounds surrealism and onto the periodicals, demonstrating the way that journals formed the armature of these

19.   Pierre Naville, "Beaux-Arts," *La Révolution surréaliste*, vol. 1 (April 1925), 27. It was in deference to Naville and others that, when later in the year Breton launched his support of the enterprise of the fine arts, he had nevertheless to begin by referring to "that lamentable expedient which is painting."

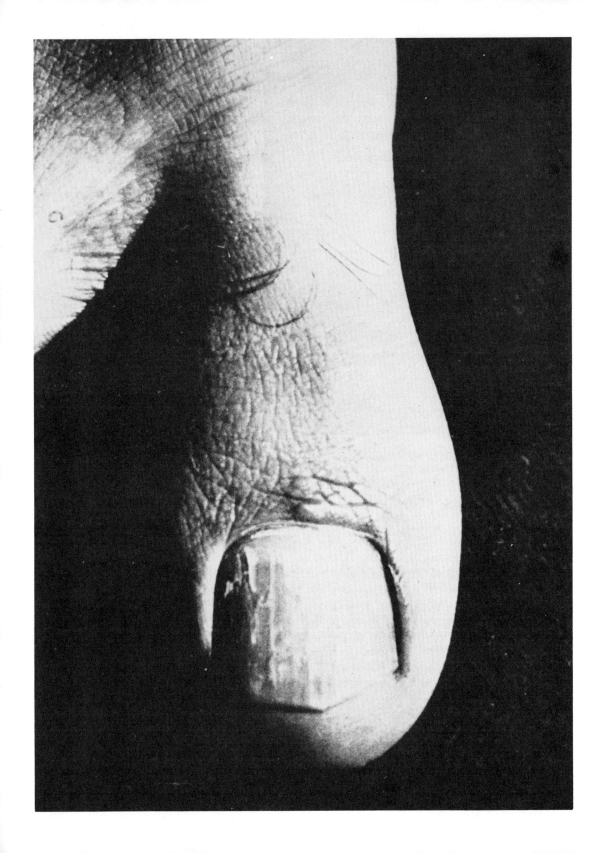

movements. Witnessing the parade of surrealist magazines—*La Révolution surréaliste, Le Surréalisme au service de la révolution, Documents, Minotaure, Marie, The International Surrealist Bulletin, VVV, Le Surréalisme, même*, and many others—one becomes convinced that *they* more than anything else are the true objects produced by surrealism. And with this conviction comes an inescapable association to the most important statement yet made about the vocation of photography: Benjamin's "The Work of Art in the Age of Mechanical Reproduction," and from there to one of the phenomena that Benjamin speaks of in the course of sketching the new terrain of art-after-photography, namely, the illustrated magazine, which is to say, photograph plus text.

At the very moment when Benjamin was making his analysis, the surrealists were quite independently putting it into practice. And that they were doing so is something that traditional art history, with its eye focused on works of fine art, has tended to miss.

If we add these two things together: namely the primacy the surrealists themselves gave to the illustrative photograph, and the failure of stylistic concepts derived from the formal, pictorial code—distinctions like linear/painterly or representational/abstract—to forge any kind of unity from the apparent diversity of surrealist production, the failure to arrive, that is, at what Rubin called an *intrinsic definition* of surrealism, we might be led to the possibility that it is within the photographic rather than the pictorial code that such a definition is to be found—that is, that issues of surrealist heterogeneity will be resolved around the semiological functions of photography rather than the formal properties operating the traditional art-historical classifications of style. What is at stake, then, is the relocation of photography from its eccentric position relative to surrealism to one that is absolutely central—definitive, one might say.

Now, it may be objected that in turning to photography for a principle of unification, one is simply replacing one set of problems with another. For the same visual heterogeneity reigns within the domain of surrealist photography as within its painting and sculpture. Quickly examining the range of surrealist photographic forms, we can think of 1) the absolutely banal images Boiffard created for Breton's *Nadja*; 2) the less banal but still straight photographs made by Boiffard for *Documents* in 1929, such as the ones made for Georges Bataille's essay on the big toe; 3) still "straight," but raising certain questions about the status of photographic evidence, the documentations of sculptural objects that have no existence apart from the photograph, which were immediately dismantled after being recorded (examples are by Hans Bellmer and Man Ray); moving, then, into the great range of processes used to manipulate the image; 4) the frequent use of negative printing; 5) the recourse to multiple exposure or sandwich printing to produce montage effects; 6) various kinds of manipulations with mirrors, as in the Kertész *Distortion* series; 7) the two processes made famous by Man Ray, namely solarization and the cameraless image of the rayograph—the latter having a rather obvious appeal to surrealist sensibilities because of the cursive, graphic quality of

J.-A. Boiffard. Illustration for Georges Bataille, "Le Gros Orteil," Documents, *no. 6, 1929.*

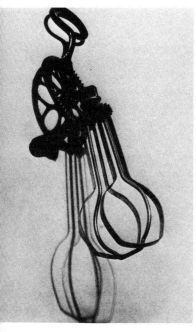

Man Ray. Man. *1918.*   *Hans Bellmer.* La Poupée. *1934.*

the images against their flattened, abstracted ground and because of the psychological status these ghosts of objects seem to have attained—Ribemont-Dessaignes
calling them "these objects of dreams," Man Ray himself locating them more
within the domain of memory by their effect of "recalling the event more or less
clearly, like the undisturbed ashes of an object consumed by flames";[20] 8) the
technique Raoul Ubac called brûlage, in which the emulsion is burned (which
literalizes Man Ray's evocative description of the rayograph), the process having
arisen from an attempt to assimilate photography fully into the domain of
automatic practice, just as the series of graphic manipulations that Brassaï made
in the mid-1930s attempted to open photographic information to a direct relationship with a kind of automatist, drawn image.

Long as this list is, there is one form still missing from it, namely, photomontage. This form, pioneered by Dada, was rarely employed by surrealist
photographers, though it was attractive to certain of the surrealist poets, who
made photomontages themselves. One important example is André Breton's 1938
self-portrait entitled *Automatic Writing.*

Breton's self-portrait, fabricated from various photographic elements, is not
only an example of photomontage—a process distinct from combination printing
insofar as the term refers, for the most part, to the cutting up and reassembling of
already printed material—but it is also an instance of construction *en abyme*. It is
the microscope as representative of a lensed instrument that places within the field
of the representation another representation that reduplicates an aspect of the first,
namely the photographic process by which the parts were originally made. And if

20.   Man Ray, *Exhibition Rayographs 1921–1928*, Stuttgart, L.G.A., 1963.

André Kertész. Distortion. *1933.*

Breton does this, it is to set up the intellectual rhyme between psychic automatism as a process of mechanical recording and the automatism associated with the camera—"that blind instrument," as Breton says. His own association of these two mechanical means of registration occurs as early as 1920, when he declared that "automatic writing, which appeared at the end of the 19th century, is a true photography of thought."[21]

But if an icon of the lens's automatism is placed inside this image entitled *Écriture-Automatique*, what, we might ask, of the concept of writing itself? Is that not entirely foreign to the purely visual experience of photography—a visuality itself symbolized as heightened and intensified by the presence of the microscope? Faced with this image and its caption, are we not confronted with yet another instance of the constant juxtaposition of writing and vision, a juxtaposition that leads nowhere but to theoretical confusion? It is my intention to show that this time it leads not to confusion but to clarity, to exactly the kind of dialectical synthesis of opposites that Breton had set out as the program for surrealism. For what I wish to claim is that the notion of *écriture* is pictured inside this work through the very fabric of the image's making, that is, through the medium of montage.

Throughout the avant-garde in the 1920s, photomontage was understood as a means of infiltrating the mere picture of reality with its meaning. This was achieved through juxtaposition: of image with image, or image with drawing, or image with text. John Heartfield said, "A photograph can, by the addition of an

21. In a text introducing Ernst's *Fatagaga* photomontages, reprinted in Max Ernst, *Beyond Painting and Other Writings by the Artist and His Friends*, New York, Wittenborn Schultz, 1948, p. 177.

unimportant spot of color, become a photomontage, a work of art of a special kind."[22] And what kind this was to be is explained by Tretyakov when he wrote, "If the photograph, under the influence of the text (or caption), expresses not simply the fact which it shows, but also the social tendency expressed by the fact, then this is already a photomontage."[23] Aragon seconded this insistence on a sense of reality bearing its own interpretation when he described Heartfield's work, "As he was playing with the fire of appearance, reality took fire around him. . . . The scraps of photographs that he formerly manoeuvred for the pleasure of stupefaction, under his fingers began to *signify*."[24]

This insistence on signification as a political act, on a revision of photography away from the surfaces of the real, was preached by Bertolt Brecht, who said, "A photograph of the Krupp works or GEC yields almost nothing about these institutions. . . . Therefore something has actively to be *constructed*, something artificial, something set-up."[25] This was a position that was uncongenial to the

22.   John Heartfield, *Photomontages of the Nazi Period*, New York, Universe Books, 1977, p. 26.
23.   *Ibid.*
24.   Louis Aragon, "John Heartfield et la beauté révolutionnaire" (1935), reprinted in Aragon, *Les Collages*, Paris, Hermann, 1965, pp. 78–79.
25.   In Walter Benjamin, "A Short History of Photography," trans. Stanley Mitchell, *Screen*, vol. 13, no. 1 (Spring 1972), 24.

DURCH LICHT ZUR NACHT

Also sprach Dr. Goebbels: Laßt uns aufs neue Brände entfachen.

proto-surrealist Max Ernst, who dismissed the Berlin dadaists with the words, "C'est vraiment allemand. Les intellectuels allemands ne peuvent pas faire ni caca ni pipi sans des idéologies."[26] But photomontage was nonetheless the medium of the *Fatagagas* and remained an abiding principal in Ernst's later work; and when Aragon wrote about the effect of the separate elements in Ernst's montages he compared them to "words."[27] By this he refers not only to the transparency of each signifying element (by contrast with the opacity of the pieces of cubist collages), but also to the experience of each element as a separate unit which, like a word, is conditioned by its placement within the syntagmatic chain of the sentence, is controlled by the condition of syntax.

Whether we think of syntax as temporal—as the pure succession of one word after another within the unreeling of the spoken sentence; or whether we think of it as spatial—as the serial progression of separate units on the printed page; syntax in either dimension reduces to the basic exteriority of one unit to another. Traditional linguistics contemplates this pure exteriority as that fissure or gap or blank that exists between signs, separating them one from the other, just as it also

26.   Cited in Dawn Ades, *Photomontage*, New York, Pantheon, 1976, p. 19.
27.   Louis Aragon, "La Peinture au défi," in *Les Collages*, p. 44.

Far left: André Breton. L'Écriture automatique. *1938.*

Left: John Heartfield. Durch Licht zur Nacht. *May 10, 1933.*

This page: Raoul Hausman. ABCD. *1923–4.*

thinks of the units of the sign itself as riven into two parts—one irremediably outside or exterior to the other. The two parts are signified and signifier—the first the meaning of the sign, a meaning transparent to thought held within consciousness; the second, the mark or sound that is the sign's material vehicle. "The order of the signified," Derrida writes, stating the position of traditional linguistics, "is never contemporary, is at best the subtly discrepant inverse or parallel—discrepant by the time of a breath—from the order of the signifier."[28] For Derrida, of course, spacing is not an exteriority that signals the outside boundaries of meaning: one signified's end before another's onset. Rather, spacing is radicalized as the precondition for meaning as such, and the outsideness of spacing is revealed as already constituting the condition of the "inside." This movement, in which spacing "invaginates" presence, will be shown to illuminate the distinction between surrealist photography and its dada predecessor.

In dada montage the experience of blanks or spacing is very strong, for between the silhouettes of the photographed forms the white page announces itself as the medium that both combines and separates them. The white page is not

28.   Derrida, *Of Grammatology*, p. 18.

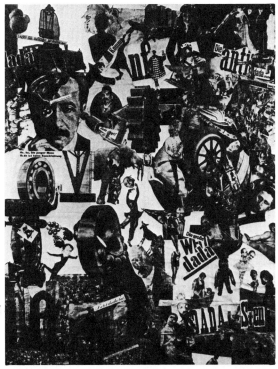

This page: Hannah Hoch. Cut with the Cake-Knife. *1919.*

Right: Man Ray. Lilies. *1930.*

Far right: Roger Parry. Illustration for Léon-Paul Fargue, Banalité, *1928.*

the opaque surface of cubist collage, asserting the formal and material unity of the visual support; the white page is rather the fluid matrix within which each representation of reality is secured in isolation, held within a condition of exteriority, of syntax, of spacing.

The photographic image, thus "spaced," is deprived of one of the most powerful of photography's many illusions. It is robbed of a sense of presence. Photography's vaunted capture of a moment in time is the seizure and freezing of presence. It is the image of simultaneity, of the way that everything within a given space at a given moment is present to everything else; it is a declaration of the seamless integrity of the real. The photograph carries on one continuous surface the trace or imprint of all that vision captures in one glance. The photographic image is not only a trophy of this reality, but a document of its unity as that-which-was-present-at-one-time. But spacing destroys simultaneous presence: for it shows things sequentially, either one after another or external to one another—occupying separate cells. It is spacing that makes it clear—as it was to Heartfield, Tretyakov, Brecht, Aragon—that we are not looking at reality, but at the world infested by interpretation or signification, which is to say, reality distended by the gaps or blanks which are the formal preconditions of the sign.

Now, as I said, the surrealist photographers rarely used photomontage. Their interest was in the seamless unity of the print, with no intrusions of the

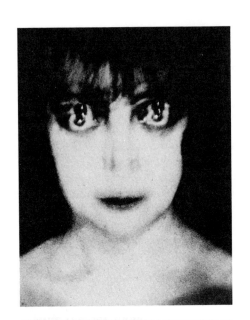

white page. By preserving the body of the print intact, they could make it read photographically, that is to say, in direct contact with reality. But without exception the surrealist photographers infiltrated the body of this print, this single page, with spacing. Sometimes they mimicked photomontage by means of combination printing. But that is the least interesting of their strategies, because it does not create, forcefully enough, an experience of the real itself as sign, the real fractured by spacing. The cloisonné of the solarized print is to a greater extent testimony to this kind of cleavage in reality. As are the momentarily unintelligible gaps created by negative printing. But more important than anything else is the strategy of doubling. For it is doubling that produces the formal rhythm of spacing—the two-step that banishes the unitary condition of the moment, that creates *within* the moment an experience of fission. For it is doubling that elicits the notion that to an original has been added its copy. The double is the simulacrum, the second, the representative of the original. It comes after the first, and in this following, it can only exist as figure, or image. But in being seen in conjunction with the original, the double destroys the pure singularity of the first. Through duplication, it opens the original to the effect of difference, of deferral, of one-thing-after-another, or within another: of multiples burgeoning within the same.

This sense of deferral, of opening reality to the "interval of a breath," we have been calling (following Derrida) *spacing*. But doubling does something else

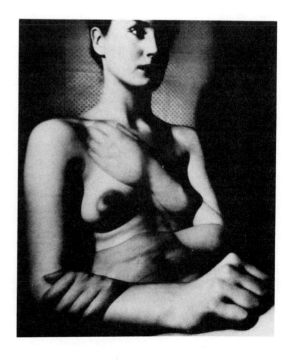

Top left: Man Ray. La Marquise Casati (1922).

Lower left: Maurice Tabard. Untitled (1929).

This page: Bill Brandt. Perspective of Nudes.

besides the transmutation of presence into succession. It marks the first in the chain as a signifying element: it transmutes raw matter into the conventionalized form of the signifier. Lévi-Strauss describes the importance of pure phonemic doubling in the onset of linguistic experience in infancy—the child's dawning knowledge of signs.

> Even at the babbling stage the phoneme group /pa/ can be heard. But the difference between /pa/ and /papa/ does not reside simply in reduplication: /pa/ is a noise, /papa/ is a word. The reduplication indicates intent on the part of the speaker; it endows the second syllable with a function different from that which would have been performed by the first separately, or in the form of a potentially limitless series of identical sounds /papapapa/ produced by mere babbling. Therefore the second /pa/ is not a repetition of the first, nor has it the same signification. It is a sign that, like itself, the first /pa/ too was a sign, and that as a pair they fall into the category of signifiers, not of things signified.[29]

Repetition is thus the indicator that the "wild sounds" of babbling have been made deliberate, intentional; and that what they intend is meaning. Doubling is in this sense the "signifier of signification."[30]

From the perspective of formed language, the phonemes /pa/ or /ma/ seem less like wild sounds and more like verbal elements *in potentia*. But if we think of the infant's production of gutturals and glottal stops, and other sounds that do not form a part of spoken English, we have a stronger sense of this babbling as the raw material of sonic reality. Thus /pa/ moving to /papa/ seems less disconnected from the case of photographic doubling, where the material of the image is the world in front of the camera.

As I said above, surrealist photography exploits the special connection to reality with which all photography is endowed. For photography is an imprint or transfer off the real; it is a photochemically processed trace causally connected to that thing in the world to which it refers in a manner parallel to that of fingerprints or footprints or the rings of water that cold glasses leave on tables. The photograph is thus generically distinct from painting or sculpture or drawing. On the family tree of images it is closer to palm prints, death masks, the Shroud of Turin, or the tracks of gulls on beaches. For technically and semiologically speaking, drawings and paintings are icons, while photographs are indexes.

Given this special status with regard to the real, being, that is, a kind of deposit of the real itself, the manipulations wrought by the surrealist

29.   Claude Lévi-Strauss, *The Raw and the Cooked*, trans. J. and D. Weightman, New York, Harper & Row, 1970, pp. 339–340.
30.   *Ibid.* See Craig Owens, "Photography *en abyme,*" *October*, no. 5 (Summer 1978), 73–88, for another use of this passage in the analysis of photography.

Hans Bellmer. La Poupée. *1934.*

Maurice Tabard. Solarized Guitar. *1933.*

photographers—the spacings and doublings—are intended to register the spacings and doublings of that very reality of which *this* photograph is merely the
faithful trace. In this way the photographic medium is exploited to produce a
paradox: the paradox of reality constituted as sign—or presence transformed into
absence, into representation, into spacing, into writing.

Now this is the move that lies at the very heart of surrealist thinking, for it is
precisely this experience of *reality as representation* that constitutes the notion of
the Marvelous or of Convulsive Beauty—the key concepts of surrealism.[31] Towards the beginning of *L'Amour fou* there is a section that Breton had published
on its own under the title "Beauty Will Be Convulsive. . . . " In this manifesto
Breton characterizes Convulsive Beauty in terms of three basic types of example.
The first falls under the general case of mimicry—or those instances in nature
when one thing imitates another—the most familiar, perhaps, being those
markings on the wings of moths that imitate eyes. Breton is enormously attracted
to mimicry, as were all the surrealists, *Documents* having, for example, published
Blossfeldt's photographs of plant life imitating the volutes and flutings of classical
architecture. In "Beauty Will Be Convulsive" the instances of mimicry Breton uses
are the coral imitations of plants on the Great Barrier Reef and "The Imperial
Mantle," from a grotto near Montpellier, where a wall of quartz offers the
spectacle of natural carving, producing the image of drapery "which forever defies
that of statuary." Mimicry is thus an instance of the natural production of signs,
of one thing in nature contorting itself into a representation of another.

Breton's second example is "the expiration of movement"—the experience of
something that should be in motion but has been stopped, derailed, or, as
Duchamp would have said, "delayed." In this regard Breton writes, "I am sorry
not to be able to reproduce, among the illustrations to this text, a photograph of a
very handsome locomotive after it had been abandoned for many years to the
delirium of a virgin forest."[32] That Breton should have wanted to show a
photograph of this object is compelling because the very idea of stop-motion is
intrinsically photographic. The convulsiveness, then, the arousal in front of the
object, is to a perception of it detached from the continuum of its natural
existence, a detachment which deprives the locomotive of some part of its physical
self and turns it into a sign of the reality it no longer possesses. The still
photograph of this stilled train would thus be a representation of an object already
constituted as a representation.

Breton's third example consists of the found-object or found verbal
fragment—both instances of objective chance—where an emissary from the
external world carries a message informing the recipient of his own desire. The
found-object is a *sign* of that desire. The particular object Breton uses at the

31.   Louis Aragon's 1925 definition of the Marvelous reads, "Le merveilleux, c'est la contradiction
qui apparaît dans le réel" ("Idées," *La Révolution surréaliste*, vol. I [April 1925] 30).
32.   André Breton, *L'Amour fou*, Paris, Gallimard, 1937, p. 13.

opening of *L'Amour fou* is a perfect demonstration of Convulsive Beauty's condition as sign. The object is a slipper-spoon that Breton found in a flea market, and which he recognized as a fulfillment of the wish spoken by the automatic phrase that had begun running through his mind some months before—the phrase *cendrier Cendrillon*, or Cinderella ashtray. The flea-market object became something that signified for him as he began to see it as an extraordinary *mise-en-abyme*: a chain of reduplications to infinity in which the spoon and handle of the object was seen as the front and last of a shoe of which the little carved slipper was the heel. Then *that* slipper was imagined as having for its heel another slipper, and so on to infinity. Breton read the natural writing of this chain of reduplicated slippers as signifying his own desire for love and thus as the sign that begins the quest of *L'Amour fou*.[33]

If we are to generalize the aesthetic of surrealism, the concept of Convulsive Beauty is at the core of that aesthetic: reducing to an experience of reality transformed into representation. Surreality *is*, we could say, nature convulsed into a kind of writing. The special access that photography has to this experience is its privileged connection to the real. The manipulations then available to photography—what we have been calling doubling and spacing—appear to document these convulsions. The photographs are not *interpretations* of reality, decoding it, as in Heartfield's photomontages. They are presentations of that very reality as configured, or coded, or written. The experience of nature as sign, or nature as representation, comes "naturally" then to photography. It extends, as well, to that domain most inherently photographic, which is that of the framing

33.   *Ibid.*, pp. 35–41.

(Photo Man Ray)

8.   DE LA HAUTEUR D'UN PETIT SOULIER FAISANT CORPS AVEC ELLE (p. 35)

Man Ray. *Illustration for André Breton,* L'Amour fou, *1937.*

BILLET D'AUTOBUS ROULÉ "SYMÉTRIQUEMENT", FORME TRÈS RARE
D'AUTOMATISME MORPHOLOGIQUE AVEC GERMES ÉVIDENTS DE STÉRÉOTYPIE.

NUMÉRO D'AUTOBUS ROULÉ, TROUVÉ DANS LA POCHE DE VESTON D'UN
BUREAUCRATE MOYEN (CRÉDIT LYONNAIS); CARACTÉRISTIQUES LES PLUS
FRÉQUENTES DE "MODERN'STYLE".

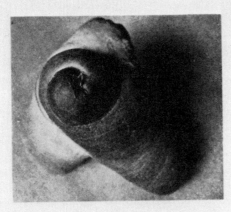

LE PAIN ORNEMENTAL ET MODERN'STYLE ÉCHAPPE A LA
STÉRÉOTYPIE MOLLE.

MORCEAU DE SAVON PRÉSENTANT DES FORMES AUTOMATIQUES
MODERN'STYLE, TROUVÉ DANS UN LAVABO.

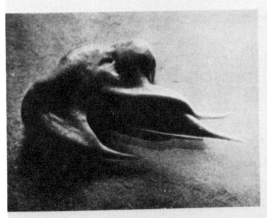
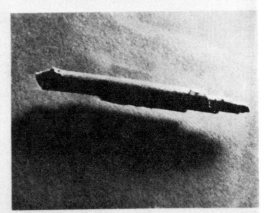

LE HASARD MORPHOLOGIQUE DU DENTIFRICE RÉPANDU N'ÉCHAPPE
PAS A LA STÉRÉOTYPIE FINE ET ORNEMENTALE.

ENROULEMENT ÉLÉMENTAIRE OBTENU CHEZ UN "DÉBILE MENTAL".

SCULPTURES INVOLONTAIRES

edge of the image experienced as cut or cropped. But I would add, though there is no space here to expand on it, that what unites *all* surrealist production is precisely this experience of nature as representation, physical matter as writing. This is of course not a morphological coherence, but a semiological one.

No account of surrealist photography would be complete if it could not incorporate the unmanipulated images that figure in the movement's publications—works like the Boiffard big toes, or the "Involuntary Sculptures" photographed by Brassaï for Salvador Dali, or the straight image of a hatted figure by Man Ray made for *Minotaure*. Because it is *this* type that is closest to the movement's heart. But the theoretical apparatus by which to assimilate this genre of photograph has already been developed. And that is the concept of spacing.

Inside the image, spacing can be generated by the cloisonné of solarization or the use of found frames to interrupt or displace segments of reality. But at the very boundary of the image the camera frame which crops or cuts the represented element out of reality-at-large can be seen as another example of spacing. Spacing is the indication of a break in the simultaneous experience of the real, a rupture that issues into sequence. Photographic cropping is *always* experienced as a rupture in the continuous fabric of reality. But surrealist photography puts enormous pressure on that frame to make it itself read as a sign—an empty sign it is true, but an integer in the calculus of meaning: a signifier of signification.

The frame announces that between the part of reality that was cut away and this part there is a difference; and that this segment which the frame frames is an example of nature-as-representation, nature-as-sign. As it signals that experience of reality the camera frame also controls it, configures it. This it does by point-of-view, as in the Man Ray example, or by focal length, as in the extreme close-ups of the Dali. And in both these instances what the camera frames and thereby makes visible is the automatic writing of the world: the constant, uninterrupted production of signs. Dali's images are of those nasty pieces of paper like bus tickets and theater stubs that we roll into little columns in our pockets, or those pieces of eraser that we unconsciously knead—these are what his camera produces through the enlargements that he publishes as involuntary sculpture. Man Ray's photograph is one of several to accompany an essay by Tristan Tzara about the unconscious production of sexual imagery throughout all aspects of culture—this particular one being the design of hats.

The frame announces the camera's ability to find and isolate what we could call the world's constant writing of erotic symbols, its ceaseless automatism. In this capacity the frame can itself be glorified, represented, as in the photograph by Man Ray that I introduced at the outset. Or it can simply be there, silently operating as spacing, as in Brassaï's seizure of automatic production in his series on graffiti.

And now, with this experience of the frame, we arrive at the supplement. Throughout Europe in the twenties and thirties, camera-seeing was exalted as a special form of vision: the New Vision, Moholy-Nagy called it. From the Inkhuk

Brassaï. Photographs for Sculptures Involontaires. *Published in* Minotaure *(1933).*

to the Bauhaus to the ateliers of Montparnasse, the New Vision was understood in the same way. As Moholy explained it, human eyesight was, simply, defective, weak, impotent. "Helmholtz," Moholy explained, "used to tell his pupils that if an optician were to succeed in making a human eye and brought it to him for his approval, he would be bound to say: 'This is a clumsy piece of work.'" But the invention of the camera has made up for this deficiency so that now "we may say that we see the world with different eyes."[34]

These, of course, are camera-eyes. They see faster, sharper, at stranger angles, closer-to, microscopically, with a transposition of tonalities, with the penetration of X ray, and with access to the multiplication of images that makes possible the writing of association and memory. Camera-seeing is thus an extraordinary extension of normal vision, one that supplements the deficiencies of the naked eye. The camera covers and arms this nakedness, it acts as a kind of prosthesis, enlarging the capacity of the human body.

But in increasing the ways in which the world can be present to vision, the

34.   László Moholy-Nagy, *Vision in Motion*, Chicago, 1947, p. 206.

Man Ray. Illustration for Tzara, "D'un Certain Automatisme du Gout," Minotaure *(1933).*

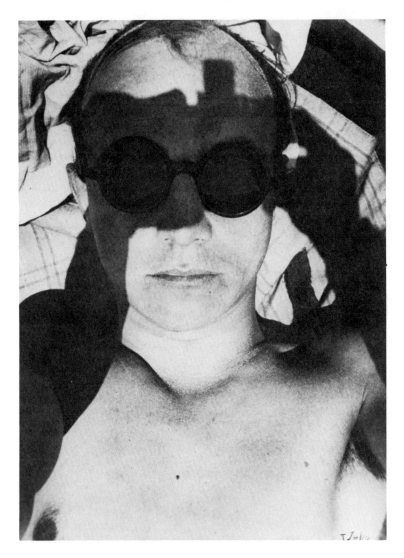

Umbo. Self-Portrait. *c. 1930.*

camera mediates that presence, gets between the viewer and the world, shapes reality according to *its* terms. Thus what supplements and enlarges human vision also supplants the viewer himself; the camera is the aid who comes to usurp.

The experience of the camera as prosthesis and the image of it figuring in the field of the photograph is everywhere to be found in the New Vision.[35] In Umbo's self-portrait the camera is represented by a cast shadow whose relationship to the photographer's eyes involves the interesting paradox of all supplementary devices, where the very thing that extends, displaces as well. In this image the camera that

35.   See my "Jump over the Bauhaus," *October*, no. 15 (Winter 1980), 103–110.

literally expands Umbo's vision, allowing him to see himself, also masks his eyes, nearly extinguishing them in shadow.

Florence Henri's self-portrait functions in similar ways. There the camera's frame is revealed as that which masters or dominates the subject, and the phallic shape she constructs for its symbol is continuous with the form that most of world culture has used for the expression of supremacy. The supplement is thus experienced emblematically, through the internalized representation of the camera frame as an image of mastery: camera-seeing essentialized as a superior power of focus and selection from within the inchoate sprawl of the real.

Throughout Europe in the 1920s there was the experience of something supplemental added to reality. That this was coherently experienced and actively configured in the photography made with the supplementary instrument accounts for the incredible coherence of European photography of this period—not, as is sometimes suggested, its diffraction into different sects. But it is my thesis that what the surrealists in particular added to that reality was the vision of it *as* representation or sign. Reality was both extended and replaced or supplanted by that master supplement which is writing: the paradoxical writing of the photograph.

Washington, D.C., 1981

This New Art: To Draw in Space

In 1932, as he is about to christen the approach to sculpture that he and Picasso have just invented, Julio Gonzalez's thoughts move backward in time and outward in space to the ancient practice of configuring the constellations. From eight points of light the Greeks and Phoenecians bodied forth the cape of Orion and behind that the phantom presence of the man and his sword; while twenty stars sufficed to suggest the mast and rigging of the ship *Argo* — although the relation of those twenty to the form of a vessel is just as inscrutable as the eight are to the shape of the hunter and his cloak. With this strange indifference to the look of things, the constellations project the natural world of ships and swans into the heavens, inscribing it there with a drawing that does not stoop to the business of tracing likenesses. To draw with the stars is to constellate, which means to employ a technique that is neither mimetic nor abstract. "In the restlessness of the night, the stars mark out points of hope in the sky," Gonzales writes. "It is these points in the infinite which are the precursors of this new art: To draw in space."

The phrase is taken from the 1932 essay that Gonzalez dedicated to the work of Picasso: "Picasso sculpteur et les cathédrales."[1] But the domain of thinking from which it emerges has less to do with Picasso's practice of the new sculptural technique than it does with Gonzalez's own.

By now the Picasso/Gonzalez collaboration is fixed in the annals of twentieth-century art. In 1928, wanting to translate a group of latticelike drawings into small three-dimensional models constructed of iron wire, Picasso called on Gonzalez, his friend and countryman. Gonzalez, who had apprenticed in the decorative metal trade under his father, had worked as a master craftsman for more than thirty years. Although for fifteen of those years he had also exhibited in Parisian galleries and salons — mostly paintings and small *repoussé* heads in bronze or silver — he identified himself on those occasions as either a jeweler or a decorative artist. This modesty and his expertise in the full range of

1.   In Josephine Withers, *Julio Gonzalez/Sculpture in Iron*, New York University Press, New York, 1978, pp. 131–138. All quotes by Gonzalez are taken from this text.

smithing procedures, including the relatively new technique of oxyacetylene welding, made him the perfect worker of Picasso's aesthetic will. Gonzalez carefully measured lengths of iron wire and, using solder for the joints, built the models according to plan. That was in 1928 and 1929. One year elapsed, and then Picasso returned to Gonzalez's studio for a new bout of work with iron.

In this second phase the sculptures were larger and less involved with the careful translation of a two-dimensional blueprint into a freestanding model. The technique was one of assemblage—the concatenation of various parts, all of them scrap iron, some of them found-objects: collanders, shoemakers' lasts, industrial springs. Gonzalez's skill in direct-metal processes permitted Picasso's collage sensibility to erupt within the three-dimensional world of sculpture. For Gonzalez the power of this eruption was, literally, earthshaking—the beginning of what he called "this new art: To draw in space."

But except for the few maquettes of 1928–29, Picasso was not really concerned with drawing in space; he was interested in assemblage: in maintaining the work's terrestrial quality by compromising its formal elegance with the quiddity and banality of the everyday object insinuated into the midst of the metal scrap. So Gonzalez's characterization of his friend's enterprise, although generous, was not quite correct. It was, instead, self-descriptive.

In 1929, through Picasso's example, Gonzalez found himself liberated into an artist of major aesthetic ambition. For the first time he realized that the techniques of which he was master could be pressed into the service of Art—that art was not invariably to be found elsewhere, higher up than the realm of Vulcan, but was to be produced there also, from the mouth of the forge. A few years later another, much younger artist was to feel the exact same sense of liberation when faced with the revelation of Picasso's tack-welded lattice constructions. That artist, David Smith, so fully sympathized with Gonzalez's position that in writing about the revelation of the aesthetic potential of direct-metal sculpture Smith simply extrapolated from his own experience to that of Gonzalez. "When a man is trained in metalworking," Smith wrote, "and has pursued it as labor with the ideal of art represented by oil painting, it is very difficult to conceive that what has been labor and livelihood is the same means by which art can be made."[2] But for Gonzalez (as was also the case for Smith by the later 1930s) the point of this revelation was not a sculpture of assemblage and a sensibility of collage. The point was the further invention of a new kind of drawing: the sculptural inscription of space. From the very outset of Gonzalez's newly established persona as Artist come works—such as the 1929 *Don Quixote*—that announce this intention.

2.   David Smith, "First Master of the Torch," *Art News,* LIV (February 1956), 36. Smith first saw Picasso's (and Gonzalez's) constructions in reproduction, in a 1936 issue of *Cahiers d'art.*

That Gonzalez's maturity as an artist should have been the product of just one year's development, so that from 1930 to 1939 there came an almost unbroken chain of masterpieces, is undoubtedly a function of the artist's age and experience at the time of his contact with Picasso—he was 52—and also of his intimate knowledge of avant-garde production during the decade that preceded their collaboration. Aside from his close friendships with Picasso and Brancusi, Gonzalez was connected, by ties that went back to his youth in Barcelona, with Torrès-Garcia, the Argentine artist who arrived via Spain and America in Paris in 1924. Polemical by nature, Torrès-Garcia was voluble in his articulation of the various factions that split the Parisian avant-garde of the 1920s. Needing to take sides (against surrealism, against neoclassicism), Torrès-Garcia joined forces with Michel Seuphor and formed the association of abstract artists, Cercle et Carré. This was in 1929, the year of Gonzalez's breakthrough. But the theoretical disputes in which Torrès-Garcia engaged and the colleagues who gathered around him were active before then, and through his friendship with Torrès-Garcia, Gonzalez knew both the issues and the protagonists. Hélion and Vantongerloo had become friends of Gonzalez's and Mondrian, Arp, Ozenfant, and Léger his acquaintances. He was thus at the center of the debate over abstraction—of abstraction as the tool to overthrow the material realm of nature and the means of instituting a reign of pure spirit or intellect. Modern man was thought to be conceptual man, and his art must reflect with greatest accuracy his power of intellection.

But militant abstraction neither convinced nor interested Gonzalez. He found the spirit of mathematics cold and unlovely and liked to quote Picasso saying, "Try to draw by hand a perfect circle—a useless task." Gonzalez would then add, "One will not produce great art in making perfect circles and squares with the aid of compass and ruler, or in drawing one's inspiration from New York skyscrapers. The truly novel works, which often look bizarre, are, quite simply, those which are directly inspired by Nature."

Thus, if the gathering forces for abstract art had advertised the conditions of twentieth-century aesthetics as a struggle between abstraction and naturalism, spirit and matter, conception and representation, culture and nature, Gonzalez was forced to acknowledge that he was unwilling to take sides against nature. Trained in the arts of decoration, and trained to think of the decorative as a modality of the frivolous, Gonzalez's term of highest praise for that which was truly art was that it was "serious." And for him, an art that completely abandoned nature could not be serious.

By committing himself to drawing from nature, Gonzalez inaugurated his sculptural activity with a process that was as far as possible from that of Picasso's improvisatory assemblage. One of his early major works, *Woman Combing Her Hair* (1931) exemplifies this procedure. To compare the finished work in iron with the pencil sketch from which it comes is to see that the one is a

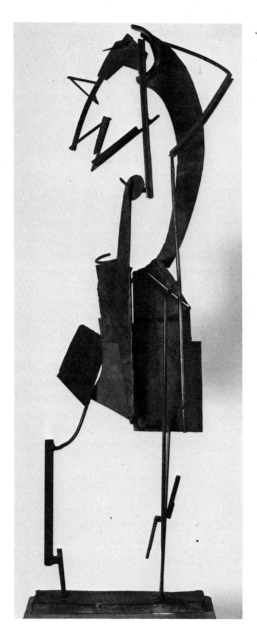

Julio Gonzalez. Woman Combing Her Hair.
*1931. Iron, 67 by 21 ¾ by 7 ⅞ inches.
Musée National d'Art Moderne, Centre Georges
Pompidou, Paris.*

 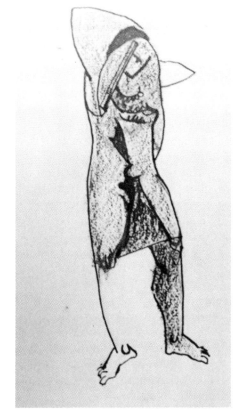

Julio Gonzalez. Study for Woman Combing Her Hair. *c. 1931. Drawing.*

Julio Gonzalez. Woman Getting Dressed. *c. 1930. Drawing.*

quite literal copy or transcription of the other. The rounded vertical plane of the drawing that profiles the woman's bowed back and neck finds its reciprocal twin — enlarged, of course — in the finished sculpture. And from this neck the drawing projects the jagged contour of hair falling forward over the face of the woman as she reaches up to comb it. Again, this contour is repeated in the sculpture.

But at this point a chasm opens between the two objects — sculpture and drawing — which is not the gap that divides two different media but that which separates two different levels of legibility. The four rods of metal that loosely configure a **W** as they project from the neck of the figure do not "read" in anything like the way the almost identical profile reads in the drawing. Unlike its penciled version, the metal **W** is unintelligible as hair tossed forward over the head; it is a gangling shape, as ineffectual as a half-clenched fist closing over a portion of empty space, its grasp on the conventions of figure/ground separation forever relaxed.

A penciled contour is easily filled in by the viewer who seeks to conjure a body from a network of lines. His perceptual faculties hasten his search for figurative completion, segregating the closed forms from the amorphous backgrounds that serve only as the matrix in which to structure completed wholes. With the page to orient him, the viewer of Gonzalez's sketch has no trouble seeing the white space within the pencilled W as materially different from the rest of the page's white expanse. He sees it as hair falling forward, and the angle projected out from its far side he easily visualizes as the elbow of the raised right arm of the woman reaching up toward her bent head. Solid is thus distinguished from void and near from far.

But in the metal translation none of this is true. The tiny iron angle that attaches itself to the outer rim of the W simply does not function for vision as the reciprocal limb to the woman's near arm and elbow. And by not functioning to configure a pair, the illegible right arm deserts the left arm to its own fate of uncertain identity.

It is not that one cannot see instantly that *Woman Combing Her Hair* is the representation of a standing figure. Two stalklike legs, a torso and erect spine guarantee, at its broadest scale, the visual mime of human presence. But in the closer detail of the metal drawing, as it translates from pencil to iron, meaning is elided, the way inept renderings of idiomatic phrases in a foreign language create a chaos of literalness in place of smooth fields of sense. The falling hair, the raised arms, are victims of the kind of literalness that changes *n'est-ce pas* to "isn't it"; and the paradoxical result of this literalness is that the upper part of this particular figure is crowned with an aureole of metal line that is completely abstract.

It would be exhausting to trace this breakdown of configurative sense over the various sites at which it occurs in the *Woman Combing Her Hair*. But the basic fact is that the sketch made in the presence of the model (and thus from nature) was able to render the body even though certain elisions, certain omissions, certain condensations were made in the depiction of the form. In the sketch the model's leg can be seen even though only the elegant curve of the calf and ankle are drawn, leaving to the viewer's imagination the projection of knee and the plane of shin. The point at which abstraction threatens complete unintelligibility is the point at which the drawing is translated to metal. Abstraction is thus a function of a specific process—in this case the process of making a copy.

One of the phenomena that fascinates students of printmaking is precisely this burgeoning of abstraction within the realm of naturalistic representation, due to the procedures of copying. Before photography, famous works of art owed their dissemination to the activities of the copyist: the man who translated the colors and textures of the painted masterpiece into the black and white line of the engraver's plate. Since the copies could circulate in ways the original obviously could not, it was from the black and white engraving that further copies would be made, for luxury albums, for example, or by student artists. Now this second copyist is often faced with a problem. Is that dark spot rendered on the side of, say, a figure's neck in the first print a patch of shadow or is it a part of the man's attire? The interpretation of the meaning of various forms, once one is at this second remove from the original, is what becomes precarious. And this is true not only for the identification of objects, like the ambiguous piece of clothing, but also for spatial relations, as foreshortened limbs lose the certainty of their original hold on space.

Every form of communication — visual, oral, textual — has its particular mode of breakdown or rupture. And as William Ivins shows in *Prints and Visual Communication*, the special breaking point for the visual arts is located in the channel of transmission that involves the translation to copies. In yet another standard text of art-historical reasoning — Ernst Gombrich's *Art and Illusion* — we are taught not to relegate copying to an accidental or marginal part of the making of art. Gombrich offers various formulae, like "making and matching" or "schema and correction," to spell for us the highly conventionalized patterns of rendering that are transmitted from master to apprentice (the patterns for "making" clouds, foliage, draperies) without much of natural appearance allowed to intervene. The pattern books that are the backbone of architectural production, so that a building can be cooked up from a detail taken from here and a ground plan drawn from there, are just one example of the extent to which aesthetic production has always been at one level the art of making copies from other art.

The copyist is not only the slave of imitation. He is also, at times, the master of invention. Needing to decide about ambiguous patches (like the clothing/shadow ambiguity in the earlier example), he conjures a reading by imagining what would make sense. This new thing is what he then delineates. The children's game Telephone is an example of how a message passed from one person to another is transformed to a wholly new invention through the very rite of transmitted passage. Furthermore, one's feeling that ritual or other kinds of repeated forms have their source of meaning in some long since forgotten referent from which the forms derived but which they no longer in any way resemble, only adds to the suggestive resonance of these forms. Their quality as coded vehicles of repetition is what gives them their aesthetic authority. They have a purely formulaic rather than a mimetic relation to their referents. In this sense the emblematic is a function of the world of the copy rather than the world of nature.

The process of copying is deeply embedded in the industry of art. It is what separates that industry from the romantic experience of art as either the continually fresh reflection of nature or the ever original product of the imagination. Copying exists in a very different place from imagination or nature. For copying can neither be situated at the mimetic pole — the imitation of nature — nor at the abstract pole — the pure projection of imagination or spirit. In this set of relationships, the copy occupies that region structuralism terms *neuter*; for the copy is a combination of exclusions: it is both nonmimetic and nonabstract.

Even though it occupies the neuter level in the structuralist disposition of terms, the copy or translation is, as we have seen, the term most centered in the processes of actual art making. It is the term that defines the industry of art rather than the effects of art: the magic tricks seen from the wings of the theater, so to speak. It is a view of the bees in their hive rather than the taste of honey. In this sense it is the term of demystification.

I have said earlier that the aesthetic battle lines of the 1920s and '30s were drawn through the mimetic/abstract axis. But further, these terms were understood as fronts for another set of terms, namely matter and spirit. Any avant-garde text from this time — constructivist, neo-plasticist, abstraction-créationist, surrealist — will describe the actual aesthetic struggle as a war between the physical and the conceptual, a duality that we have no trouble translating further into mind/body. Gonzalez was, intellectually, a creature of his time, and when setting out to verbalize his aesthetic invention he used the current terms of the debate. "The real problem to be solved here," he writes, "is not only to wish to make a harmonious work, of a fine and perfectly balanced whole — No! But to get this [result] by the marriage of material and space, by the union of real forms with imagined forms, obtained or suggested by established points, or by perforations, and, according to the natural law of love, to mingle and make them inseparable one from another, as are the body and the spirit." This combination, this marriage of body and spirit, Gonzalez goes on to call "ennobling," a term that is entirely appropriate for the marriage in question. For like the yolk and white of the Platonic image, the noble offspring of this marriage is Man.

Thus the aesthetic field, as it was structured by the thinking of the twenties and thirties, was the collective semantic marker not for Art but for Man. The field was both thoroughly humanized and psychologized; its obsessive subjects either biological or psychic creation. Although a field agonized by the warring rights of abstraction and representation might seem to be defining the domain of the aesthetic, those terms functioned in fact to define the combined terrain of psyche and soma, the structural unity of Man. Furthermore, this was man in his essential or natural state, man as a function of nature rather than a product of culture. This is why the structural diagram places *copy* on a different level from the couple *mimetic/abstract*. The neutral term has nothing to do with the definition of natural man; it characterizes an exclusion of nature, a release into artifice. The copy does not occupy the "noble" realm of struggle. But it does reveal that the terms of that struggle are not aesthetically definitive but are instead psychological in kind. This is the sense in which *copy* is a demystifying term. It unmasks the definitive condition of art in the postwar period, to show that it functioned constantly to produce a mystique of culture-as-nature. Arp speaks for this mystification: "Art is fruit growing out of man like the fruit out of a plant, like the child out of the womb." The surrealist exfoliations of the unconscious (the mind in its natural state) by means of automatism were further attempts to mystify the cultural and parade it as nature.

Gonzalez, as I have said, mostly spoke the language of his time when he was writing about art. And why would he not? He was not by profession a theorist or critic. But certain of his expressions betray another level of his thinking and do not fit into the easy flow of that part of his argument that is simply borrowed from the collective text of the postwar avant-garde. In the passage by Gonzalez just cited, the aberrant phrase is the one that qualifies "imagined forms" as those "obtained or suggested by established points, or by perforations." Reading this we might wonder, what established points? How, in the fluidity of imaginative space, are points established? And we might then associate this to the image Gonzalez reaches for earlier in his text, when he has to characterize the inventiveness of his art. There the established points in space are stars, stars that draw cursive figures to which names are given and from whose abstract spines whole figures are imaginatively projected: the constellations. These points are indeed "established." But they are a function of ritual drawing. Only a cultural repetition can supply the phantom cape for the invisible Orion. The constellations translate the man, and in the terms of this translation they can be spoken of as "drawing in space."

Gonzalez's metaphorical use of the constellations is more eloquent and more precise in defining what had emerged from his use of direct-metal process than any of his constructivist cant about body and spirit. For the space defined by Gonzalez's sculptural drawing is the procedural space of transcription, of the translation of one medium (the sketch) into another (the three-dimensional construction). Abstraction is the almost effortless, because inevitable, product of this method—an abstraction that feels uncanny because the buried memory of the original model seems still to be active within the newly coded forms. The 1932 *Dream* is a powerful example of this eloquent indecipherability, as is *Head on a Long Stem* of the same year and *The Lovers II* of the next.

The openness of Gonzalez's metal drawing is a further product of his method, an openness made possible by the suggestiveness of the "established points." Unlike Picasso, Gonzalez was not working with the metaphors of bodies — with one object (a bicycle seat) employed because it resembled another (a bull's skull). He was not substituting one body for another to produce a sculpture of substantive collage: chains of metaphors fantastically agglutinated. Instead he was employing the baffles of translation, a process that moved him further and further from the corporeal object (the collander/head) and closer to a cursiveness that space itself (the space of Gonzalez's process: copying) would render abstract: the deep ambiguity of the **W** of *Woman Combing Her Hair.*

The kind of drawing in which Gonzalez engaged — this constellating — with its natural tendency to the nonphysical, without the doctrinaire quality of Cercle et Carré abstraction, was shared by a very few of Gonzalez's contemporaries. And in their hands, also, constellating became a powerful cursive mode. The most notable example is Miró, whose work in the 1930s was given over to this process.

In the domain of sculpture the seminal position of Gonzalez is certain. Had he no other follower but David Smith, his position as the disseminator of a new process would be secure. But there were others as well. Anthony Caro's "table sculptures" would be unthinkable without the brilliant series of seated figures that Gonzalez began in 1935 — a group that inspired Smith's "Albany" series as well. In both those later artists one feels the effects of the figurative underpinnings of Gonzalez's drawing in space as well as its peculiar drive toward abstraction.

In ending this discussion it might be interesting to confront, straight on, one of the conclusions to be drawn from what I have been saying about Gonzalez's process, his immersion in the modalities of transcription and copying, his distance from the metaphoric conditions of assemblage. Although he used metal scrap and the occasional found-object as well, the exigencies of Gonzalez's process meant that many of his shapes had to be obtained by reworking the scrap through forging and certainly relegating the industrial readymade parts — bolts or springs — to minor areas of the work. Gonzalez's sculpture was not about the transformations rung by perceptual association on the quotidian object. Therefore the uniqueness of that object — just this collander or this bicycle seat — was irrelevant to his work. Thus many of the issues of direct-metal working that would theoretically prohibit its translation into bronze are also irrelevant.

In the case of assemblage in direct-metal, the production of copies or multiples in bronze violates the *conceptual* uniqueness of the original; for it is born of a unique perceptual moment for which the specific process of direct-metal is the technical equivalent. But Gonzalez took direct-metal in another direction, which operated through the very channels of transcriptions and copies. Theoretically, then, the bronze editions that the Gonzalez Estate has been issuing during the last decades are not as deeply at variance with the character of his work as editions of Picasso's constructions would be of his.

The question of sculptural editions, of sculpture as having the potential for a multiple existence that goes quite against the grain of the resolute uniqueness of painting, is a growing problem for criticism. But the question of the copy is not simply a moral issue — as in the French term for aesthetic copyright: *droit moral.* The question of the copy is fully an aesthetic question — although one that an avant-garde born of the romantic drive for originality has largely repressed.[3] The copy is simultaneously a term of demystification and process, or rather of demystification because of process.

New York, 1981

3.   See my "The Originality of the Avant-Garde," this volume.

Let us start with two images, identically titled *Tufa Domes, Pyramid Lake, Nevada*. The first is a (recently) celebrated photograph made by Timothy O'Sullivan in 1868 that functions with special insistence within the art-historical construction of nineteenth-century landscape photography. The second is a lithographic copy of the first, produced for the publication of Clarence King's *Systematic Geology* in 1878.[1]

Twentieth-century sensibility welcomes the original O'Sullivan as a model of the mysterious, silent beauty to which landscape photography had access during the early decades of the medium. In the photograph, three bulky masses of rock are seen as if deployed on a kind of abstract, transparent chessboard, marking by their separate positions a retreating trajectory into depth. A fanatical descriptive clarity has bestowed on the bodies of these rocks a hallucinatory wealth of detail, so that each crevice, each granular trace of the original volcanic heat finds its record. Yet the rocks seem unreal and the space dreamlike, the tufa domes appear as if suspended in a luminous ether, unbounded and directionless. The brilliance of this undifferentiated ground, in which water and sky connect in an almost seamless continuum, overpowers the material objects within it, so that if the rocks seem to float, to hover, they do so merely as shape. The luminous ground overmasters their bulk, making them instead the functions of design. The mysterious beauty of the image is in this opulent flattening of its space.

By comparison, the lithograph is an object of insistent visual banality. Everything mysterious in the photograph has been explained with supplemental, chatty detail. Clouds have been massed in the sky; the far shore of the lake has been given a definitive shape; the surface of the lake has been characterized by little eddies and ripples. And most important for the demotion of this image from strange to commonplace, the reflections of the rocks in the water have

1.   Clarence King, *Systematic Geology*, 1878, is vol. 1 of *Professional Papers of the Engineer Department U.S. Army*, 7 vols. & atlas, Washington, D.C., U.S. Government Printing Office, 1877–78.

Timothy O'Sullivan. Tufa Domes, Pyramid Lake (Nevada). *1868.*

Photolithograph after O'Sullivan, Tufa Domes, Pyramid Lake. (*Published in King Survey report, 1875*).

been carefully re-created, so that gravity and direction are restored to this space formerly awash with the vague luminosity of too rapidly exposed collodion.

But it is clear, of course, that the difference between the two images — the photograph and its translation — is not a function of the inspiration of the photographer and the insipidity of the lithographer. They belong to two separate domains of culture, they assume different expectations in the user of the image, they convey two distinct kinds of knowledge. In a more recent vocabulary, one would say that they operate as representations within two distinct discursive spaces, as members of two different discourses. The lithograph belongs to the discourse of geology and, thus, of empirical science. In order for it to function within this discourse, the ordinary elements of topographical description had to be restored to the image produced by O'Sullivan. The coordinates of a continuous homogeneous space, mapped not so much by perspective as by the cartographic grid, had to be reconstructed in terms of a coherent recession along an intelligibly horizontal plane retreating toward a definite horizon. The geological data of the tufa domes had to be grounded, coordinated, mapped. As shapes afloat on a continuous, vertical plane, they would have been useless.[2]

2.   The cartographic grid onto which this information is reconstructed has other purposes besides the collation of scientific information. As Alan Trachtenberg argues, the government-sponsored Western surveys were intended to gain access to the mineral resources needed for industrialization. It was an industrial as well as a scientific program that generated this photography, which "when viewed outside the context of the reports it accompanied seems to perpetuate the landscape tradition." Trachtenberg continues: "The photographs represent an essential aspect of the enterprise, a form of record keeping; they contributed to the federal government's policy of supplying fundamental needs of industrialization, needs for reliable data concerning raw materials, and promoted a public willingness to support government policy of conquest, settlement, and exploitation." Alan Trachtenberg, *The Incorporation of America*, New York, Hill and Wang, 1982, p. 20.

And the photograph? Within what discursive space does it operate?

Aesthetic discourse as it developed in the nineteenth century organized itself increasingly around what could be called the space of exhibition. Whether public museum, official salon, world's fair, or private showing, the space of exhibition was constituted in part by the continuous surface of wall—a wall increasingly structured solely for the display of art. The space of exhibition had other features besides the gallery wall. It was also the ground of criticism: on the one hand, the ground of a written response to the works' appearance in that special context; on the other, the implicit ground of choice (of either inclusion or exclusion), with everything excluded from the space of exhibition becoming marginalized with regard to its status as Art.[3] Given its function as the physical vehicle of exhibition, the gallery wall became the signifier of inclusion and, thus, can be seen as constituting in itself a representation of what could be called *exhibitionality,* or that which was developing as the crucial medium of exchange between patrons and artists within the changing structure of art in the nineteenth century. And in the last half of the century, painting—particularly landscape painting—responded with its own corresponding set of depictions. It began to internalize the space of exhibition—the wall—and to represent it.

The transformation of landscape after 1860 into a flattened and compressed experience of space spreading laterally across the surface was extremely rapid. It began with the insistent voiding of perspective, as landscape painting counteracted perspectival recession with a variety of devices, among them sharp value contrast, which had the effect of converting the orthogonal penetration of depth—effected, for example, by a lane of trees—into a diagonal ordering of the surface. No sooner had this compression occurred, constituting within the single easel painting a representation of the very space of exhibition, than other means of composing this representation were employed: serial landscapes, hung in succession, mimed the horizontal extension of the wall, as in Monet's Rouen Cathedral paintings; or landscapes, compressed and horizonless, expanded to become the absolute size of the wall. The synonymy of landscape and wall (the one a representation of the other) of Monet's late waterlilies is thus an advanced moment in a series of operations in which aesthetic discourse resolves itself around a representation of the very space that grounds it institutionally.

This constitution of the work of art as a representation of its own space of exhibition is in fact what we know as the history of modernism. It is now fascinating to watch historians of photography assimilating their medium to the

---

3.   In his important essay "L'espace de l'art," Jean-Claude Lebensztejn discusses the museum's function, since its relatively recent inception, in determining what will count as Art: "The museum has a double but complementary function: to exclude everything else, and through this exclusion to constitute what we mean by the word art. It does not overstate the case to say that the concept of art underwent a profound transformation when a space, fashioned for its very definition, was opened to contain it." In Lebensztejn, *Zigzag*, Paris, Flammarion, 1981, p. 41.

logic of that history. For if we ask, once again, within what discursive space
does the original O'Sullivan — as I described it at the outset — function, we have
to answer: that of the aesthetic discourse. And if we ask what it is a representation *of*, the answer must be that within this space it is constituted as a representation of the plane of exhibition, the surface of the museum, the capacity of
the gallery to constitute the objects it selects for inclusion as Art.

But did O'Sullivan in his own day, the 1860s and 1870s, construct his
work for the aesthetic discourse and the space of exhibition? Or did he create it
for the scientific/topographical discourse that it more or less efficiently serves?
Is the interpretation of O'Sullivan's work as a representation of aesthetic
values — flatness, graphic design, ambiguity, and, behind these, certain intentions toward aesthetic significations: sublimity, transcendence — not a retrospective construction designed to secure it as art?[4] And is this projection not
illegitimate, the composition of a false history?

This question has a special methodological thrust from the vantage of the
present, as a newly organized and energized history of photography is at work
constructing an account of the early years of the medium. Central to this account is the photography, most of it topographical, originally undertaken for
the purposes of exploration, expedition, and survey. Matted, framed, labeled,
these images now enter the space of historical reconstruction through the museum. Decorously isolated on the wall of exhibition, the objects can be read
according to a logic that insists on their representational character within the
discursive space of art, in an attempt to "legitimate" them. The term is Peter
Galassi's, and the issue of legitimacy was the focus of the Museum of Modern

4.   The treatment of Western survey photography as continuous with painterly depictions of
nature is everywhere in the literature. Barbara Novak, Weston Naef, and Elisabeth Lindquist-
Cock are three specialists who see this work as an extension of the landscape sensibilities operative in American nineteenth-century painting, with transcendentalist fervor constantly condi-
tioning the way nature is seen. Thus, the by-now standard argument about the King/O'Sullivan
collaboration is that this visual material amounts to a proof-by-photography of creationism and
the presence of God. King, it is argued, resisted both Lyell's geological uniformitarianism and
Darwin's evolutionism. A catastrophist, King read the geological records of the Utah and Nevada
landscape as a series of acts of creation in which all species were given their permanent shape by a
divine creator. The great upheavals and escarpments, the dramatic basalt formations were all
produced by nature and photographed by O'Sullivan as proof of King's catastrophist doctrine.
With this mission to perform, O'Sullivan's Western photography becomes continuous with the
landscape vision of Bierstadt or Church.
        There is equal support for the opposite argument: King was a serious scientist, who made
great efforts to publish as part of the findings of his survey Marsh's palaeontological finds, which
he knew full well provided one of the important "missing links" needed to give empirical support
to Darwin's theory. Furthermore, as we have seen, O'Sullivan's photographs in their lithographic
form function as neutralized, scientific testimony in the context of King's report; the transcen-
dentalists' God does not inhabit the visual field of *Systematic Geology*. See Barbara Novak, *Nature
and Culture*, New York, Oxford University Press, 1980; Weston Naef, *Era of Exploration*, New
York, the Metropolitan Museum of Art, 1975; and Elisabeth Lindquist-Cock, *Influence of Photography on American Landscape Painting*, New York, Garland Press, 1977.

Art exhibition *Before Photography*, which he organized. In a sentence that was repeated by every reviewer of his argument, Galassi sets up this question of photography's position with respect to the aesthetic discourse: "The object here is to show that photography was not a bastard left by science on the doorstep of art, but a legitimate child of the Western pictorial tradition."[5]

The legitimation that follows depends on something far more ambitious than proving that certain nineteenth-century photographers had pretensions to being artists, or theorizing that photographs were as good as, or even superior to, paintings, or showing that photographic societies organized exhibitions on the model of Establishment salons. Legitimations depend on going beyond the presentation of apparent membership in a given family; they demand the demonstration of the internal, generic necessity of such membership. Galassi wants, therefore, to address internal, formal structures rather than external, circumstantial details. To this end he wishes to prove that the perspective so prominent in nineteenth-century outdoor photography—a perspective that tends to flatten, to fragment, to generate ambiguous overlap, to which Galassi gives the name "analytic," as opposed to the "synthetic" constructive perspective of the Renaissance—was fully developed by the late eighteenth century within the discipline of painting. The force of this proof, Galassi maintains, will be to rebut the notion that photography is essentially a "child of technical rather than aesthetic traditions" and an outsider to the internal issues of aesthetic debate and to show, instead, that it is a product of that same spirit of inquiry *within the arts* that welcomed and developed both "analytic" perspective and an empiricist vision. The radically fore-shortened and elliptical sketches by Constable (and even Degas) can then be used as models for a subsequent photographic practice, which in Galassi's presentation turns out overwhelmingly to be that of topography: Samuel Bourne, Felice Beato, Auguste Salzmann, Charles Marville, and, of course, Timothy O'Sullivan.

And the photographs respond as they are bid. The Bourne of a road in Kashmir, in its steep split in values, empties perspective of its spatial significance and reinvests it with a two-dimensional order every bit as powerfully as does a contemporary Monet. The Salzmann, in its fanatical recording of the texture of stone on a wall that fills the frame with a nearly uniform tonal continuum, assimilates its depiction of empirical detail to a representation of the pictorial infrastructure. And the O'Sullivans, with their rock formations engulfed by that passive, blank, collodion sky, flatten into the same hypnotically seen but two-dimensionally experienced order that characterized the *Tufa Domes* of Pyramid Lake. When viewing the evidence on the walls of the museum, we have no doubt that Art has not only been intended but has also been represented—in the flattened, decoratively unifying drawing of "analytic" perspective.

5.   Peter Galassi, *Before Photography*, New York, The Museum of Modern Art, 1981, p. 12.

Samuel Bourne. A Road Lined with Poplars,
Kashmir. *1863–70. Albumen-silver print from
a glass negative, 8-15/16 by 11 inches. Collection,
Paul F. Walter, New York.*

But here the demonstration runs into difficulty. For Timothy O'Sullivan's
photographs were not published in the nineteenth century and their only public
distribution was through the medium of stereography. Most of the famous
O'Sullivans — the Canyon de Chelly ruins from the Wheeler Expedition, for example — exist as stereographic views, and it was to these that, in O'Sullivan's
case, as in William Henry Jackson's, the wider public had access.[6] Thus, if we
began with a comparison between two images — the photograph and the lithographic translation — we can continue with a comparison between two cameras:
a 9 × 12 plate camera and a camera for stereoscopic views. These two pieces of
equipment mark distinct domains of experience.

Stereographic space is perspectival space raised to a higher power.
Organized as a kind of tunnel vision, the experience of deep recession is insistent and inescapable. This experience is heightened by the fact that the viewer's
own ambient space is masked out by the optical instrument he must hold before

6.   See the chapter "Landscape and the Published Photograph," in Naef, *Era of Exploration.* In
1871 the Government Printing Office published a catalogue of Jackson's work, *Catalogue of
Stereoscopic, 6 × 8 and 8 × 10 Photographs by Wm. H. Jackson.*

Auguste Salzmann. Jerusalem, The Temple Wall, West Side. *1853–54. Salt print from a paper negative, 9-3/16 by 13⅛ inches. Collection, The Museum of Modern Art, New York.*

his eyes. As he views the image in an ideal isolation, his own surrounds, with their walls and floors, are banished from sight. The apparatus of the stereoscope mechanically focuses all attention on the matter at hand and precludes the visual meandering experienced in the museum gallery as one's eyes wander from picture to picture and to surrounding space. Instead, the refocusing of attention can occur only within the spectator's channel of vision constructed by the optical machine.

The stereographic image appears multilayered, a steep gradient of different planes stretching away from the nearby space into depth. The operation of viewing this space involves scanning the field of the image, moving from its lower left corner, say, to its upper right. That much is like looking at a painting. But the actual experience of this scan is something wholly different. As one moves, visually, through the stereoscopic tunnel from inspecting the nearest ground to attending to an object in the middle distance, one has the sensation of refocusing one's eyes. And then again, into the farthest plane, another effort is made, and felt, to refocus.[7]

7.   The eye is not actually refocusing. Rather, given the nearness of the image to the eyes and the fixity of the head in relation to it, in order to scan the space of the image a viewer must readjust and recoordinate the two eyeballs from point to point as vision moves over the surface.

Timothy O'Sullivan. Shoshone Falls
(Idaho). *1868.*

These micromuscular efforts are the kinesthetic counterpart to the sheerly
optical illusion of the stereograph. They are a kind of enactment, on a very reduced scale, of what happens when a deep channel of space is opened before
one. The actual readjustment of the eyes from plane to plane within the stereoscopic field is the representation by one part of the body of what another part of
the body (the feet) would do in passing through real space. From this physio-
optical traversal of the stereo field derives another difference between it and
pictorial space. This difference concerns the dimension of time.

The contemporary accounts of what it was like to look at stereographs all
dilate on the length of time spent examining the contents of the image. For
Oliver Wendell Holmes, Sr., a passionate advocate of stereography, this peru-
sal was the response appropriate to the "inexhaustible" wealth of detail provided
by the image. As he picks his way over this detail in his writing on stereography
— in describing, for example, his experience of an E.&H.T. Anthony view up
Broadway — Holmes enacts for his readers the protracted engagement with the
spectacle demanded by stereo viewing. By contrast, paintings do not require
(and as they become more modernist, certainly do not support) this temporal
dilation of attention, this minute-by-minute examining of every inch of the
ground.

When Holmes characterizes this special modality of viewing, where "the
mind feels its way into the very depths of the picture," he has recourse to extreme mental states, like hypnotism, "half-magnetic effects," and dream. "At
least the shutting out of surrounding objects, and the concentration of the
whole attention which is a consequence of this, produce a dream-like exalta-
tion," he writes, "in which we seem to leave the body behind us and sail away
into one strange scene after another, like disembodied spirits."[8]

8.   Oliver Wendell Holmes, "Sun-Painting and Sun-Sculpture," *Atlantic Monthly*, VIII (July
1861), 14–15. The discussion of the view of Broadway occurs on p. 17. Holmes's other two essays
appeared as "The Stereoscope and the Stereograph," *Atlantic Monthly*, III (June 1859), 738–748;
and "Doings of the Sunbeam," *Atlantic Monthly*, XII (July 1863), 1–15.

The phenomenology of the stereoscope produces a situation not unlike that of looking at cinema. Both involve the isolation of the viewer with an image from which surrounding interference is masked out. In both, the image transports the viewer optically, while his body remains immobile. In both, the pleasure derives from the experience of the simulacrum: the appearance of reality from which any testing of the real-effect by actually, physically, moving through the scene is denied. And in both, the real-effect of the simulacrum is heightened by a temporal dilation. What has been called the *apparatus* of cinematic process had, then, a certain proto-history in the institution of stereography, just as stereography's own proto-history is to be found in the similarly darkened and isolating but spectacularly illusionistic space of the diorama.[9] And in the case of the stereograph, as was later the case for film, the specific pleasures that seem to be released by that apparatus — the desires that it seems to gratify — accounted for the instantly wild popularity of the instrument.

The diffusion of stereography as a truly mass medium was made possible by mechanized printing techniques. Beginning in the 1850s but continuing almost unabated into the 1880s, the figures for stereo sales are dizzying. As early as 1857 the London Stereoscopic Company had sold 500,000 stereoscopes and, in 1859, was able to claim a catalogue listing more than 100,000 different stereo views.[10]

It is in this very term — *view* — by which the practice of stereoscopy identified its object, that we can locate the particularity of that experience. First of all, *view* speaks to the dramatic insistence of the perspectively organized depth I have been describing. This was often heightened, or acknowledged, by the makers of stereo views by structuring the image around a vertical marker in fore- or middle ground that works to *center* space, forming a representation within the visual field of the eyes' convergence at a vanishing point. Many of Timothy O'Sullivan's images organize themselves around such a center — the staff of a bare tree trunk, the sheer edge of a rock formation — whose compositional sense derives from the special sensations of the *view*. Given O'Sullivan's tendency to compose around the diagonal recession and centering of the *view*, it

9.   See, Jean-Louis Baudry, "The Apparatus," *Camera Obscura*, no. 1 (1976), 104–126, originally published as "Le Dispositif," *Communications*, no. 23 (1975), 56–72; and Baudry, "Cinéma: Effects idéologiques produits par l'appareil de base," *Cinéthique*, no. 7–8 (1979), 1–8.

10.   Edward W. Earle, ed., *Points of View: The Stereograph in America: A Cultural History*, Rochester, N.Y., The Visual Studies Workshop Press, 1979, p. 12. In 1856 Robert Hunt in the *Art Journal* reported, "The stereoscope is now seen in every drawing-room; philosophers talk learnedly upon it, ladies are delighted with its magic representation, and children play with it." *Ibid.*, p. 28.

11.   "Photographs from the High Rockies," *Harper's Magazine*, XXXIX (September 1869), 465–475. In this article *Tufa Domes, Pyramid Lake* finds yet one more place of publication, in a crude translation of the photograph, this time as an illustration to the author's adventure narrative. Thus one more imaginative space is projected onto the blank, collodion screen. This time, in response to the account of the near capsize of the exploration party's boat, the engraver whips the waters into a darkened frenzy and the sky into banks of lowering storm clouds.

is not surprising to find that in his one published account of his work as a Western photographer he consistently speaks of what he makes as "views" and what he does when making them as "viewing." Writing of the expedition to Pyramid Lake, he describes the provisions, "among which may be mentioned the instruments and chemicals necessary for our photographer to 'work up his view.'" Of the Humboldt Sink, he says, "It was a pretty location to work in, and viewing there was as pleasant work as could be desired."[11] *View* was the term consistently used in the photographic journals, as it was overwhelmingly the appellation photographers gave to their entries in photographic salons in the 1860s. Thus, even when consciously entering the space of exhibition, they tended to choose *view* rather than *landscape* as their descriptive category.

Further, *view* addresses a notion of authorship in which the natural phenomenon, the point of interest, rises up to confront the viewer, seemingly without the mediation of an individual recorder or artist, leaving "authorship" of the views to their publishers rather than to the operators (as they were called) who took the pictures. Thus, authorship is characteristically made a function of publication, with copyright held by the various companies, e.g., Keystone Views, while the photographers remain anonymous. In this sense the phenomenological character of the view, its exaggerated depth and focus, opens onto a second feature, which is the isolating of the object of that view. Indeed, it is a "point of interest," a natural wonder, a singular phenomenon that comes to occupy this centering of attention. This experience of the *singular* is, as Barbara Stafford has shown in an examination of singularity as a special category associated with travel accounts beginning in the late eighteenth century, founded on the transfer of authorship from the subjectivity of the artist to the objective manifestations of nature.[12] For this reason, the institution of the view does not claim the imaginative projection of an author so much as the legal protection of property in the form of the copyright.

12.   Stafford writes, "The concept that true history is natural history emancipates the objects of nature from the government of man. For the idea of singularity it is significant . . . that geological phenomena—taken in their widest sense to include specimens from the mineral kingdom—constitute landscape forms in which natural history finds aesthetic expression. . . . The final stage in the historicizing of nature sees the products of history naturalized. In 1789, the German *savant* Samuel Witte—basing his conclusions on the writings of Desmarets, Duluc and Faujas de Saint-Fond—annexed the pyramids of Egypt for nature, declaring that they were basalt eruptions; he also identified the ruins of Peresepolis, Baalbek, Palmyra, as well as the Temple of Jupiter at Agrigento and the Palace of the Incas in Peru, as lithic outcroppings." Barbara M. Stafford, "Towards Romantic Landscape Perception: Illustrated Travels and the Rise of 'Singularity' as an Aesthetic Category," *Art Quarterly*, n.s. I (1977), 108–109. She concludes her study of "the cultivation of taste for the natural phenomenon as singularity," by insisting that "the lone natural object . . . need not be interpreted as human surrogates; on the contrary, [the nineteenth-century Romantic landscape painter's] isolated, detached monoliths should be placed within the vitalist aesthetic tradition—emerging from the illustrated voyage—that valued the natural singular. One might refer to this tradition as that of a 'neue Sachlichkeit' in which the regard for the specifics of nature produces a repertory of animate particulars" (117–118).

Finally, *view* registers this singularity, this focal point, as one moment in a complex representation of the world, a kind of complete topographical atlas. For the physical space within which the "views" were kept was invariably a cabinet in whose drawers were catalogued and stored a whole geographical system. The file cabinet is a different object from the wall or the easel. It holds out the possibility of storing and cross-referencing bits of information and of collating them through the particular grid of a system of knowledge. The elaborate cabinets of stereo views that were part of the furnishing of nineteenth-century middle-class homes as well as of the equipment of public libraries comprise a compound representation of geographic space. The spatiality of the view, its insistent penetration, functions as the sensory model for a more abstract system whose subject also is space. View and land survey are interdetermined and interrelated.

What emerges from this analysis is a system of historically specific requirements that were satisfied by the view and in relation to which *view* formed a coherent discourse. I hope it is apparent that this discourse is disjunct from what aesthetic discourse intends by the term *landscape*. Just as the view's construction of space cannot be assimilated, phenomenologically, to the compressed and fragmented space of what *Before Photography* calls analytic perspective,[13] so the representation formed by the collectivity of these views cannot be likened to the representation organized by the space of exhibition. The one composes an image of geographic order; the other represents the space of an autonomous Art and its idealized, specialized History, which is constituted by aesthetic discourse. The complex collective representations of that quality called style—period style, personal style—are dependent upon the space of exhibition; one could say they are a function of it. Modern art history is in that sense a product of the most rigorously organized nineteenth-century space of exhibition: the museum.[14]

André Malraux has explained to us how the museum, with its succession of (representations of) styles, collectively organizes the master representation of Art. Having updated themselves through the institution of the modern art book, Malraux's museums are now "without walls," the galleries' contents collectivized by means of photographic reproduction. But this serves only to intensify the reductiveness of the process:

13.   For another discussion of Galassi's argument with relation to the roots of "analytic perspective" in seventeenth-century optics and the *camera obscura*, see Svetlana Alpers, *The Art of Describing: Dutch Art in the Seventeenth Century*, University of Chicago Press, 1983, pp. 243–244, fn. 37.
14.   Michel Foucault opens a discussion of the museum in "Fantasia of the Library," in *Language, Counter-Memory, Practice*, trans. D. F. Bouchard and S. Simon, Ithaca, N.Y., Cornell University Press, 1977, pp. 87–109. See also Eugenio Donato, "The Museum's Furnace: Notes toward a Contextual Reading of *Bouvard and Pécuchet*," *Textual Strategies: Perspectives in Post-Structuralist Criticism*, ed. Josué V. Harari, Ithaca, Cornell University Press, 1979; and Douglas Crimp, "On the Museum's Ruins," *October*, no. 13 (Summer 1980), 41–57.

Thus it is that, thanks to the rather specious unity imposed by the photographic reproduction on a multiplicity of objects, ranging from the statue to the bas-relief, from bas-reliefs to seal-impressions, and from these to the plaques of the nomads, a "Babylonian style" seems to emerge as a real entity, not a mere classification — as something resembling, rather the life-story of a great creator. Nothing conveys more vividly and compellingly the notion of a destiny shaping human ends than do the great styles, whose evolutions and transformations seem like long scars that Fate has left, in passing, on the face of the earth.[15]

Having decided that nineteenth-century photography belongs in a museum, having decided that the genres of aesthetic discourse are applicable to it, having decided that the art-historical model will map nicely onto this material, recent scholars of photography have decided (ahead of time) quite a lot. For one thing, they have concluded that given images are *landscapes* (rather than *views*) and they are thus certain about the discourse these images belong to and what they are representations of. For another (but this conclusion is reached simultaneously with the first), they have determined that other fundamental concepts of aesthetic discourse will be applicable to this visual archive. One of these is the concept *artist*, with its correlative notion of sustained and intentional progress to which we give the term *career*. The other is the possibility of coherence and meaning that will unfold through the collective body of work so produced, this constituting the unity of an *oeuvre*. But, it can be argued, these are terms that nineteenth-century topographic photography not only tends not to support but in fact opens to question.

The concept *artist* implies more than the mere fact of authorship; it suggests that one must go through certain steps to earn the right to claim the condition of being an author, the word *artist* being somehow semantically connected with the notion of vocation. Generally, "vocation" implies an apprenticeship, a juvenilia, a learning of the tradition of one's craft and the gaining of an individuated view of that tradition through a process that includes both success and failure. If this, or at least some part of it, is what is necessarily included in the term *artist*, can we then imagine someone being an artist for just one year? Would this not be a logical (some would say, grammatical) contradiction, like the example adduced by Stanley Cavell in relation to aesthetic judgments, where he repeats Wittgenstein's question: "Could someone have a feeling of ardent love or hope for the space of one second — *no matter what* preceded or followed this second?"[16]

---

15.   André Malraux, "Museum without Walls," *The Voices of Silence*, Princeton, Princeton University Press, Bollingen Series XXIV, 1978, p. 46.
16.   Stanley Cavell, *Must We Mean What We Say?*, New York, Scribners, 1969, p. 91, fn. 9.

But this is the case with Auguste Salzmann, whose career as a photographer began in 1853 and was over in less than a year. Little else on the horizon of nineteenth-century photography appeared only to vanish quite so meteorically. But other major figures within this history enter this métier and then leave it in less than a decade. This is true of Roger Fenton, Gustave LeGray, and Henri LeSecq, all of them acknowledged "masters" of the art. Some of these desertions involved a return to the more traditional arts; others, like Fenton's, meant taking up a totally different field such as the law. What do the span and nature of these engagements with the medium mean for the concept of *career*? Can we study these "careers" with the same methodological presuppositions, the same assumptions of personal style and its continuity, that we bring to the careers of another sort of artist?[17]

And what of the other great aesthetic unity: *oeuvre*? Once again we encounter practices that seem difficult to bring into conformity with what the term comprises, with its assumptions that the oeuvre is the result of sustained intention and that it is organically related to the effort of its maker: that it is coherent. One practice already mentioned was the imperious assumption of copyright, so that certain oeuvres, like Matthew Brady's and Francis Frith's, are largely a function of the work of their employees. Another practice, related to the nature of photographic commissions, left large bodies of the oeuvre unachieved. An example is the Heliographic Mission of 1851, in which LeSecq, LeGray, Baldus, Bayard, and Mestral (which is to say some of the greatest figures in early photographic history in France) did survey work for the Commission des Monuments Historiques. Their results, some 300 negatives recording medieval architecture about to be restored not only were never published or exhibited by the commission but were never even printed. This is analogous to a director shooting a film but never having the footage developed, hence never seeing the rushes. How would the result fit into the oeuvre of this director?[18]

17.   Students of photography's history are not encouraged to question whether art-historical models might (or might not) apply. The session on the history of photography at the 1982 College Art Association meeting (a session proudly introduced as the fruits of real scholarly research at last applied to this formerly unsystematically studied field) was a display of what can go wrong. In the paper "Charles Marville, Popular Illustrator: Origins of a Photographic Aesthetic," presented by Constance Kane Hungerford, the model of the necessary internal consistency of an oeuvre encouraged the idea that there had to be a stylistic connection between Marville's early practice as an engraver and his later work as a photographer. The characterizations of style this promoted with regard to Marville's photographic work (e.g., sharp contrasts of light and dark, hard, crisp contours) were not only hard to see, consistently, but when these did apply they did not distinguish him in any way from his fellows on the Heliographic Mission. For every "graphic" Marville, it is possible to find an equally graphic LeSecq.
18.   An example of this is the nearly four miles of footage shot by Eisenstein in Mexico for his project *Que Viva Mexico*. Sent to California, where it was developed, this footage was never seen by Eisenstein, who was forced to leave the United States immediately upon his return from Mex-

There are other practices, other exhibits, in the archive that also test the applicability of the concept *oeuvre*. One of these is the body of work that is too meager for this notion; the other is the body that is too large. Can we imagine an oeuvre consisting of one work? The history of photography tries to do this with the single photographic effort produced by Auguste Salzmann, a lone volume of archaeological photographs (of great formal beauty), some portion of which are known to have been taken by his assistant.[19] And, at the opposite extreme, can we imagine an oeuvre consisting of 10,000 works?

Eugène Atget's labors produced a vast body of work, which he sold over the years of its production (roughly 1895 to 1927) to various historical collections, such as the Bibliothèque de la Ville de Paris, the Musée de la Ville de Paris (Musée Carnavalet), the Bibliothèque Nationale, the Monuments Historiques, as well as to commercial builders and artists. The assimilation of this work of documentation into a specifically aesthetic discourse began in 1925 with its notice and publication by the surrealists and was followed, in 1929, by its placement within the photographic sensibility of the German New Vision.[20] Thus began the various partial viewings of the 10,000-piece archive; each view the result of a selection intended to make a given aesthetic or formal point.

The repetitive rhythm of accumulation that interested the Neue Sachlichkeit could be found and illustrated within this material, as could the collage sensibility of the surrealists, who were particularly drawn to the Atget shopfronts, which they made famous. Other selections sustain other interpretations of the material. The frequent visual superimpositions of object and agent, as when Atget captures himself as a reflection in the glazed entrance of the café he is photographing, permit a reading of the work as reflexive, picturing its own conditions of making. Other readings of the images are more architectonically

ico. The footage was then cannibalized by two American editors to compose *Thunder over Mexico* and *Time in the Sun*. Neither of these is supposed to be part of Eisenstein's oeuvre. Only a "shooting chronology" assembled by Jay Leyda in the Museum of Modern Art now exists. Its status in relation to Eisenstein's oeuvre is obviously peculiar. But given Eisenstein's nearly ten years of filmmaking experience at the time of the shooting (given also the state of the art of cinema in terms of the body of material that existed by 1930 and the extent to which this had been theorized), it is probable that Eisenstein had a more complete sense, from the script and his working conception of the film, of what he had made as a "work"—even though he never saw it—than the photographers of the Heliographic Mission could have had of theirs. The history of Eisenstein's project is fully documented in Sergei Eisenstein and Upton Sinclair, *The Making and Unmaking of "Que Viva Mexico,"* eds. Harry M. Geduld and Ronald Gottesman, Bloomington, Indiana University Press, 1970.
19.   See Abigail Solomon-Godeau, "A Photographer in Jerusalem, 1955: Auguste Salzmann and His Times," *October*, no. 18 (Fall 1981), 95. This essay raises some of the issues about the problematic nature of Salzmann's work considered as *oeuvre*.
20.   Man Ray arranged for publication of four photographs by Atget in *La Révolution Surréaliste*, three in the June 1926 issue and one in the December 1926 issue. The exhibition *Film und Foto*, Stuttgart, 1929, included Atget, whose work was also reproduced in *Foto-Auge*, Stuttgart, Wedekind Verlag, 1929.

formal. They see Atget managing to locate a point around which the complex spatial trajectories of the site will unfold with an especially clarifying symmetry. Most often images of parks and rural scenes are used for such analyses.

But each of these readings is partial, like tiny core samples that are extracted from a vast geological field, each displaying the presence of a different ore. Or like the blind men's elephant. Ten thousand pieces are a lot to collate. Yet, if Atget's work is to be considered art, and he an artist, this collation must be made; we must acknowledge ourselves to be in the presence of an oeuvre. The Museum of Modern Art's four-part exhibition of Atget, assembled under the already loaded title *Atget and the Art of Photography*, moves briskly toward the solution of this problem, always assuming that the model that will serve to ensure the unity for this archive is the concept of an *artist's oeuvre*. For what else could it be?

John Szarkowski, after recognizing that, from the point of view of formal invention, the work is extremely uneven, speculates on why this should be so:

> There are a number of ways to interpret this apparent incoherence. We could assume that it was Atget's goal to make glorious pictures that would delight and thrill us, and that in this ambition he failed as often as not. Or we could assume that he began photographing as a novice and gradually, through the pedagogical device of work, learned to use his peculiar, recalcitrant medium with economy and sureness, so that his work became better and better as he grew older. Or we could point out that he worked both for others and for himself and that the work he did for himself was better, because it served a more demanding master. Or we could say that it was Atget's goal to explain in visual terms an issue of great richness and complexity — the spirit of his own culture — and that in service to this goal he was willing to accept the results of his own best efforts, even when they did not rise above the role of simple records.
>
> I believe that all of these explanations are in some degree true, but the last is especially interesting to us, since it is so foreign to our understanding of artistic ambition. It is not easy for us to be comfortable with the idea that an artist might work as a servant to an idea larger than he. We have been educated to believe, or rather, to assume, that no value transcends the value of the creative individual. A logical corollary of this assumption is that no subject matter except the artist's own sensibility is quite worthy of his best attention.[21]

21.   Maria Morris Hambourg and John Szarkowski, *The Work of Atget: Volume 1, Old France*, New York, The Museum of Modern Art, and Boston, New York Graphic Society, 1981, pp. 18–19.

This inching forward from the normal categories of description of aesthetic production—formal success/formal failure; apprenticeship/maturity; public commission/personal statement—toward a position that he acknowledges as "foreign to our understanding of artistic ambition," namely, work "in the service of an issue larger than self-expression," evidently troubles Szarkowski. Just before breaking off this train of thought he meditates on why Atget revisited sites (sometimes after several years) to choose different aspects of, say, a given building to photograph. Szarkowski's answer resolves itself in terms of formal success/formal failure and the categories of artistic maturation that are consistent with the notion of oeuvre. His own persistence in thinking about the work in relation to this aesthetic model surfaces in his decision to continue to treat it in terms of stylistic evolution: "The earlier pictures show the tree as complete and discrete, as an object against a ground; as centrally positioned within the frame; as frontally lighted, from behind the photographer's shoulder. The later pictures show the tree radically cut by the frame, asymetrically positioned, and more obviously inflected by the quality of light that falls upon it."[22] This is what produces the "elegiac" mood of some of the late work.

But this whole matter of artistic intention and stylistic evolution must be integrated with the "idea larger than he" that Atget can be thought to have served. If the 10,000 images form Atget's picture of the larger idea, then that idea can inform us of Atget's aesthetic intentions, for there will be a reciprocal relation between the two, one inside, the other outside the artist.

To get hold, simultaneously, of this larger idea and of Atget's elusive intentions in making this vast archive ("It is difficult," Szarkowski writes, "to name an important artist of the modern period whose life and intention have been so perfectly withheld from us as those of Eugène Atget"), it was long believed to be necessary to decipher the code provided by Atget's negative numbers. Each of the 10,000 plates is numbered. Yet the numbers are not strictly successive; they do not organize the work chronologically; they sometimes double back on each other.[23]

For researchers into the problem of Atget's oeuvre, the numbers were seen as providing the all-important code to the artist's intentions and the work's meaning. Maria Morris Hambourg has finally and most definitively deciphered this code, to find in it the systematization of a catalogue of topographic

22.   *Ibid.*, p. 21.
23.   The first published discussion of this problem characterizes it as follows: "Atget's numbering system is puzzling. His pictures are not numbered in a simple serial system, but in a confusing manner. In many cases, low-numbered photographs are dated later than high-numbered photographs, and in many cases numbers are duplicated." See Barbara Michaels, "An Introduction to the Dating and Organization of Eugène Atget's Photographs," *The Art Bulletin*, LXI (September 1979), 461.

subjects, divided into five major series and many smaller subseries and groups.[24] The names given to the various series and groupings (Landscape-Documents, Picturesque Paris, Environs, Old-France) establish as the master, larger idea for the work a collective picture of the spirit of French culture—similar, we could say, to Balzac's undertaking in the *Comédie Humaine.* In relation to this master subject, Atget's vision can be organized around a set of intentions that are socio-aesthetic, so to speak; he becomes photography's great visual anthropologist. The unifying intention of the oeuvre can be understood as a continuing search for the representation of the moment of interface between nature and culture, as in the juxtaposition of the vines growing beside a farmhouse window curtained in a lace representation of schematized leaves. But this analysis, interesting and often brilliant as it is, is once again only partial. The desire to represent the paradigm nature/culture can be traced in only a small fraction of the images and then, like the trail of an elusive animal, it dies out, leaving the intentions as mute and mysterious as ever.

What is interesting in this case is that the Museum of Modern Art and Maria Morris Hambourg hold in their hands the solution to this mystery, a key that will not so much unlock the system of Atget's aesthetic intentions as dispel them. And this example seems all the more informative as it demonstrates the resistance of the museological and art-historical disciplines to using that key.

The coding system Atget applied to his images derives from the card files of the libraries and topographic collections for which he worked. His subjects are often standardized, dictated by the established categories of survey and historical documentation. The reason many of Atget's street images uncannily resemble the photographs by Marville taken a half-century earlier is that both are functions of the same documentary master plan.[25] A catalogue is not so much an idea as it is a mathesis, a system of organization. It submits not so much to intellectual as to institutional analysis. And it seems clear that Atget's work is the *function* of a catalogue that he had no hand in inventing and for which *authorship* is an irrelevant term.

The normal conditions of authorship that the museum wishes to maintain tend to collapse under this observation, leading us to a rather startling reflection. The museum undertook to crack the code of Atget's negative numbers in order to discover an aesthetic anima. What they found, instead, was a card catalogue.

With this in mind we get different answers to various earlier questions, like the problem of why Atget photographed certain subjects piecemeal, the im-

24.   Maria Morris Hambourg, "Eugène Atget, 1857–1927: The Structure of the Work," unpublished Ph.D. dissertation, Columbia University, 1980.
25.   See *Charles Marville, Photographs of Paris 1852–1878*, New York, The French Institute/Alliance Française, 1981. This contains an essay, "Charles Marville's Old Paris," by Maria Morris Hambourg.

Eugène Atget. Verrières, coin pittoresque.
*1922. Printing-out paper, 9-7/16 by 7-1/16
inches. Collection, The Museum of Modern Art,
New York.*

Eugène Atget. Sceaux. *1922. Printing-out
paper, 9-7/16 by 7-1/16 inches. Collection, The
Museum of Modern Art, New York.*

age of a façade separated by months or even years from the view of the same
building's doorway or window mullions or wrought-iron work. The answer, it
seems, lies less in the conditions of aesthetic success or failure than in the requirements of the catalogue and its categorical spaces.

   Subject is the fulcrum in all of this. Are the doorways and the ironwork bal-
conies Atget's subjects, his choices, the manifest expression of him as active *subject*, thinking, willing, intending, creating? Or are they simply (although there
is nothing simple in this) *subjects*, the functions of the catalogue, to which Atget
himself is *subject*? What possible price of historical clarity are we willing to pay
in order to maintain the former interpretation over the latter?

   Everything that has been put forward about the need to abandon or at
least to submit to a serious critique the aesthetically derived categories of

authorship, oeuvre, and genre (as in *landscape*) obviously amounts to an attempt to maintain early photography as an archive and to call for the sort of archaeological examination of this archive that Michel Foucault both theorizes and provides a model for. Describing the analysis to which archaeology submits the archive in order to reveal the conditions of its discursive formations, Foucault writes:

> [They] must not be understood as a set of determinations imposed from the outside on the thought of individuals, or inhabiting it from the inside, in advance as it were; they constitute rather the set of conditions in accordance with which a practice is exercised, in accordance with which that practice gives rise to partially or totally new statements, and in accordance with which it can be modified. [The relations established by archaeology] are not so much limitations imposed on the initiative of subjects as the field in which that initiative is articulated (without however constituting its center), rules that it puts into operation (without it having invented or formulated them), relations that provide it with a support (without it being either their final result or their point of convergence). [Archaeology] is an attempt to reveal discursive practices in their complexity and density; to show that to speak is to do something—something other than to express what one thinks.[26]

Everywhere at present there is an attempt to dismantle the photographic archive—the set of practices, institutions, and relationships to which nineteenth-century photography originally belonged—and to reassemble it within the categories previously constituted by art and its history.[27] It is not hard to conceive of what the inducements for doing so are, but it is more difficult to understand the tolerance for the kind of incoherence it produces.

Cambridge, New York, 1982

26.   Michel Foucault, *The Archaeology of Knowledge*, trans. A. M. Sheridan Smith, New York, Harper and Row, 1976, pp. 208–209.
27.   Thus far the work of Alan Sekula has been the one consistent analysis of the history of photography to attack this effort. See Alan Sekula, "The Traffic in Photographs," *Art Journal*, XLI (Spring 1981), 15–25; and "The Instrumental Image: Steichen at War," *Artforum*, XIII (December 1975). A discussion of the rearrangement of the archive in relation to the need to protect the values of modernism is mounted by Douglas Crimp's "The Museum's Old/The Library's New Subject," *Parachute* (Spring 1981).

The Originality of the Avant-Garde

This summer the National Gallery in Washington installed what it proudly describes as "the largest Rodin exhibition, ever." Not only was this the greatest public gathering of Rodin's sculpture, but it included, as well, much of his work never before seen. In certain cases the work had not been seen because it consisted of pieces in plaster that had lain on the shelves in storage at Meudon since the artist's death, closed off to the prying eyes of scholars and public alike. In other instances the work had not been seen because it had only just been made. The National Gallery's exhibition included, for example, a brand new cast of *The Gates of Hell*, so absolutely recent that visitors to the exhibition were able to sit down in a little theater provided for the occasion to view a just completed movie of the casting and finishing of this new version.

To some—though hardly all—of the people sitting in that theater watching the casting of *The Gates of Hell*, it must have occurred that they were witnessing the making of a fake. After all, Rodin has been dead since 1918, and surely a work of his produced more than sixty years after his death cannot be the genuine article, cannot, that is, be an original. The answer to this is more interesting than one would think; for the answer is neither yes nor no.

When Rodin died he left the French nation his entire estate, which consisted not only of all the work in his possession, but also all of the rights of its reproduction, that is, the right to make bronze editions from the estate's plasters. The Chambre des Députés, in accepting this gift, decided to limit the posthumous editions to twelve casts of any given plaster. Thus *The Gates of Hell*, cast in 1978 by perfect right of the State, is a legitimate work: a real original we might say.

But once we leave the lawyer's office and the terms of Rodin's will, we fall immediately into a quagmire. In what sense is the new cast an original? At the time of Rodin's death *The Gates of Hell* stood in his studio like a mammoth plaster chessboard with all the pieces removed and scattered on the floor. The arrangement of the figures on *The Gates* as we know it reflects the most current notion the sculptor had about its composition, an arrangement documented by numbers penciled on the plasters corresponding to numbers located at various stations on *The Gates*. But these numbers were regularly changed as Rodin played with and

Auguste Rodin. The Three Nymphs.

recomposed the surface of the doors; and so, at the time of his death, *The Gates* were very much unfinished. They were also uncast. Since they had originally been commissioned and paid for by the State, they were, of course, not Rodin's to issue in bronze, even had he chosen to do so. But the building for which they had been commissioned had been cancelled; *The Gates* were never called for, hence never finished, and thus never cast. The first bronze was made in 1921, three years after the artist's death.

So, in finishing and patinating the new cast there is no example completed during Rodin's lifetime to use for a guide to the artist's intentions about how the finished piece was to look. Due to the double circumstance of there being no lifetime cast *and*, at time of death, of there existing a plaster model still in flux, we could say that *all* the casts of *The Gates of Hell* are examples of multiple copies that exist in the absence of an original. The issue of authenticity is equally problematic for each of the existing casts; it is only more conspicuously so for the most recent.

But, as we have constantly been reminding ourselves ever since Walter Benjamin's "Work of Art in the Age of Mechanical Reproduction," authenticity empties out as a notion as one approaches those mediums which are inherently multiple. "From a photographic negative, for example," Benjamin argued, "one can make any number of prints; to ask for the 'authentic' print makes no sense."

Auguste Rodin. The Two Dancers *(left).* The Three
Shades *(right).*

For Rodin, the concept of the "authentic bronze cast" seems to have made as little
sense as it has for many photographers. Like Atget's thousands of glass negatives
for which, in some cases, no lifetime prints exist, Rodin left many of his plaster
figures unrealized in any permanent material, either bronze or marble. Like
Cartier-Bresson, who never printed his own photographs, Rodin's relation to the
casting of his sculpture could only be called remote. Much of it was done in
foundries to which Rodin never went while the production was in progress; he
never worked on or retouched the waxes from which the final bronzes were cast,
never supervised or regulated either the finishing or the patination, and in the end
never checked the pieces before they were crated to be shipped to the client or
dealer who had bought them. From his position deep in the ethos of mechanical
reproduction, it was not as odd for Rodin as we might have thought to have willed
his country posthumous authorial rights over his own work.

   The ethos of reproduction in which Rodin was immersed was not limited, of
course, to the relatively technical question of what went on at the foundry. It was
installed within the very walls, heavy with plaster dust—the blinding snow of
Rilke's description—of Rodin's studio. For the plasters that form the core of
Rodin's work are, themselves, casts. They are thus potential multiples. And at the
core of Rodin's massive output is the structural proliferation born of this multiplicity.

Auguste Rodin. The Prodigal Son *(left).* Gates of Hell *(center and right).*

In the tremulousness of their balance, *The Three Nymphs* compose a figure of spontaneity—a figure somewhat discomposed by the realization that these three are identical casts of the same model; just as the magnificent sense of improvisatory gesture is strangely bracketed by the recognition that *The Two Dancers* are not simply spiritual, but mechanical twins. *The Three Shades,* the composition that crowns *The Gates of Hell,* is likewise a production of multiples, three identical figures, triple-cast, in the face of which it would make no sense—as little as with the nymphs or dancers—to ask which of the three is the original. *The Gates* themselves are another example of the modular working of Rodin's imagination, with the same figure compulsively repeated, repositioned, recoupled, recombined.[1] If bronze casting is that end of the sculptural spectrum which is inherently multiple, the forming of the figurative originals is, we would have thought, at the *other* end—the pole consecrated to uniqueness. But Rodin's working procedures force the fact of reproduction to traverse the *full length* of this spectrum.

1.   For a discussion of Rodin's figural repetitions, see my *Passages in Modern Sculpture*, New York, Viking, 1977, chapter 1; and Leo Steinberg, *Other Criteria*, New York, Oxford University Press, pp. 322–403.

Auguste Rodin. Fugit Amor.

Now, nothing in the myth of Rodin as the prodigious form giver prepares us for the reality of these arrangements of multiple clones. For the form giver is the maker of originals, exultant in his own originality. Rilke had long ago composed that incantatory hymn to Rodin's originality in describing the profusion of bodies invented for *The Gates*:

> . . . bodies that listen like faces, and lift themselves like arms; chains of bodies, garlands and single organisms; bodies that listen like faces and lift tendrils and heavy clusters of bodies into which sin's sweetness rises out of the roots of pain. . . . The army of these figures became much too numerous to fit into the frame and wings of *The Gates of Hell*. Rodin made choice after choice and eliminated everything that was too solitary to subject itself to the great totality; everything that was not necessary was rejected.[2]

This swarm of figures that Rilke evokes is, we are led to believe, composed of *different* figures. And we are encouraged in this belief by the cult of originality that

2.   Rainer Maria Rilke, *Rodin*, trans. Jessie Lemont and Hans Frausil, London, Grey Walls Press, 1946, p. 32.

grew up around Rodin, one that he himself invited. From the kind of reflexively intended hand-of-God imagery of Rodin's own work, to his carefully staged publicity—as in his famous portrait as genius progenitor by Edward Steichen—Rodin courted the notion of himself as form giver, creator, crucible of originality. Rilke chants,

> One walks among these thousand forms, overwhelmed with the imagination and the craftsmanship which they represent, and involuntarily one looks for the two hands out of which this world has risen. . . . One asks for the man who directs these hands.[3]

Henry James, in *The Ambassadors*, had added,

> With his genius in his eyes, his manners on his lips, his long career behind him and his honors and rewards all round, the great artist affected our friend as a dizzying prodigy of type . . . with a personal lustre almost violent, he shone in a constellation.

What are we to make of this little chapter of the *comédie humaine*, in which the artist of the last century most driven to the celebration of his own originality and of the autographic character of his own kneading of matter into formal life, *that* artist, should have given his own work over to an afterlife of mechanical reproduction? Are we to think that in this peculiar last testimony Rodin acknowledged the extent to which his was an art of reproduction, of multiples without originals?

But at a second remove, what are we to make of our own squeamishness at the thought of the future of posthumous casting that awaits Rodin's work? Are we not involved here in clinging to a culture of originals which has no place among the reproductive mediums? Within the current photography market this culture of the original—the vintage print—is hard at work. The vintage print is specified as one made "close to the aesthetic moment"—and thus an object made not only by the photographer himself, but produced, as well, contemporaneously with the taking of the image. This is of course a mechanical view of authorship—one that does not acknowledge that some photographers are less good printers than the printers they hire; or that years after the fact photographers reedit and recrop older images, sometimes vastly improving them; or that it is possible to re-create old papers and old chemical compounds and thus to resurrect the look of the nineteenth-century vintage print, so that authenticity need not be a function of the history of technology.

But the formula that specifies a photographic original as a print made "close to the aesthetic moment" is obviously a formula dictated by the art historical notion of period style and applied to the practice of connoisseurship. A period style is a special form of coherence that cannot be fraudulently breached. The

3.   *Ibid.,* p. 2.

authenticity folded into the concept of *style* is a product of the way style is conceived as having been generated: that is, collectively and unconsciously. Thus an individual could not, by definition, consciously will a style. Later copies will be exposed precisely because they are not of the period; it is exactly that shift in sensibility that will get the chiaroscuro wrong, make the outlines too harsh or too muddy, disrupt the older patterns of coherence. It is this concept of period style that we feel the 1978 cast of *The Gates of Hell* will violate. We do not care if the copyright papers are all in order; for what is at stake are the aesthetic rights of style based on a culture of originals. Sitting in the little theater, watching the newest *Gates* being cast, watching this violation, we want to call out, "Fraud."

*

Now why would one begin a discussion of avant-garde art with this story about Rodin and casts and copyrights? Particularly since Rodin strikes one as the very last artist to introduce to the subject, so popular was he during his lifetime, so celebrated, and so quickly induced to participate in the transformation of his own work into kitsch.

The avant-garde artist has worn many guises over the first hundred years of his existence: revolutionary, dandy, anarchist, aesthete, technologist, mystic. He has also preached a variety of creeds. One thing only seems to hold fairly constant in the vanguardist discourse and that is the theme of originality. By originality, here, I mean more than just the kind of revolt against tradition that echoes in Ezra Pound's "Make it new!" or sounds in the futurists' promise to destroy the museums that cover Italy as though "with countless cemeteries." More than a rejection or dissolution of the past, avant-garde originality is conceived as a literal origin, a beginning from ground zero, a birth. Marinetti, thrown from his automobile one evening in 1909 into a factory ditch filled with water, emerges as if from amniotic fluid to be born—without ancestors—a futurist. This parable of absolute self-creation that begins the first *Futurist Manifesto* functions as a model for what is meant by originality among the early twentieth-century avant-garde. For originality becomes an organicist metaphor referring not so much to formal invention as to sources of life. The self as origin is safe from contamination by tradition because it possesses a kind of originary naiveté. Hence Brancusi's dictum, "When we are no longer children, we are already dead." Or again, the self as origin has the potential for continual acts of regeneration, a perpetuation of self-birth. Hence Malevich's pronouncement, "Only he is alive who rejects his convictions of yesterday." The self as origin is the way an absolute distinction can be made between a present experienced *de novo* and a tradition-laden past. The claims of the avant-garde are precisely these claims to originality.

Now, if the very notion of the avant-garde can be seen as a function of the discourse of originality, the actual practice of vanguard art tends to reveal that "originality" is a working assumption that itself emerges from a ground of repetition and recurrence. One figure, drawn from avant-garde practice in the visual arts, provides an example. This figure is the grid.

Aside from its near ubiquity in the work of those artists who thought of themselves as avant-garde—their numbers include Malevich as well as Mondrian, Léger as well as Picasso, Schwitters, Cornell, Reinhardt and Johns as well as Andre, LeWitt, Hesse, and Ryman—the grid possesses several structural properties which make it inherently susceptible to vanguard appropriation. One of these is the grid's imperviousness to language. "Silence, exile, and cunning," were Stephen Dedalus's passwords: commands that in Paul Goodman's view express the self-imposed code of the avant-garde artist. The grid promotes this silence, expressing it moreover as a refusal of speech. The absolute stasis of the grid, its lack of hierarchy, of center, of inflection, emphasizes not only its anti-referential character, but—more importantly—its hostility to narrative. This structure, impervious both to time and to incident, will not permit the projection of language into the domain of the visual, and the result is silence.

This silence is not due simply to the extreme effectiveness of the grid as a barricade against speech, but to the protectiveness of its mesh against all intrusions from outside. No echoes of footsteps in empty rooms, no scream of birds across open skies, no rush of distant water—for the grid has collapsed the spatiality of nature onto the bounded surface of a purely cultural object. With its proscription of nature as well as of speech, the result is still more silence. And in this new-found quiet, what many artists thought they could hear was the beginning, the origins of Art.

For those for whom art begins in a kind of originary purity, the grid was emblematic of the sheer disinterestedness of the work of art, its absolute purpose-lessness, from which it derived the promise of its autonomy. We hear this sense of the originary essence of art when Schwitters insists, "Art is a primordial concept, exalted as the godhead, inexplicable as life, indefinable and without purpose." And the grid facilitated this sense of being born into the newly evacuated space of an aesthetic purity and freedom.

While for those for whom the origins of art are not to be found in the idea of pure disinterest so much as in an empirically grounded unity, the grid's power lies in its capacity to figure forth the material ground of the pictorial object, si-multaneously inscribing and depicting it, so that the image of the pictorial surface can be seen to be born out of the organization of pictorial matter. For these artists, the grid-scored surface is the image of an absolute beginning.

Perhaps it is because of this sense of a beginning, a fresh start, a ground zero, that artist after artist has taken up the grid as the medium within which to work, always taking it up as though he were just discovering it, as though the origin he had found by peeling back layer after layer of representation to come at last to this schematized reduction, this graph-paper ground, were *his* origin, and his finding it an act of originality. Waves of abstract artists "discover" the grid; part of its

Agnes Martin. Play. *1966.*

structure one could say is that in its revelatory character it is always a new, a unique discovery.

And just as the grid is a stereotype that is constantly being paradoxically re-discovered, it is, as a further paradox, a prison in which the caged aritst feels at liberty. For what is striking about the grid is that while it is most effective as a badge of freedom, it is extremely restrictive in the actual exercise of freedom. Without doubt the most formulaic construction that could possibly be mapped on a plane surface, the grid is also highly inflexible. Thus just as no one could claim to have invented it, so once one is involved in deploying it, the grid is extremely difficult to use in the service of invention. And thus when we examine the careers of those artists who have been most committed to the grid, we could say that from the time they submit themselves to this structure their work virtually ceases to develop and becomes involved, instead, in repetition. Exemplary artists in this respect are Mondrian, Albers, Reinhardt, and Agnes Martin.

But in saying that the grid condemns these artists not to originality but to repetition, I am not suggesting a negative description of their work. I am trying instead to focus on a pair of terms—originality and repetition—and to look at their coupling unprejudicially; for within the instance we are examining, these two terms seem bound together in a kind of aesthetic economy, interdependent and mutually sustaining, although the one—originality—is the valorized term and the other—repetition or copy or reduplication—is discredited.

We have already seen that the avant-garde artist above all claims originality as his right—his birthright, so to speak. With his own self as the origin of his work, that production will have the same uniqueness as he; the condition of his own singularity will guarantee the originality of what he makes. Having given himself this warrant, he goes on, in the example we are looking at, to enact his originality in the creation of grids. Yet as we have seen, not only is he—artist *x*, *y*, or *z*—*not* the inventor of the grid, but *no one* can claim this patent: the copyright expired sometime in antiquity and for many centuries this figure has been in the public domain.

Structurally, logically, axiomatically, the grid *can only be repeated*. And, with an act of repetition or replication as the "original" occasion of its usage within the experience of a given artist, the extended life of the grid in the unfolding progression of his work will be one of still more repetition, as the artist engages in repeated acts of self-imitation. That so many generations of twentieth-century artists should have maneuvered themselves into this particular position of paradox—where they are condemned to repeating, as if by compulsion, the logically fraudulent original—is truly compelling.

But it is no more compelling than that other, complementary fiction: the illusion not of the originality of the artist, but of the originary status of the pictorial surface. This origin is what the genius of the grid is supposed to manifest to us as viewers: an indisputable zero-ground beyond which there is no further model, or referent, or text. Except that this experience of originariness, felt by generations of artists, critics, and viewers is itself false, a fiction. The canvas surface and the grid that scores it do not fuse into that absolute unity necessary to the notion of an origin. For the grid *follows* the canvas surface, doubles it. It is a representation of the surface, mapped, it is true, onto the same surface it represents, but even so, the grid remains a figure, picturing various aspects of the "originary" object: through its mesh it creates an image of the woven infrastructure of the canvas; through its network of coordinates it organizes a metaphor for the plane geometry of the field; through its repetition it configures the spread of lateral continuity. The grid thus does not reveal the surface, laying it bare at last; rather it veils it through a repetition.

As I have said, this repetition performed by the grid must follow, or come after, the actual, empirical surface of a given painting. The representational text of the grid however also precedes the surface, comes *before* it, preventing even that literal surface from being anything like an origin. For behind it, logically prior to it, are all those visual texts through which the bounded plane was collectively organized as a pictorial field. The grid summarizes all these texts: the gridded overlays on cartoons, for example, used for the mechanical transfer from drawing to fresco; or the perspective lattice meant to contain the perceptual transfer from three dimensions to two; or the matrix on which to chart harmonic relationships, like proportion; or the millions of acts of enframing by which the picture was reaffirmed as a regular quadrilateral. All these are the texts which the "original" ground plane of a Mondrian, for example, repeats—and, by repeating, represents. Thus the very ground that the grid is thought to reveal is already riven from within by a process of repetition and representation; it is always already divided and multiple.

What I have been calling the fiction of the originary status of the picture surface is what art criticism proudly names the opacity of the modernist picture plane, only in so terming it, the critic does not think of this opacity as fictitious. Within the discursive space of modernist art, the putative opacity of the pictorial field must be maintained as a fundamental concept. For it is the bedrock on which a whole structure of related terms can be built. All those terms—singularity, authenticity, uniqueness, originality, original—depend on the originary moment of which this surface is both the empirical and the semiological instance. If modernism's domain of pleasure is the space of auto-referentiality, this pleasure dome is erected on the semiological possibility of the pictorial sign as nonrepresentational and nontransparent, so that the signified becomes the redundant condition of a reified signifier. But from *our* perspective, the one from which we see that the signifier cannot be reified; that its objecthood, its quiddity, is only a fiction; that every signifier is itself the transparent signified of an already-given decision to carve it out as the vehicle of a sign—from *this* perspective there is no opacity, but only a transparency that opens onto a dizzying fall into a bottomless system of reduplication.

This is the perspective from which the grid that signifies the pictorial surface, by representing it, only succeeds in locating the signifier of another, prior system of grids, which have beyond them, yet another, even earlier system. This is the perspective in which the modernist grid is, like the Rodin casts, logically multiple: a system of reproductions without an original. This is the perspective from which the real condition of one of the major vehicles of modernist aesthetic practice is seen to derive not from the valorized term of that couple which I invoked earlier—the doublet, *originality/repetition*—but from the discredited half of the pair, the one that opposes the multiple to the singular, the reproducible to the unique, the fraudulent to the authentic, the copy to the original. But this is the negative half of the set of terms that the critical practice of modernism seeks to repress, *has* repressed.

From this perspective we can see that modernism and the avant-garde are functions of what we could call the discourse of originality, and that that discourse serves much wider interests—and is thus fueled by more diverse institutions—than the restricted circle of professional art-making. The theme of originality, encompassing as it does the notions of authenticity, originals, and origins, is the shared discursive practice of the museum, the historian, and the maker of art. And throughout the nineteenth century all of these institutions were concerted, together, to find the mark, the warrant, the certification of the original.[4]

*

That this would be done despite the ever-present reality of the copy as the *underlying condition of the original* was much closer to the surface of consciousness in the early years of the nineteenth century than it would later be permitted to be. Thus, in *Northanger Abbey* Jane Austen sends Catherine, her sweetly provincial young heroine, out for a walk with two new, rather more sophisticated friends; these friends soon embark on viewing the countryside, as Austen says, "with the eyes of persons accustomed to drawing, and decided on its capability of being formed into pictures, with all the eagerness of real taste." What begins to dawn on Catherine is that her countrified notions of the natural— "that a clear blue sky" is for instance "proof of a fine day"—are entirely false and that the natural, which is to say, the landscape, is about to be constructed for her by her more highly educated companions:

> . . . a lecture on the picturesque immediately followed, in which his instructions were so clear that she soon began to see beauty in every

4.   On the discourse of origins and originals, see Michel Foucault, *The Order of Things*, New York, Pantheon, 1970, pp. 328-335: "But this thin surface of the original, which accompanies our entire existence . . . is not the immediacy of a birth; it is populated entirely by those complex mediations formed and laid down as a sediment in their own history by labor, life and language so that . . . what man is reviving without knowing it, is all the intermediaries of a time that governs him almost to infinity."

thing admired by him. . . . He talked of fore-grounds, distances, and second distances—side-screens and perspectives—lights and shades;—and Catherine was so hopeful a scholar that when they gained the top of Beechen Cliff, she voluntarily rejected the whole city of Bath, as unworthy to make part of a landscape.[5]

To read any text on the picturesque is instantly to fall prey to that amused irony with which Austen watches her young charge discover that nature itself is constituted in relation to its "capability of being formed into pictures." For it is perfectly obvious that through the action of the picturesque the very notion of landscape is constructed as a second term of which the first is a representation. Landscape becomes a reduplication of a picture which preceded it. Thus when we eavesdrop on a conversation between one of the leading practitioners of the picturesque, the Reverend William Gilpin, and his son, who is visiting the Lake District, we hear very clearly the order of priorities.

In a letter to his father, the young man describes his disappointment in the first day's ascent into the mountains, for the perfectly clear weather insured a total absence of what the elder Gilpin constantly refers to in his writings as effect. But the second day, his son assures him, there was a rainstorm followed by a break in the clouds.

> Then what effects of gloom and effulgence. I can't describe [them]—nor need I—for you have only to look into your own store house [of sketches] to take a view of them—It gave me however a very singular pleasure to see your system of effects so compleatly confirmed as it was by the observations of that day—wherever I turned my eyes, I beheld a drawing of yours.[6]

In this discussion, it is the drawing—with its own prior set of decisions about *effect*—that stands behind the landscape authenticating its claim to represent nature.

The 1801 Supplement to Johnson's Dictionary gives six definitions for the term *picturesque*, the six of them moving in a kind of figure eight around the question of the landscape as originary to the experience of itself. According to the Dictionary the picturesque is: 1) what pleases the eye; 2) remarkable for singularity; 3) striking the imagination with the force of paintings; 4) to be expressed in painting; 5) affording a good subject for a landscape; 6) proper to take a landscape from.[7] It should not be necessary to say that the concept of singularity, as in the part of the definition that reads, "remarkable for singularity," is at odds semantically with other parts of the definition, such as "affording a good subject for a

---

5. Jane Austen, *Northanger Abbey*, 1818, Vol. I, Chapter XIV.
6. In Carl Paul Barbier, *William Gilpin*, Oxford, The Clarendon Press, 1963, p. 111.
7. See Barbier, p. 98.

landscape," in which *a landscape* is understood to mean a type of painting. Because that pictorial type—in all the formulaic condition of Gilpin's "effects"— is not single (or singular) but multiple, conventional, a series of recipes about roughness, chiaroscuro, ruins and abbeys, and therefore, when the effect is found in the world at large, that natural array is simply felt to be repeating another work—a "landscape"—that already exists elsewhere.

But the *singularity* of the Dictionary's definition deserves even further examination. Gilpin's *Observations on Cumberland and Westmorland* addresses this question of singularity by making it a function of the beholder and the array of singular moments of his perception. The landscape's singularity is thus not something which a bit of topography does or does not possess; it is rather a function of the images it figures forth at any moment in time and the way these pictures register in the imagination. That the landscape is not static but constantly recomposing itself into different, separate, or singular pictures, Gilpin advances as follows:

> He, who should see any one scene, as it is differently affected by the lowering sky, or a bright one, might probably see two very different landscapes. He might not only see distances blotted out; or splendidly

William Gilpin. Sketch for A Fragment. *1764.*

exhibited; but he might even see variations produced in the very objects themselves; and that merely from the different times of the day, in which they were examined.[8]

With this description of the notion of singularity as the perceptual-empirical unity of a moment of time coalesced in the experience of a subject, we feel ourselves entering the nineteenth-century discussion of landscape and the belief in the fundamental, originary power of nature dilated through subjectivity. That is, in Gilpin's two-different-landscapes-because-two-different-times-of-day, we feel that the prior condition of landscape as being already a picture is being let go of. But Gilpin then continues, "In a warm sunshine the purple hills may skirt the horizon, and appear broken into numberless pleasing forms; but under a sullen sky a total change may be produced," in which case, he insists, "the distant mountains, and all their beautiful projection may disappear, and their place be

8.   William Gilpin, *Observations on Cumberland and Westmorland*, Richmond, The Richmond Publishing Co., 1973, p. vii. The book was written in 1772 and first published in 1786.

William Gilpin. The Waterfall. *1774.*

occupied by a dead flat." Gilpin thus reassures us that the patent to the "pleasing forms" as opposed to the "dead flat" has already been taken out by painting.

Thus what Austen's, Gilpin's, and the Dictionary's picturesque reveals to us is that although the *singular* and the *formulaic* or repetitive may be semantically opposed, they are nonetheless conditions of each other: the two logical halves of the concept *landscape*. The priorness and repetition of pictures is necessary to the singularity of the picturesque, because for the beholder singularity depends on being recognized as such, a re-cognition made possible only by a prior example. If the definition of the picturesque is beautifully circular, that is because what allows a given moment of the perceptual array to be seen as singular is precisely its conformation to a multiple.

Now this economy of the paired opposition—singular and multiple—can easily be examined within the aesthetic episode that is termed *the Picturesque*, an episode that was crucial to the rise of a new class of audience for art, one that was focused on the practice of taste as an exercise in the recognition of singularity, or—in its application within the language of romanticism—originality. Several decades later into the nineteenth century, however, it is harder to see these terms still performing in mutual interdependence, since aesthetic discourse—both official and nonofficial—gives priority to the term originality and tends to suppress the notion of repetition or copy. But harder to see or not, the notion of the copy is still fundamental to the conception of the original. And nineteenth-century practice was concerted towards the exercise of copies and copying in the creation of that same possibility of recognition that Jane Austen and William Gilpin call taste. Thiers, the ardent Republican who honored Delacroix's originality to the point of having worked on his behalf in the awarding of important government commissions, had nevertheless set up a museum of copies in 1834. And forty years later in the very year of the first impressionist exhibition, a huge Musée des Copies was opened under the direction of Charles Blanc, then the Director of Fine Arts. In nine rooms the museum housed 156 newly commissioned full-scale oil copies of the most important masterpieces from foreign museums as well as replicas of the Vatican Stanze frescoes of Raphael. So urgent was the need for this museum, in Blanc's opinion, that in the first three years of the Third Republic, *all* monies for official commissions made by the Ministry of Fine Arts went to pay for copyists.[9] Yet, this insistence on the priority of copies in the formation of taste hardly prevented Charles Blanc, no less than Thiers, from deeply admiring Delacroix, or from providing the most accessible explanation of advanced color theory then available in print. I am referring to the *Grammar of the Arts of Design*, published in 1867, and certainly the obvious text in which the budding impressionists could read about simultaneous contrast, complementarity, or achromatism, and be introduced to the theories and diagrams of Chevreul and Goethe.

9.   For details, see Albert Boime, "Le Musée des Copies," *Gazette des Beaux-Arts*, LXIV (1964), 237-247.

   This is not the place to develop the truly fascinating theme of the role of the copy within nineteenth-century pictorial practice and what is emerging as its necessity to the concept of the original, the spontaneous, the new.[10] I will simply say that the copy served as the ground for the development of an increasingly organized and codified sign or seme of spontaneity—one that Gilpin had called roughness, Constable had termed "the chiaroscuro of nature"—by which he was referring to a completely conventionalized overlay of broken touches and flicks of pure white laid in with a palette knife—and Monet later called instantaneity, linking its appearance to the conventionalized pictorial language of the sketch or *pochade*. *Pochade* is the technical term for a rapidly made sketch, a shorthand notation. As such, it is codifiable, recognizable. So it was both the rapidity of the *pochade* and its abbreviated language that a critic like Chesnaud saw in Monet's work and referred to by the way it was produced: "the chaos of palette scrapings," he called it.[11] But as recent studies of Monet's impressionism have made explicit, the sketchlike mark, which functioned as the *sign* of spontaneity, had to be prepared for through the utmost calculation, and in this sense spontaneity was the most fakable of signifieds. Through layers of underpainting by which Monet developed the thick corrugations of what Robert Herbert calls his texture-strokes, Monet patiently laid the mesh of rough encrustation and directional swathes that would signify speed of execution, and from this speed, mark both the singularity of the perceptual moment and uniqueness of the empirical array.[12] On top of this constructed "instant," thin, careful washes of pigment establish the actual relations of color. Needless to say, these operations took—with the necessary drying time—many days to perform. But the illusion of spontaneity—the burst of an instantaneous and originary act—is the unshakable result. Rémy de Gourmont falls prey to this illusion when he speaks in 1901 of canvases by Monet as "the work of an instant," the specific instant being "that flash" in which "genius collaborated with the eye and the hand" to forge "a personal work of absolute originality."[13] The illusion of unrepeatable, separate instants is the product of a fully calculated procedure that was necessarily divided up into stages and sections and worked on piecemeal on a variety of canvases at the same time, assembly-line style. Visitors to Monet's studio in the last decades of his life were startled to find the master of instantaneity at work on a line-up of a dozen or more canvases. The production of spontaneity through the constant overpainting of canvases (Monet kept back the Rouen Cathedral series from his dealer, for

10.   For a discussion of the institutionalization of copying within nineteenth-century artistic training, see Albert Boime, *The Academy and French Painting in the 19th Century*, London, Phaidon, 1971.
11.   Cited by Steven Z. Levine, "The 'Instant' of Criticism and Monet's Critical Instant," *Arts Magazine*, vol. 55, no. 7 (March 1981), 118.
12.   See Robert Herbert, "Method and Meaning in Monet," *Art in America*, vol. 67, no. 5 (September 1979), 90–108.
13.   Cited by Levine, p. 118.

example, for three years of reworking) employs the same aesthetic economy of the pairing of singularity and multiplicity, of uniqueness and reproduction, that we saw at the outset in Rodin's method. In addition, it involves that fracturing of the empirical origin that operates through the example of the modernist grid. But as was true in those other cases as well, the discourse of originality in which impressionism participates represses and discredits the complementary discourse of the copy. Both the avant-garde and modernism depend on this repression.

*

What would it look like not to repress the concept of the copy? What would it look like to produce a work that acted out the discourse of reproductions without originals, that discourse which could only operate in Mondrian's work as the inevitable subversion of his purpose, the residue of representationality that he could not sufficiently purge from the domain of his painting? The answer to this, or at least one answer, is that it would look like a certain kind of play with the notions of photographic reproduction that begins in the silkscreen canvases of Robert Rauschenberg and has recently flowered in the work of a group of younger artists whose production has been identified by the critical term *pictures*.[14] I will focus on the example of Sherrie Levine, because it seems most radically to question the concept of origin and with it the notion of originality.

Levine's medium is the pirated print, as in the series of photographs she made by taking images by Edward Weston of his young son Neil and simply rephotographing them, in violation of Weston's copyright. But as has been pointed out about Weston's "originals," these are already taken from models provided by others; they are given in that long series of Greek kouroi by which the nude male torso has long ago been processed and multiplied within our culture.[15] Levine's act of theft, which takes place, so to speak, in front of the surface of Weston's print, opens the print from behind to the series of models from which it, in turn, has stolen, of which it is itself the reproduction. The discourse of the copy, within which Levine's act must be located has, of course, been developed by a variety of writers, among them Roland Barthes. I am thinking of his characterization, in *S/Z*, of the realist as certainly not a copyist from nature, but rather a "pasticher," or someone who makes copies of copies. As Barthes says:

> To depict is to . . . refer not from a language to a referent, but from one code to another. Thus realism consists not in copying the real but in copying a (depicted) copy. . . . Through secondary mimesis [realism] copies what is already a copy.[16]

14.   The relevant texts are by Douglas Crimp; see his exhibition catalogue *Pictures*, New York, Artists Space, 1977; and "Pictures," *October*, no. 8 (Spring 1979), 75–88.
15.   See Douglas Crimp, "The Photographic Activity of Postmodernism," *October*, no. 15 (Winter 1980), 98–99.
16.   Roland Barthes, *S/Z*, trans. Richard Miller, New York, Hill and Wang, 1974, p. 55.

Sherrie Levine. Photograph by Eliot Porter. *1981.*

In another series by Levine in which the lush, colored landscapes of Eliot Porter are reproduced, we again move through the "original" print, back to the origin in nature and—as in the model of the picturesque—through another trap door at the back wall of "nature" into the purely textual construction of the sublime and its history of degeneration into ever more lurid copies.

Now, insofar as Levine's work explicitly deconstructs the modernist notion of origin, her effort cannot be seen as an *extension* of modernism. It is, like the discourse of the copy, postmodernist. Which means that it cannot be seen as avant-garde either.

Because of the critical attack it launches on the tradition that precedes it, we might want to see the move made in Levine's work as yet another step in the forward march of the avant-garde. But this would be mistaken. In deconstructing the sister notions of origin and originality, postmodernism establishes a schism between itself and the conceptual domain of the avant-garde, looking back at it from across a gulf that in turn establishes a historical divide. The historical period that the avant-garde shared with modernism is over. That seems an obvious fact. What makes it more than a journalistic one is a conception of the discourse that has brought it to a close. This is a complex of cultural practices, among them a demythologizing criticism and a truly postmodernist art, both of them acting now to void the basic propositions of modernism, to liquidate them by exposing their fictitious condition. It is thus from a strange new perspective that we look back on the modernist origin and watch it splintering into endless replication.

Washington, D.C., 1981

Introductory Note to **Sincerely Yours**

After its initial publication, "The Originality of the Avant-Garde" drew an immediate response from Professor Albert Elsen, the organizer of the National Gallery of Art's Rodin Rediscovered. *In a four-page letter to the editors of* October, *Elsen attacked the essay's discussion of Rodin's relation to the question of originals and originality, dismissing any possibility that the status of these concepts might be problematic. Writing that my text seemed to have ignored the exhibition's catalogue, "which includes essays by the former director of the Louvre on 'An Original in Sculpture,' Dan Rosenfeld's on 'Rodin's Carved Sculpture,' and my own on 'The Gates of Hell,'" Elsen went on to repeat what he feels should by now be obvious: "Jean Chatelain shows that in France editions of bronzes have been traditionally considered original. One could add that just as with prints, then and now, bronze editions were and are originals. To speak of an original Rembrandt print is no different from speaking of an original Rodin bronze."*

Having decided that for me originality "means unique, one of a kind," Elsen was anxious to counter this definition with Rodin's own. "Rodin's view of originality lay in his conceptions," Elsen insists, "such as his interpretation of the story of the Burghers of Calais or his ideas of what a public monument could be, such as his Balzac. . . . In his time, Rodin's acclaim as an original artist did not rest on making one-of-a-kind sculptures. He considered his authorized bronzes and carvings, reproduced by others, as 'authograph' works, because they were his conceptions carried out to his standards. If a client wanted a totally distinctive marble, he would stipulate to Rodin that the commissioned work must differ in some visible, unalterable way from any subsequent carvings of the same theme. Rodin's public knew well the system of a division of labor that he inherited and relied upon to be productive and creative."

If originality can be rendered entirely unproblematic for us, so can authenticity. Describing Rodin's relation to Jean Limet, the sculptor's "favorite patineur," Elsen adds: "Contrary to Krauss, Rodin had very strong and consistent views on authenticity. He recognized as authentic only those bronze casts he had authorized. All others he condemned as counterfeit."

Equally unproblematic, within this context of reproduction, is the question of repetition. Thus, "Contrary to Krauss, Rodin's contemporaries were aware of his reutilization of the same figure, not only in The Gates, *but in his free-standing work. In 1900, review-ing Rodin's retrospective and* The Gates of Hell, *a critic named Jean E. Schmitt wrote about* The Gates, *'The same figure, the same group, inverted, modified, accentuated, sim-plified, combined with others arranged in a shadow, placed in the light, revealed to their author the secrets of sculpture, the mysteries of composition, the beauties of which he had only confused dreamed.' Krauss would have us believe that she and not Rilke, who as Rodin's secretary was in the studio daily for seven months, has recognized the same figure in* The Three Shades.*"*

Having set the historical record straight by this series of inversions ("contrary to Krauss"), Elsen then attacked two more recent issues. One was my account of the film docu-menting the casting of The Gates of Hell, *which had been scheduled for the exhibition but was not finished in time to be shown within the context of* Rodin Rediscovered, *inval-idating my reference to it in "The Originality of the Avant-Garde." The other was my po-sition in the essay "Julio Gonzalez: This New Art: To Draw in Space," which he saw as failing to "condemn the posthumous casting of Julio Gonzalez's unique welded iron works." Regarding this as an evasion of the very issues I had raised in relation to Rodin, Elsen went on to present as my position on Gonzalez, "that since the use of found materials by Gonzalez was not metaphoric as in Picasso's work, and what he did with welded iron was 'a process,' many of the issues of direct metal working that would theoretically prohibit translation into bronze are also irrelevant." Expressing his indignation over this idea, as well as everything else to be found in "The Originality of the Avant-Garde," Elsen demands, "Just what do we call out when a critic invents issues, makes up contradictions, promotes a double standard, and reviews an event that has not yet happened?"*

It was, presumably, this sense of outrage that directed the close of his letter. After a postscript to the readers of October, *directing them to the "view of experts" registered in the "Standards for Sculptural Reproduction and Preventive Measures Against Unethical Cast-ing," a view "adopted by the Art Museum Directors Association, Artists Equity, the Art Dealers Association, and the College Art Association," Elsen then gave notice to* October's *editors as follows: "cc: Leo Steinberg, Kirk Varnedoe, Henry Millon, Arthur Danto." Somewhat puzzled, the editors printed his letter in full, with the exception of that final, cen-sorious, tag. Published in* October, *no. 20 (Spring 1982), Elsen's letter was followed by my "Sincerely Yours."*

National Gallery installation of Rodin
Rediscovered, *Section VII: "The Gates of Hell
and Their Offspring." (Photo: James Pipkin.)*

Where to begin? Perhaps contrarywise: at the end. We could begin with the final paragraph of Professor Elsen's discussion of "Rodin's 'Perfect Collaborator,' Henri Lebossé," published in the catalogue for *Rodin Rediscovered*:

> Why did Lebossé accept Bénédite's commission to make the huge posthumous version of *The Defense*? *Did pride vanquish prudence*? . . . Lebossé's decision is more understandable, *if not condonable*, when one reads of his problems just after the war in putting his business back on its feet, even with the help of his son who had been demobilized. Finally, Bénédite had the *legal, if not ethical authority* as director of the Musée Rodin, and Lebossé *had money coming to him* after Rodin's death for other unfinished projects.[1]

These questions and their speculative replies cap the episode with which Elsen chooses to close his description of the career of Rodin's favorite *reproducteur*—a man whose letterhead bore the information "that he engaged in reducing and enlarging objects of 'art and industry' by a 'mathematically perfected process' and employed a 'special machine' for making these 'counterparts' in 'editions.' "[2] (Throughout this essay Professor Elsen's most frequently used terms for Lebossé's marbles is not *counterpart* but *reproduction*—a term to which we will return.)

The episode was a "scandal" in which Lebossé was "tragically" involved, although with the complicity of the first director of the Musée Rodin, who as beneficiary of Rodin's will had, of course, "the legal, if not ethical authority" in this matter. After Rodin's death Lebossé began an enlargement of *The Defense*, increasing the original scale of the work fourfold, which is to say, beyond that ever commissioned by Rodin himself. This was done at Bénédite's instructions

1.   Albert E. Elsen, ed., *Rodin Rediscovered*, Washington, D.C., The National Gallery of Art, 1981, p. 256 (italics added).
2.   *Ibid.*, p. 249.

for sale to the Dutch government as a monument to be erected at Verdun. Upon completion, we learn, "there was a storm of criticism directed at Bénédite for undertaking the posthumous enlargement," and further, "tragically for Rodin's 'perfect collaborator', the Verdun enlargement became part of a 1920 scandal involving fake works, marble carvers who continued to turn out sculpture signed with Rodin's name, and unauthorized bronze casts of the Barbedienne foundry."[3]

Now the major difference between Lebossé and the other "marble carvers who continued to turn out sculpture signed with Rodin's name" seems to be that their "fake" was illegal and his wasn't—by virtue of the authorization of "the artist or his beneficiaries" (General Code of Taxes, Appendix iii, Article 17), in this case the Musée Rodin, which is by law the sole, proper "holder of the artist's rights of authorship," and thus the source of "legal, if not ethical authority."[4] The director of the Musée Rodin, no less than Lebossé, approaches this question of authorship with money on his mind; for the museum's endowment *is* the right of reproduction and its income is derived from the continuing flow of originals.

The "legal if not ethical authority" is, indeed, central to the concept of the original edition and its careful buttressing not only by the Penal Code but also by the General Code of Taxes. For the law interests itself greatly in the question of the way originality opens directly onto the matter of contracts.

As Elsen assures us in his letter, Jean Chatelain is very illuminating on the whole problem of the sculptural original, particularly the issue to which he mainly limits himself, that of "original editions." "The special worth of an original edition," Chatelain writes, "does not come from an objective character of its originality, in the etymological meaning of the term, since every edition is in itself an operation of reproducing a model which is really the original, nor does this come about for want of a legal or customary definition. It arises from the agreements made by the edition's author with the buyers."[5] The *buyers*? What do they have to do with the matter of authorship or the status of the original?

Linking as it does "the revolutionary upheaval which shattered the traditional workshop system and the advent of an individualistic philosophy, followed by the rise of romanticism and the development of the art market and speculation,"[6] Chatelain's account of the development of the idea of the "original edition" has everything to do with consumption. The nineteenth-century buyer, he explains, was infected by the notion of originality—by which was understood innovation, creativity, inspiration. And, conflating originality with the condition of the physical original, he desired to possess the object that most

3.   *Ibid.*, p. 256.
4.   Jean Chatelain quotes from the relevant statues in *Rodin Rediscovered*, p. 281.
5.   *Ibid.*, p. 279.
6.   *Ibid.*, p. 275.

directly bore the traces of this spontaneous, unrepeatable process. Because of this new condition of desire, "any reproduction of an artist's work made by someone else, no matter what the process might be, is without real artistic value and therefore of an inconsequential price, for it no longer gives direct evidence of the creative impulse."[7]

For the compound arts (such as bronze sculpture), which are "arts of repetition," this new economy of desire threatened an absolute fall in value and required an immediate response. The "original edition" was the form of that response, a formula that Chatelain is quick to tell us "defies logic and linguistic accuracy [since] originality implies uniqueness; [while] an edition implies diffusion, multiplication, and series."[8] But as in most economic processes the logic has little to do with semantics, or "etymological meaning," and is instead a function of supply and demand, of what Chatelain calls "systematic rarefaction." Again and again Chatelain stresses that the "original edition" is a juridical fiction set up to create what could be called the *originality-effect*: "The effectiveness of this formula remains such in the eyes of the public at large that we can see it used to give greater value to editions which, for want of being originals, will at least have the appearance of being so, by being numbered."[9]

At first, reading this, we feel that Chatelain is being facetious, or perhaps is writing out of a scarcely veiled cynicism. But this is the effect of extracting pieces of his prose from the full context of his presentation, where his discussion is at pains to explain the reasonableness of the system and thus to account for the drift of his argument as it moves inexorably away from "etymological meaning" and into the determinations of the marketplace. Thus, dismissing the possibility of "competent authorities to . . . define what is an original edition at a given moment and for a given art," and viewing their indecision as something that "only reinforces this feeling of relativism," this former director of the Louvre throws the question into the arena of commerce:

> Once again, as is the usual formula in a liberal rights system, there remains the will of the parties involved: it is up to both sides to define what they mutually agree to. . . . In our field it is quite clear that the bidder, the seller that is to say, eventually the holder of the copyright of a certain work — be he the creating artist or his beneficiaries — he alone is in a position to set the characteristics of an edition about to be undertaken. He decides how many copies are to be made, what the technical characteristics are to be, and which specialists are to be called in. The buyer cannot help but take or leave, the conditions thus layed out. The most he can do, aside from simply saying yes or no, is to try to bargain down the price or ask for some

7. *Ibid.*, p. 276.
8. *Ibid.*, p. 277.
9. *Ibid.*, p. 278.

special secondary characteristic — in bronze, for example, for a certain type of socle.[10]

The beneficiary is thus truly the holder of the artist's "authorship," for he alone, once the artist is dead, "is in a position to set the characteristics of an edition. . . ." And the buyer? Desiring an original — the object of his desire — he must do what he can "to bargain down the price."

For Chatelain the wholly commercial/conventional nature of the "original edition" — which, in ordei to stress the oxymoronic quality of the formula, he sometimes changes to "original copy" — raises logical problems such that interpretation of the relevant legal instruments can often pose difficulties. As an example he examines a recent decree bearing on the Tax Code and treating the suppression of frauds in transactions involving works of art. This decree mandates that all reproductions of an original work carry the indelible notation "reproduction"; included in this category are "casts of casts." Now, the problem, as Chatelain sees it, arises from the fact that the term "casts of casts" seems to limit itself to casts not made from the original matrix — that is, in the case of bronze sculpture, not made from the original plaster. What that would mean is that any cast made from the original plaster *even after* the threshold of the "original edition" had been reached (in the case of Rodin, twelve casts) would *not* be a reproduction, but would be part of an "edition" and in some sense — "legal, if not ethical"? — an original. This possibility does not seem compatible with the principle of "systematic rarefaction," and so another reading of "casts of casts" is imagined by Chatelain. In *this* interpretation (which he calls "more stringent") *all* casts made once the limit of the "original edition" is reached, whether from the original plaster or not, would be considered "reproductions" and would have to be so labeled. Which of these interpretations should we adopt?

> Technically, only the first interpretation seems to us to be justified since it rests on a criterion which is itself technical. That which is made from the original plaster is a proof, an edition; that which is not made from the original plaster is a reproduction.
>
> On the other hand, the overall spirit of the decree of 3 March 1981 is evidently *to impose strict limits on the art trade* as to the designation of objects. One can therefore think that the second interpretation, *because it is restrictive*, conforms more than the first to this spirit.[11]

The spirit of this decree is to impose limits on the art trade, which seems among other things to mean shoring up that fallible market for the compound arts by the operations of "systematic rarefaction." The decrees and codes to which Chatelain refers are of course articles of French law made with particular re-

10. *Ibid.*, p. 279.
11. *Ibid.*, pp. 281–282 (italics added).

gard to a French art market that is taken seriously indeed. On this subject no one could suspect Chatelain of being facetious. Nor the French government. In October 1981 a tax on wealth passed by the Socialist controlled parliament was to have included privately held works of art. At the eleventh hour, however, Mitterrand, apparently convinced of the serious blow that would have thereby been dealt to the art market in France, exempted works of art from the bill. The following day the newspaper *Libération* carried the headline: "Vendez vos yachts! Achetez des Picassos!" No one here but the most heterodox left is going to joke about a market's production of rarefaction, systematic or otherwise.

But Elsen, who distinguishes between "legal" and "ethical authority," seems to want definitions that go beyond this commercial/conventional notion of the authenticity of "original editions." In his introduction to *Rodin Rediscovered* he refers to the American *Statement of Standards on the Reproduction of Sculptures* (which he also cites at the end of his letter) for a criterion that goes beyond authenticity: namely, desirability. And there he writes that although "posthumous casts by the Musée Rodin are unquestionably authentic in the terms of the sculptor's intent and his grant of the right of reproduction to the state," they are viewed by these *Standards* "as less desirable than those made in Rodin's lifetime."[12]

This viewing, with its lessening of desire, is Elsen's, not mine. Contrary to his notion that I regard the production of posthumous casts through the lens of condemnation, worry, and dismissal, I welcome the opportunity it affords us (who are we here?) to experience the conundrum posed by the "original"-by-convention in cases of the compound arts; because, contrary to Elsen's reading of my argument, I wish to explore the possibility that this convention is no less operative within the simple arts, thus raising the possibility that all claims to originality are equally conventional/juridical. Contrary to Elsen, this is not a worry, but a welcome: welcoming theory.

With those three contraries, we move into the series of statements made in Elsen's letter which often take the form "contrary to Krauss": for example, "contrary to Krauss, Rodin had very strong and consistent views on authenticity"; or "contrary to Krauss, Rodin's contemporaries were aware of his reutilization of the same figure." Indignant at my seeming contrariness, Elsen accuses me of inventing issues, making up contradictions, promoting a double standard, and reviewing an event that has not yet happened, all of this adding up to fraud. But what of the contraries to his contraries? What if his disclaimers make false claims about mine? Would that be fraud? Or would it be argument of the kind that theory often elicits from disciplinary orthodoxy? Let us begin *a contrario*.

Contrary to Elsen, I did not condemn the recent casting of Rodin's *Gates of*

---

12. *Ibid.*, p. 15.

Hell as "fake." I specifically called it a "legitimate work" and a "real original." But I also imagined confusion arising in viewers' minds which would lead them to brand the work as fake or counterfeit. After all, this confusion has, historically, arisen in relation to Rodin's own standard shop practices. Elsen himself cites instances of it: "There was a storm of criticism directed at Bénédite for undertaking the posthumous enlargement. Many people misunderstood the enlarging process and did not realize that for Rodin it was not to be strictly mechanical. There was published criticism that Lebossé had betrayed Rodin. . . ."[13] If this misunderstanding could have arisen in Rodin's day, despite the fact that, as Elsen tells us, "Rodin's public knew well the system of a division of labor that he inherited and relied upon to be productive and creative," how could it not occur even more insistently now? That it *does* occur is mentioned over and over by Elsen and his collaborators in the catalogue *Rodin Rediscovered*. They cannot seem to shake off the nag of this ("uninformed") public doubt. In discussing "Rodin's Carved Sculpture" Daniel Rosenfeld describes the corps of workmen that surrounded the master in his studio — "between 1900 and 1910 nearly fifty individuals were involved with the execution of Rodin's marble sculptures" — and begins his account of the atelier with the sentence: "The multiple marble examples of *Eve* [12 or more] raise the question of originality and authenticity in Rodin's carved sculpture."[14] Like Elsen, he feels certain that this question is an anachronism and would not have troubled Rodin's contemporaries. But that it *does* disturb us *now* is acknowledged, for example, by asides like "the issue of their authenticity as products of the artist's hand, so disquieting to some modern critics. . . ."[15]

By imagining the scene of this kind of disquietude and confusion, in which multiple appellations could be appended to an object — could be, and *are* — appellations that range across a wide spectrum: counterfeit . . . legitimate . . . authentic . . . desirable, a scene that is repeated not just by some uninformed member of the public but by art-historical experts, like Jean Chatelain in his arresting indecision about what to call those unfortunate proofs that have been pulled past the legal limit of the "original edition" — are they reproductions? they're not really *reproductions*! — by imagining this scene in all the intensity of its indecision, I wished to inaugurate a discussion that could not be solved in the confines of a courtroom or even the chambers of the College Art Association or the Art Dealers of America.[16]

13. *Ibid.*, p. 256.
14. *Ibid.*, p. 90.
15. *Ibid.*, p. 95.
16. This imaginary scene, with its onset of doubt, could be staged anywhere: in the galleries of a Rodin exhibition, in a darkened room where a movie of the casting of *The Gates* is shown, or in a meeting with the education department of a museum where a discussion about how to explain very late posthumous casts to a possibly dubious public takes place. It was at the last of these three possibilities (but there are many more, of course) that I first learned of the existence of the

This is a question of what could be called an "irreducible plurality"—a condition of multiplicity that will *not* reduce to the unit *one*, to the singular or unique—a condition that is inside the very existence of the unique or singular instance, multiplying it. Under this condition the compound arts are, simply, compound and no amount of systematic rarefaction will change this. The transfer of the idea from medium to medium in the production of the final "original" guarantees that inside that ultimate oneness is such a state of fission that the locus of singularity keeps receding from us.

Take, for example, the testimony of George Bernard Shaw. Like everyone else, he was conversant with the facts of Rodin's production and the paradox that the sculptor with the "inimitable touch" was famous for works that he himself had never laid hands on. (Elsen: "No sculptor in history is more famous for having an inimitable touch than Auguste Rodin. Yet big public works like the *Monument to Balzac* and *The Thinker*, on which much of Rodin's reputation is based, in fact issued from the hands of Henri Lebossé.")[17] Shaw was also aware that Rodin himself firmly located the "original" of a work in the clay model: "People say that all modern sculpture is done by Italian artisans who mechanically reproduce the sculptor's plaster model in the stone. Rodin himself says so." But Shaw begged to differ on this point. "The particular qualities that Rodin gets in his marbles are not in the clay models," Shaw writes, insisting

<hr/>

movie of the casting of *The Gates of Hell*. Professor Elsen was at the National Gallery of Art in the early Spring of 1981 to describe the contents and layout of the forthcoming exhibition to the gallery's staff. It was he who spoke of the film and the little theater that would be constructed for its screening. (The exhibition was specifically conceived as a suite of separate rooms, or imaginative spaces, in which different aspects of the problem—the atelier, the salon, the photographic dissemination of the work, etc.—could be gathered and collectively projected.)

"The Originality of the Avant-Garde" was written for *The Theory of the Avant-Garde*, a conference held at the University of Iowa, April 9–11, 1981. It was therefore conceived and composed months before the opening of *Rodin Rediscovered*. The inclusion in the essay of the film and its screening as the imaginary mise-en-scène for the little drama of doubt depended on Professor Elsen's own earlier description of the show. *October* 18 was going to press at the time of the opening of the exhibition, at which point it was observable that there was no film. But since I knew from other sources about the existence of footage for this film, I assumed that the project was late but that it would be screened in conjunction with *Rodin Rediscovered* later in the course of the exhibition. However, the inclusion of the scene of the "film" in the published essay was, reportorially, journalistically, an error.

And yet . . . and yet . . . "the staging of the film" is part of the staging of *The Gates* as a theoretical entity at the beginning of a general inquiry on originality within the conceptual frame of modernism. As such, "the staging of the film" within the theoretical setting of "The Originality of the Avant-Garde" bounced off someone else's imaginary "staging of the film," namely, Professor Elsen's, as he informed a group of curators of the series of imaginary spaces by means of which Rodin would be rediscovered. These imaginary projections, these settings within which we locate the object of our inquiry, are important, and they are real. The variety of their actualizations is something else. Let us just say that in March 1981 Professor Elsen admitted to looking forward to that little theater and its "technicolor" projection of the forging of *The Gates of Hell* every bit as avidly as I did, although undoubtedly for different reasons.

17. *Rodin Rediscovered*, p. 249.

that the magical qualities of "Rodin" are somehow *in* the marbles and not *in* the other materials: "He gave me three busts of myself: one in bronze, one in plaster, one in marble. The bronze is me . . . The plaster is me. But the marble has quite another sort of life: it glows; and light flows over it. It does not look solid: it looks luminous; and this curious glowing and flowing keeps people's fingers off it."[18] The magic is what Shaw prizes. But it was not put there by Rodin, because it was not *in* Rodin's model. It is, we could say, the product of a collaborative effort between the artist, the artisan, and the physical properties of the material, but even that is too simple.

If the compound arts are irreducibly compound, that is because at every moment there is the intervention of choices and of skills. The laying on of hands? But even if there is only one hand—Rodin's from start to finish—there is still the slippage that is inevitable in transfer, the multiplicity inside the choice-repertory of the single creator. Working in a compound art Rodin had choices about how to produce the final versions of his works, both in terms of scale and material. For many years now critical opinion has been that Rodin's choices with regard to many of his marbles were a betrayal of his art. "Dulcified replicas made by hired hands," Leo Steinberg called them in the opening of his extraordinary study of Rodin, by way of meditating on the reasons for the nearly total eclipse of the artist's fame during the 1930s, '40s, and '50s.[19] Even Elsen in those days acknowledged that the marbles were a problem. Writing to Steinberg in 1969 he said, "Admittedly the marbles are not his best. Much of the stone carving is hack work. We know that there has been no editing of his marbles on view in Paris."[20] Would it be an exaggeration to say that inside Rodin there were at least two artists and that one, collaborating with the least exigent tastes of his own time (Shaw's perhaps?), betrayed the other? And in that case would we not speak not only of a divided or compound original, but also of a divided intention: at one end of the scale, the intention determinedly to withhold work from finalization and production, at war with the intention at the other end—the intention toward manufacture? Thus even within the notion of the artist's intention, which Elsen seems to think is so univocal—"Contrary to Krauss, Rodin had very strong and consistent views on authenticity. He recognized as authentic only those bronze casts he had authorized. All others he condemned as counterfeit." But "neither Rodin's nor Gonzalez's intentions[21] count with Krauss"—there may be a multiplicity.

18.   *Ibid.*, p. 95.
19.   Leo Steinberg, "Rodin," in *Other Criteria*, New York, Oxford University Press, 1972, p. 331. The core of this essay was initially published as a catalogue by the Slatkin Gallery, New York, 1963.
20.   *Ibid.*, p. 329.
21.   A word here about my high-handed treatment of Gonzalez's intentions in the catalogue essay for Pace Gallery, 1980: Speaking in his letter of my "evasions" and "double standards" with regard to Gonzalez casts, Elsen gives my position on this issue with a curious elision. He quotes

In the war that can develop between divided intentions is there not the possibility of an internal fraudulence, a sense that in doing a certain thing an artist has betrayed aspects of his own work? Informed taste feels this way about the mammoth concrete blowups of little matchbook maquettes that Picasso produced as sculpture during his waning years. This is a kind of fraudulence that is internal to an artist, seeming to be the inescapable result of the fact that an aesthetic idea cannot simply be externalized, as such, from the artist's brain. It (itself a fictitious unity) goes through stages and at any one of them it can be betrayed. By the artist himself. By his intentions. By his very notions of authenticity.

It was this kind of internal betrayal that I had in mind when I wrote that Rodin "participated in the transformation of his own work into kitsch." Contrary to Elsen, I did not use this label for the Musée Rodin casts. I had in mind not only the bulk of the marbles ("dulcified replicas"? "hack work"?), but the kind of output described in *Rodin Rediscovered* in the section devoted to "Rodin and His Founders." The following concerns the fate of a marble bust titled *Suzon*, which was worked by the Brussels firm Compagnie des Bronzes beginning in 1875:

> In 1927, she was still found among the pieces offered by the Compagnie des Bronzes in five sizes, either the original one (0.30 meters) or four mechanical reductions of 0.26, 0.21, 0.16, and 0.12 meters. These bronzes of diverse formats and also the numerous examples in marble, terra cotta, and biscuit instigated many decorative combinations, such as mounting above clocks or on fanciful bases, found most often in Belgian and Dutch private collections.[22]

Did Rodin, we wonder, design the clocks? or the fanciful bases? Did he authorize this unlimited edition? in 1875? in 1927? At some point did it *become* "counterfeit"?

This authorization, the warrant of Rodin's intentions with regard to

---

me as saying that what Gonzalez did with welded iron was "a process" and thus "many of the issues of direct metal working that would theoretically prohibit translation into bronze are also irrelevant." What I wrote in the essay concerned the *process of copying* (not the truncated "a process") as it shapes Gonzalez's formal vocabulary — a procedure that involved making life drawings, translating them into more stylized versions of the life-model, and then, through a literal copy, rendering this second two-dimensional representation as a three-dimensional version in metal, a "drawing in space." Gonzalez's access to "abstraction," I argued, was thus a function of a *process of copying* that translates form from one material to another and from one dimensional space to another. On these *conceptual* grounds I think that Gonzalez's work opens itself to further translation and copying in a way that sculptures which enter the conceptual domain of the found object do not. What I think of the actual practice of casting Gonzalezes I did not say, but it would seem to exist in the same "legal, if not ethical" domain as certain of Bénédite's choices, given that French law vests "authorship" in the beneficiaries of an artist's estate.

22. *Rodin Rediscovered*, p. 286.

authenticity—his *undivided* intentions—led in certain cases to unlimited permissiveness: "He contracted with bronze editors," writes Elsen, "for unlimited replicas of popular works such as *The Kiss, Eternal Spring*, and *Victor Hugo.* Consistent with his peers, Rodin did not usually cast in limited editions, a practice that seems to have been introduced at the turn of the century by art dealers such as Ambroise Vollard."[23] In other cases, such as the *Suzon*, it led to the authorized manufacture of *objets d'art*, sculpture-plus-clocks, the industrialization of the artisanal experience, the corruption of the aesthetics of handicraft by the processes of mechanical reproduction. The commonly used appellation for this corruption is *kitsch*.

But even where we are not talking about the extremes of mechanical reproduction bearing the authorized patent "Rodin,"[24] we have ample evidence of Rodin's submission to the internal logic of the reproductive mediums, which is indeed, as Elsen tells us, "the division of labor." This division, which had led one nineteenth-century writer to ask, "Is the artist one man or a collection of people?" was equally applicable to carving as to casting. "Yet," we read in *Rodin Rediscovered*, "bronze casting made supervision more difficult since it was done outside of the artist's studio."[25] During the course of Rodin's career at least twenty-eight separate foundries were employed in the business of casting his work, making supervision difficult indeed.

As one of its contributions to our knowledge of nineteenth-century artistic practice, *Rodin Rediscovered* provides us with evidence about the degree to which the master acceded to the logic of divided labor necessary to the reproduction of his art. Elsen is able to report, "To the best of our knowledge Rodin did no actually participate in the casting and finishing of his bronzes. He left that to specialists who knew his high standards. . . . For more than fifteen years, he trusted Jean Limet to patinate most of his important casts and report on their quality."[26] This report was needed, we learn, because of Rodin's absence from the foundries particularly after 1900 and thus his ignorance of the state of the casts: "Since the castings were sent directly by the founders to Limet, Rodin, who had not seen them, asked about the quality of the casts as this letter of 3 September 1903 [from Limet] bears witness: 'I was waiting for the bronzes which Autin sent me to examine the head of Mme. Rodin. The cast is not bad, but the chiseling in my opinion leaves much to be desired. One can judge this piece, which is very simple, with difficulty. . . .' " Having so quoted, the author of this study of Rodin's casting procedures then adds, "It can be remarked,

---

23.   *Ibid.*, p. 15.
24.   "The study of the handwriting of Rodin's signatures hardly allows the assignment of a cast to one or another period since the signatures were traced by the founders and not by the artist himself" (*Rodin Rediscovered*, p. 292).
25.   *Ibid.*, p. 90.
26.   *Ibid.*, p. 15.

therefore, that the notion of strict control of the casts and the patinas by Rodin himself needs to be shaded, at least from 1900."[27]

What, we wonder, then happened to this head of Mme. Rodin, the chiseling of which, in the view of Jean Limet, left "much to be desired"? For Rodin, Limet was one of the specialists "who knew his high standards," and Limet's opinion was that the chiseling left much to be desired. Was the work issued anyway? Is this what is meant by the *shading* that is needed for the "notion of strict control of the casts"? Does such shading also need to be applied to the notion of Rodin's "standards," Rodin's "consistent views," Rodin's "intentions"?

This shading is required because of the extent to which Rodin participated in what I called (in "The Originality of the Avant-Garde"), "the ethos of reproduction." Contrary to Elsen, I did not write, *tout court*, that Rodin "never supervised or regulated either the finishing or the patination, and in the end, never checked the pieces before they were shipped to the client. . . ." I said, "Much of it [the casting] was done in foundries to which Rodin never went while the production was in progress; he never . . . (etc.)," a view that is wholly supported by *Rodin Rediscovered* and is only rendered false by omitting the qualifying phrase "much of it." Why would Elsen wish to misquote?

But Elsen's contrariness increases as we penetrate more deeply the territory of this ethos of reproduction, which is, we could say, aesthetically trivial with regard to the master's supervision of casts but formally quite material when we approach Rodin's "conceptions," such as his "rethinking how to compose a figure or a group. . . ." At that point Rodin's frequent practice of composing by what Leo Steinberg has called *multiplication* becomes extremely interesting to consider.[28] The plasters, cast from the clay models, which had before Rodin been the formally neutral vehicle of reproduction, became for him a medium of composition. If there can be, *must* be, one plaster, why not three? And if three. . . . Thus the multiple, we could say, became the medium.

With the recognition of this absorption of multiples into the core of Rodin's "conceptions," this representation of the very means of reproduction, we begin to cross the bridge that both separates and links the material/legal/etymological original—Elsen's one of a kind—and the imaginative/conceptual original, which is to say, originality: a function of the powers of imagination. But we are only beginning to cross the bridge, and still within its structure, we have a view of both sides. We can see the transition as the material aspects shade into the conceptual. We can spot the sublime creative confusion engendered by Rodin's move to heighten the representation of movement—the breathlessness of each unique, fleeting moment of temporality—through the stutter of mechanical replicas, lined up side by side.

27. *Ibid.*, p. 292.
28. Steinberg, "Rodin," pp. 353–361.

Contrary to Elsen, I never claimed priority in the observation that *The Three Shades* presents us with the same figure in triplicate. My reference to Leo Steinberg's prior discussion of this phenomenon throughout Rodin's work makes this obvious.[29] But the recognition of this aspect that Professor Elsen vests in Rodin's contemporaries is not the same thing as interpretation. And thus the question of what this triplication might mean — with all the variety of its possible answers and possible denials — remains.

Its experience in 1900 by "a critic named Jean E. Schmitt" (did he earn his obscurity? we wonder) is entirely hostage to the nineteenth-century view that artistic greatness is the function of an ecstatic imagination: "The same figure, the same group, inverted, modified, accentuated, simplified, combined with others, arranged in a shadow, placed in the light, revealed to their author the secrets of sculpture, the mysteries of composition, the beauties of which he had only confusedly dreamed."

In its effort to rescue Rodin's art from the enthusiasm of sentiment and make it available to the rather sterner assessment of modernism, Leo Steinberg's reading of this manipulation of sameness regards the phenomenon of multiplication through the lens of process. The revelation of process works to expose the means of representation; in formalist terms, it bares the device. It is the intentional, shocking construction of a surface that will report not on "the secrets of sculpture," but on the banalities of making: in addition to sheer multiplication, there is the whole panoply of casting "error" courted and magnified by Rodin, as there is also the phenomenon of modeling strategies (like the little clay pellets added to a given plane to further the buildup of the form) left in their most primitive state to be recorded by the final cast.[30] This baring of the device is not discussed by Rilke, nor by Jean E. Schmitt. It was, it would seem, not visible to them. Are we then forced to abandon it as an illegitimate reading, surpassing as it does the critical powers of the viewer of Rodin's own time? Are we thereby compelled to say that because he didn't, or couldn't articulate this view of his art, Rodin didn't intend these "accidents" that support Steinberg's reading? But the accidents are too profuse and too stunning in their seeming perversity for us to dismiss them as unintentional. A view of intentionality entirely limited to contemporary documents is, it would seem, an unusable view: too rigid, too narrow to support the evidence of the work. It is also a curiously naive view, insisting that all intentions must be *conscious* causes.

If "The Originality of the Avant-Garde" adds my reading to Steinberg's, this is because the concept of multiples explored there is not the same as the notion of multiplication (though my conception is not intended to *refute* his).

---

29.   See "The Originality of the Avant-Garde," *October*, no. 18 (Fall 1981), 50, fn. 1.
30.   Steinberg: "The little clay pellets or trial lumps which a sculptor lays down where he considers raising a surface — even if the decision is no, they stay put and, in a dozen portraits of the mature period, get cast in bronze" ("Rodin," p. 393).

Multiplication, as I have said, is a feature of a more general revelation of the particularity of the artist's means. It is this particularity that is welcome to modernist sensibilities and restores an experience of uniqueness to the work. In this experience of uniqueness is married the surprise (the originality) of the strategy by which the material vehicle of the work is manifested and the sensuous immediacy of that revealed physicality. But the notion of multiples does not resolve itself into this revised, modernist experience of the absolute uniqueness of the object. As I said above, it is grounded on a perception of an irreducible plurality, the condition of the multiple without an original.

Multiplication, as Steinberg develops it, opens our perception onto process, or production. Multiples are a function, rather, of *re*production. Rodin's work was continually moving between production (the tiny clay pellets of the master's modeling) and reproduction (the authorized "Rodin"). If Rodin was able (consciously? unconsciously?)[31] to manifest the processes of production within his work, why not equally the terms of reproduction? But these are terms that are deeply disturbing to the art historian because he cannot imagine a situation of irreducible plurality: a multiple without an original.

It is to this failure of imagination that the story of *The Gates of Hell* addresses itself. It is the story that Elsen's letter is so anxious to deny, even though it is, in fact, told by Elsen in the pages of *Rodin Rediscovered*.

For the huge exhibition of Rodin's work in the summer of 1900, *The Gates of Hell* were shipped dismantled, their montage to take place at the time of installation. But this reassembly did not take place; and so, as Judith Cladel reported, "The day of the opening arrived before the master had been able to have placed on the *fronton* and on the panels of his monument the hundreds of great and small figures destined for their ornamentation."[32] And then? *The Gates* were never again reassembled under Rodin's supervision: not during the time of the exhibition nor afterward at Meudon. Cladel believed that the work was not reassembled in 1900 because "he had seen it too much during the twenty years in which it had been before his eyes. He was tired of it, weary of it."[33] But that this weariness should have extended for the next sixteen years does bear some explanation. One of these explanations has been that Rodin never considered the work to be finished, and it was for this reason that visitors to Rodin's studio had to deal with *The Gates* in their disassembled state. Elsen's explanation is different. "Rodin's refusal to reassemble his portal after June first, 1900," he suggests, "may have resulted from the view that as it was, the work

31.   To say that an artist's intentions may not be conscious is not to claim that they are therefore unconscious. It is to question a notion of causality which an easy recourse to the "unconscious" continues to serve. See Stanley Cavell, *Must We Mean What We Say?*, New York, Scribners, 1969, p. 233.
32.   *Rodin Rediscovered*, p. 72.
33.   *Ibid.*, p. 73.

had a greater breadth and unity of form."[34] If this is so, then Rodin's "undivid-ed" intention bifurcates, pointing in at least two directions: one of them, *The Gates* as we now know it; the other, the idealized unity wrested from a heaving, nearly barren ground.

Before his death Rodin "presumably" agreed to a new cast of *The Gates* that would be placed in the Rodin Museum in Paris. "This second, full plaster model was not personally assembled or directed by Rodin before his death in November 1917; it was done under the direction of the museum's ambitious first director, Léonce Bénédite."[35] Elsen continues, "We know that from some time in 1916 until his death, Rodin was physically incapable of doing even the smallest amount of work with his hands, due probably to a stroke." But what Rodin could do with his hands is not really the issue, for the likelihood is that the work of reassembly was not even conducted in his presence. "Bénédite in-sisted that the montage was done under 'the master's direction,' but from what we know of Rodin's health, this is extremely doubtful. If the montage was done at the Dépôt des Marbres, it is even more doubtful, as Rodin was very much restricted to Meudon the last year of his life."[36]

Elsen's scholarship leads him to the conclusion that Bénédite undertook this assemblage on his own initiative and that he even violated certain of Rodin's own ideas in the course of the reconstruction. Since Elsen's letter insists that the posthumous casts — all of which were made from molds taken from this new Musée Rodin plaster — are "of Rodin's realization of *The Gates of Hell* in 1900," we can only assume that in his eagerness to argue for the authorized original object of Rodin's undivided intentions he had forgotten his own description of the "liberties" taken in this "presumably" authorized final cast. Elsen's presentation of these liberties is worth quoting in full:

> Surely, if Rodin had initiated the final assembly, his first director would have so indicated to the world in 1917 rather than in 1921. Bénédite took a large number of initiatives without Rodin's knowledge and consent, and, *ethics aside, he seems to have had the legal authority to do so.* Disturbing evidence of Bénédite's meddling with Rodin's arrangement of *The Gates of Hell* is given by Judith Cladel when writing with bitterness during the years 1933–1936 about the last weeks of Rodin's life and the insensitive removal of the artist's sculpture from Meudon to Paris: "Some of Rodin's scandalized assistants who cast his plasters made it known to me that charged with the reassembly of *The Gates of Hell* they received orders to place certain figures in a different arrangement than that which the artist

34. *Ibid.*, p. 76.
35. *Ibid.*, p. 74.
36. *Ibid.*, p. 79.

wanted, because 'that would be better,' or because the figure of a woman representing a spring (*une source*) 'must not have the head below.' 'The sense of the cube (*la raison cubique*) is the mistress of things and not appearances,' Rodin used to say. But does a shockingly brusque functionary have the time to meditate on such an axiom?" (*Rodin: Sa Vie Glorieuse et Inconnue*, p. 397.) Cladel's clear accusation is that Rodin no longer had any say in what happened to his portal and that Bénédite was taking uncalled for and insensitive liberties with its reconstruction. "La raison cubique" refers to Rodin's view that one should imagine a well-made sculpture as existing within a cube.[37]

The "uncalled for and insensitive liberties" taken by this "shockingly brusque functionary" (is this what Elsen means by "ambitious"?) create the high probability that the 1917 plaster, the matrix from which all the bronze casts of *The Gates* have been taken, differs in aesthetically material ways from the 1900 plaster. Further, as Elsen himself records, after 1900 Rodin's own relationship to *The Gates* had become sufficiently complex that he refused to have them reassembled (preferring, perhaps, the "greater breadth and unity of form" of the naked doors?), and may or may not have authorized Bénédite's actions in 1917. It is this richly multiplex set of doubts raised by the history of *The Gates* that makes the work so perfect an example, on both a technical and conceptual level, of multiples without an original. As we try to move from the plurality of the casts to the unity of the model, we find this unity, this original, splintering, compounding.

And the *simple*, as distinct from the *compound*, arts? What of them? Jean Chatelain notes the "feeling of relativism" excited by the compound arts' relation to the notion of the original. This is not the case, he seems to argue, with the simple arts—those with the most immediate, direct relationship between conception and visual mark.

But we have reason to wonder whether this simplicity with its accompanying notions of immediacy and directness is not, itself, a product of that very same shift in desire that made the "original edition" necessary. For just as the compound arts—sculpture, tapestries, marquetry, porcelain, illustrated books, etc.—are the functions of workshops and the collaborative results of many skills and many hands, painting is also the product of workshops. The large decorative cycles demanded by patrons in the sixteenth, seventeenth, and eighteenth centuries could not be accomplished in any other way. The great studios, of which Rubens's is only the most well published example, necessitated an experience of the "compound" in the carrying out of the work.

---

37.   *Ibid.* (italics added).

Art history, a discipline which is an intellectual partner of those newly conceived forces of desire that Jean Chatelain sees rising in the nineteenth century — art history is committed to the marks of *simplicity*, to the establishment of the autograph work, and to the sorting out of hands. The existence of the shop can be admitted in the study of painting only as long as the shop itself can be analyzed to produce its elementary components, among them the indisputably autographic *work* of the master. The finding and constituting of this work will in fact be the task of the art historian. For his empirical unity is this unity — which he takes to be irreducibly simple or singular — of the master's mark.

Thus, for example, the analysis of the Ghent Altarpiece has often turned on the problem of locating the autographic presence of each of its masters, since it was known that both Hubert and Jan van Eyck had been responsible for its making. Even Panofsky understood that his task as art historian would be — given this dual authorship — the sorting out of hands. Two linked assumptions operate within this notion of the scholarly task. The first is that the painting is a physical simple and thus is ideally made by one hand; if it is known in a given case to be the work of more than one author, then it can be somehow analyzed into a set of simples (for this reason, the sorting of hands). The second is that as a simple a painting is what would normally function within a claim to authorship; authorship is part of the grammar of executing a painting as it is not in, say, executing marquetry. It is in relationship to its seeming naturalness as an object of the claim to authorship (and thus its greater insistency with regard to the experience of authenticity) that painting is taken to be a unitary object, a simple. As such it has clear boundaries: it is everything that is *inside* the frame. (The frame on the other hand is a function of the decorative or compound arts. The frame is what both links and separates the painting from the complex decorative/architectural system that formed its original context. But for the art historian there is no confusion between painting and frame.)[38] Thus, when Lotte Brand Philip undertook to reorient the analytical task with regard to the Ghent Altarpiece, the resistance was intense. Her argument was that Hubert van Eyck was an author of the alterpiece, only not of its painted surfaces, but rather of its frame.[39]

The idea that authorship might displace itself outward to the frame does terrible things to the system of positivist relationships out of which the art historian works. Because authorship would then be made to flow from the bounded pictorial image into that great sea of anonymous artisanal practice

38.   Jacques Derrida contests the possibility of these distinctions which ground the theory of Western art, for which it is assumed that a separation can be made between what is proper to a work and what is improper, extrinsic, outside. See "The Parergon," *October*, no. 9 (Summer 1979), 3–40.
39.   Lotte Brand Philip, *The Ghent Altarpiece and the Art of Jan van Eyck*, Princeton, Princeton University Press, 1971.

that formed the shop systems of the arts. Authorship, with all its decorum and priorities, would collapse under this weight. Authorship assumes that paintings have an absolute firstness in the hierarchy of the arts and that their frames, which are adjuncts after all, must follow after, being made to fit. But it is perfectly possible to imagine a case where the frame comes first and the painted panel, like so much decorative filler, comes afterward, tailored to the measure of the more opulent, resplendent frame. This situation, with all its implication for a collapse of the notions of a hierarchy "natural" to the arts, is the news that is being delivered to art history with increasing frequency. It is the situation that Creighton Gilbert, for example, has discovered in the relation between panel painters and the carvers of frames in early Renaissance practice in Italy.[40]

The notion of the painting as a function of the frame (and not the reverse) tends to shift our focus from being exclusively, singularly, riveted on the interior field. Our focus must begin to dilate, to spread. As the boundary between inside (painting) and outside (frame . . .) begins to blur and to break down, room is made for the possibility of experiencing the degree to which painting-as-simple is a constructed category, constructed on the basis of desire, not unlike the "original edition." Just as we can also catch ourselves in the act of constructing frames in order illicitly to excise an image from the nonsimple context of the obviously compound arts, so as to assert it as pictorial, unitary, framed.

A common enough example of this is to be found in the museum displays of ancient seal rings, where photographic enlargements of the impressions made by the seals allow the imagery and forms of the carving to be seen. But by their very transformation of the signet into a framed, enlarged, two-dimensional image, the photographs pictorialize the object, endowing it with a different kind of presence, investing it with an experience of singularity. Photography used to transform the decorative object into a picture and thus to raise its status occurs with increasing frequency in museums. In the exhibition *The Search for Alexander*, mounted by the National Gallery in Washington, for example, one of the major objects was a bronze krater from Derveni, a vessel over thirty-five inches high with continuous reliefs of extraordinary quality. Set freestanding within a vitrine in the gallery the krater was perfectly visible from all sides. Yet the designers of the exhibition felt the need to supplement this object with photographic enlargements of some of its narrative components, fragmenting and composing aspects of the decorative object into . . . pictures. It would seem that the only experience that could correspond to our sense of the

40. Creighton Gilbert, "Peintres et menuisiers au début de la renaissance en Italie," *La Revue de l'art*, no. XXXVII (1977), 9–28. My attention to these examples of the problematic of the frame was drawn by Andrée Hayum.

National Gallery installation of The Search for Alexander, *"The Tombs of Derveni."*

object's value from the point of view of its antiquity and rarity would be an adaptation of it to fit the *aesthetic* measure of singularity, which means to reconstrue it in terms of the frame. Within the exhibition the Derveni krater existed twice, once as a decorative object and once as a series of pictures, larger than itself, framed and mounted on a wall.

This institution of the frame is a function of what could be called the Institution of the Frame. It is an act of excision that simultaneously establishes and reaffirms given conceptual unities — the unity of formal coherence, the unity of the enframed simple, the unity of the artist's personal style, his oeuvre, his intentions — and these turn out to be the very unities on which the institution of art (and its history) presently depends. As research uncovers more and more information about given practices this new data is poured through the slots of old categories to fill the unitary spaces. Thus Elsen can begin his introduction to *Rodin Rediscovered* by declaring, "Our aim in preparing this catalogue was to present the latest Rodin research."[41] He never imagines that this latest research might in fact provide the ammunition to place those unities through which research was formerly collated and valued under fire. All of the information needed to open Rodin's *Gates of Hell* to the experience of the multiple without an original is to be found in *Rodin Rediscovered*. Elsen and his fellow researchers provide it.

Contrary to Elsen, I no more consider myself to be "invent[ing] issues" — in the sense of originating them — than to be laying claim to a first view of Rodin's use of triplication. These issues, through which the physical original along with the originary act are rendered a *problem* for history and criticism and not the goal of their endeavors, have long been the shared concern of scholars and writers in many fields and countries. At the end of the 1960s Michel Foucault described this collective inquiry:

> What one is seeing, then, is the emergence of a whole field of questions, some of which are already familiar, by which this new form of history is trying to develop its own theory: how is one to specify the different concepts that enable us to conceive of discontinuity (threshold, rupture, break, mutation, transformation)? By what criteria is one to isolate the unities with which one is dealing; what is *a* science? What is an *oeuvre*? What is *a* theory? What is *a* concept? What is *a* text? How is one to diversify the levels at which one may place oneself, each of which possesses its own divisions and form of analysis? What is the legitimate level of formalization? What is that of interpretation? Of structural analysis? Of attributions of causality?[42]

41. *Rodin Rediscovered*, p. 11.
42. Michel Foucault, *The Archaeology of Knowledge*, trans. A. M. Sheridan Smith, New York, Harper & Row, 1972, pp. 5–6.

But contemporary practice in the visual arts provides its critics with a special perspective on the problematic of one of these unities, which is that of *a* work, *an* aesthetic original. For we can watch the frantic attempts to reconstitute this unity even as all the activities of late modernism dramatize its dissolution as a mode of experience.

As the work of a depleted modernism becomes increasingly porous, admitting more and more citations from past art to enter the field of the image, this open terrain of eclecticism must be recontained or reunified in some way if it is to retain its "art" value (and thus its market value). Two ways are employed at present. First: frames. The work of Julian Schnabel, for example, resurrects the heavy, ornamented wooden frame of the old-master painting in order to reconstitute the interiority of the objects he makes, to shore up their identity as simples, an identity that would otherwise be contested by his recourse to imitation and pastiche. Second: the authorial mark of emotion—expressionism, psychological depth, sincerity. *Feeling* is the mark of the pictorial original. Much recent painting is both executed and received as though there were nothing problematic about the formulas of feeling and their continual reuse. The critical term *expressionism* is applied to these pictorial objects of manufacture with as little thought for its appropriateness as if it were to be appended to any of those conventions that operate the terms of polite address, like this one with which I will close my reply to Professor Elsen: "sincerely yours."

New York, 1982

II Toward Postmodernism

1. Almost everyone is agreed about '70s art. It is diversified, split, factional-ized. Unlike the art of the last several decades, its energy does not seem to flow through a single channel for which a synthetic term, like Abstract-Expressionism, or Minimalism, might be found. In defiance of the notion of collective effort that operates behind the very idea of an artistic 'movement', '70s art is proud of its own dispersal. "Post-Movement Art in America" is the term most recently applied.[1] We are asked to contemplate a great plethora of possibilities in the list that must now be used to draw a line around the art of the present: video; performance; body art; conceptual art; photo-realism in painting and an associated hyper-realism in sculpture; story art; monumental abstract sculpture (earthworks); and abstract painting, characterized, now, not by rigor but by a willful eclecticism. It is as though in that need for a list, or proliferating string of terms, there is prefigured an image of personal freedom, of multiple options now open to individual choice or will, whereas before these things were closed off through a restrictive notion of historical style.

Both the critics and practitioners of recent art have closed ranks around this 'pluralism' of the 1970s. But what, really, are we to think of that notion of multiplicity? It is certainly true that the separate members of the list do not look alike. If they have any unity, it is not along the axis of a traditional notion of 'style'. But is the absence of a collective style the token of a real difference? Or is there not something else for which all these terms are possible manifestations? Are not all these separate 'individuals' in fact moving in lockstep, only to a rather different drummer from the one called style?

2. My list began with video, which I've talked about before, attempting to detail the routines of narcissism which form both its content and its structure.[2] But now I am thinking about *Airtime*, the work that Vito Acconci made in 1973, where for 40 minutes the artist sits and talks to his reflected image. Referring to himself,

1.   This is the title of a book by Alan Sondheim, *Individuals: Post Movement Art in America*, New York, Dutton, 1977.
2.   See my "Video: The Structure of Narcissism," *October*, no. 1 (Spring 1976).

he uses 'I', but not always. Sometimes he addresses his mirrored self as 'you'. 'You' is a pronoun that is also filled, within the space of his recorded monologue, by an absent person, someone he imagines himself to be addressing. But the referent for this 'you' keeps slipping, shifting, returning once again to the 'I' who is himself, reflected in the mirror. Acconci is playing out the drama of the shifter—in its regressive form.

3. The shifter is Jakobson's term for that category of linguistic sign which is "filled with signification" only because it is "empty."[3] The word 'this' is such a sign, waiting each time it is invoked for its referent to be supplied. "This chair," "this table," or "this . . ." and we point to something lying on the desk. "Not that, *this*," we say. The personal pronouns 'I' and 'you' are also shifters. As we speak to one another, both of us using 'I' and 'you', the referents of those words keep changing places across the space of our conversation. I am the referent of 'I' only when I am the one who is speaking. When it is your turn, it belongs to you.

The gymnastics of the "empty" pronominal sign are therefore slightly complicated. And though we might think that very young children learning language would acquire the use of 'I' and 'you' very early on, this is in fact one of the last things to be correctly learned. Jakobson tells us, as well, that the personal pronouns are among the first things to break down in cases of aphasia.

4. *Airtime* establishes, then, the space of a double regression. Or rather, a space in which linguistic confusion operates in concert with the narcissism implicit in the performer's relationship to the mirror. But this conjunction is perfectly logical, particularly if we consider narcissism—a stage in the development of personality suspended between auto-eroticism and object-love—in the terms suggested by Lacan's concept of the "mirror stage." Occurring sometime between the ages of six and 18 months, the mirror stage involves the child's self-identification *through* his double: his reflected image. In moving from a global, undifferentiated sense of himself towards a distinct, integrated notion of selfhood—one that could be symbolized through an individuated use of 'I' and 'you'—the child recognizes himself as a separate object (a psychic *gestalt*) by means of his mirrored image. The self is felt, at this stage, only as an *image* of the self; and insofar as the child initially recognizes himself as an other, there is inscribed in that experience a primary alienation. Identity (self-definition) is primally fused with identification (a felt connection to someone else). It is within that condition of alienation—the attempt to come to closure with a self that is physically distant—that the Imaginary takes root. And in Lacan's terms, the Imaginary is the realm of fantasy, specified as a-temporal, because disengaged from the conditions of history. For the child, a sense of history, both his own and particularly that of others, wholly independent of himself, comes only with the full acquisition of language. For, in joining himself to language, the child enters

3. See, Roman Jakobson, "Shifters, verbal categories, and the Russian verb," *Russian Language Project*, Harvard University Press, 1957; also, Émile Benveniste, "La nature des pronoms," in *Problèmes de linguistique générale*, Paris, Gallimard, 1966.

a world of conventions which he has had no role in shaping. Language presents him with an historical framework pre-existent to his own being. Following the designation of spoken or written language as constituted of that type of sign called the symbol, Lacan names this stage of development the Symbolic and opposes it to the Imaginary.

5. This opposition between the Symbolic and the Imaginary leads us to a further comment on the shifter. For the shifter is a case of linguistic sign which partakes of the symbol even while it shares the features of something else. The pronouns are part of the symbolic code of language insofar as they are arbitrary: 'I' we say in English, but *'je'* in French, *'ego'* in Latin, *'ich'* in German . . . But insofar as their meaning depends on the existential presence of a given speaker, the pronouns (as is true of the other shifters) announce themselves as belonging to a different type of sign: the kind that is termed the index. As distinct from symbols, indexes establish their meaning along the axis of a physical relationship to their referents. They are the marks or traces of a particular cause, and that cause is the thing to which they refer, the object they signify. Into the category of the index, we would place physical traces (like footprints), medical symptoms, or the actual referents of the shifters. Cast shadows could also serve as the indexical signs of objects. . . .

6. *Tu m'* is a painting Marcel Duchamp made in 1918. It is, one might say, a panorama of the index. Across its ten-foot width parade a series cast shadows, as Duchamp's readymades put in their appearance via the index. The readymades themselves are not depicted. Instead the bicycle wheel, the hatrack, and a corkscrew, are projected onto the surface of the canvas through the fixing of cast shadows, signifying these objects by means of indexical traces. Lest we miss the point, Duchamp places a realistically painted hand at the center of the work, a hand that is pointing, its index finger enacting the process of establishing the

Marcel Duchamp. Tu M'. 1918. Oil and pencil on canvas with bottle brush, three safety pins, and a bolt. 27½ × 122¾ inches. (Yale University Art Gallery, New Haven, Bequest of Katherine S. Dreier, 1952.)

connection between the linguistic shifter 'this . . .' and its referent. Given the role of the indexical sign within this particular painting, its title should not surprise us. *Tu m'* is simply 'you'/'me'—the two personal pronouns which, in being shifters, are themselves a species of index.

7. In contributing an essay to the catalogue of the recent Duchamp retrospective, Lucy Lippard chose to write a mock short story about a personage she characterized in the title as "ALLREADYMADESOMUCHOFF."[4] Indeed, the seemingly endless stream of essays on Duchamp that have appeared over the last several years certainly does discourage one from wanting to add yet another word to the accumulating mass of literature on the artist. Yet Duchamp's relationship to the issue of the indexical sign, or rather, the way his art serves as a matrix for a related set of ideas which connect to one another through the axis of the index, is too important a precedent (I am not concerned here with the question of 'influence') for '70s art, not to explore it. For as we will see, it is Duchamp who first establishes the connection between the index (as a type of sign) and the photograph.

8. A breakdown in the use of the shifter to locate the self in relation to its world is not confined to the onset of aphasia; it also characterizes the speech of autistic children. Describing the case of Joey, one of the patients in his Chicago clinic, Bruno Bettelheim writes, "He used personal pronouns in reverse, as do most autistic children. He referred to himself as you and to the adult he was speaking to as I. A year later he called this therapist by name, though still not addressing her as 'you', but saying 'Want Miss M. to swing you.'"[5] In an

4.   In *Marcel Duchamp*, ed. Anne d'Harnoncourt and Kynaston McShine, New York, The Museum of Modern Art, 1973.
5.   Bruno Bettelheim, *The Empty Fortress, Infantile Autism and the Birth of the Self*, New York, 1967, p. 234. My attention to this passage was called by Annette Michelson in the essay cited below.

important essay drawing the parallels between those symptoms that form the psychopathological syndrome of autism and specific aspects of Duchamp's art, Annette Michelson pointed to the autist's characteristic fascination with revolving disks, the fantasy (in some cases) that he is a machine, and the withdrawal from language as a form of communication by means of speaking in private allusions and riddles.[6] All of these features occur, of course, in Duchamp's art with a vengeance. But for the moment I would like to focus on the autist's problem with the shifter—the problem of naming an individuated self—a dramatization of which is also to be found throughout the later work of Duchamp.

Tu m' is one way of signaling this. Another is the division of the self into an 'I' and a 'you' through the adoption of an alter-ego. "Rrose Sélavy and I," Duchamp writes as the beginning of the phrase he inscribes around the revolving disk of the *Machine Optique* (1920). Duchamp's photographic self-portraits in drag, as Rrose Sélavy, announce a self that is split, doubled, along the axis of sexual identity. But the very name he uses for his 'double' projects a strategy for infecting language itself with a confusion in the way that words denote their referents. "Rrose Sélavy" is a homophone suggesting to its auditors two entirely different meanings. The first is a proper name; the second a sentence: the first of the double Rs in Rrose would have to be pronounced (in French) 'er', making Er-rose Sélavy into *Éros, c'est la vie*, a statement inscribing life within a circle of eroticism which Duchamp has elsewhere characterized as "vicious."[7] The rest of the sentence from the *Machine Optique* performs another kind of indignity on the body of language—at least in terms of its capacity for meaning. Overloaded with internal rhyme, the phrase *"estimons les ecchymoses des Esquimaux aux mots exquis"* (we esteem the bruises of the Eskimos with beautiful language) substitutes sheer musicality for the process of signification. The elisions and inversions of the *es*, *ex*, and *mo* sounds upset the balance of meaning through an outrageous formalism. The confusion in the shifter couples then with another kind of breakdown, as form begins to erode the certainty of content.

9. The collapsed shifter announced itself through a specific use of language, and through the doubled self-portrait. But then, up to 1912 Duchamp had been concerned as a painter almost exclusively with autobiography. Between 1903 and 1911 his major subject was that of his family, and life as it was lived within the immediate confines of his home. This series of explicit portraiture—his father, his brothers playing chess, his sisters playing music—climaxes with the artist's own self-portrait as *The Sad Young Man on a Train* (1911).[8] In most of these portraits there is an insistent naturalism, a direct depiction of the persons who formed the

6.   Annette Michelson, "'Anemic Cinema' Reflections on an Emblematic Work," *Artforum*, XII (October 1973), 64–69.
7.   This is from "the litanies of the Chariot" one of the notes from the *Green Box*. See, *The Bride Stripped Bare by Her Bachelors, Even*. A typographical version by Richard Hamilton of Duchamp's *Green Box*, trans. George Heard Hamilton, London, Lund, Humphries, 1960, n. p.
8.   The inscription on the back of this painting reads: *Marcel Duchamp nu (esquisse) Jeune homme triste dans un train/Marcel Duchamp*.

Marcel Duchamp. Machine optique. *1920.*

*Duchamp as Rrose Sélavy, photographed by Man Ray
in New York. c. 1920–21.*

extensions of Duchamp's most intimate world. Only by the end, in *The Sad Young Man* . . . do we find that directness swamped by the adoption of a cubist-informed pictorial language, a language Duchamp was to continue to use for just six more months and then to renounce, with a rather bitter and continuing series of castigations, forever. It was as if cubism forced for Duchamp the issue of whether pictorial language could continue to signify directly, could picture a world with anything like an accessible set of contents. It was not that self-portraiture was displaced within Duchamp's subsequent activity. But only that the project of depicting the self took on those qualities of enigmatic refusal and mask with which we are familiar.

10. The *Large Glass* is of course another self-portrait. In one of the little sketches Duchamp made for it and included in the *Green Box* he labels the upper register "MAR" and the lower half "CEL." And he retains these syllables of his own name in the title of the finished work: *La mariée mise à nu par ses célibataires même*; the MAR of *mariée* linked to the CEL of *célibataires*; the self projected as double. Within this field of the split self-portrait we are made to feel the presence of the index. The "Sieves," for example, are colored by the fixing of dust that had fallen on the prone surface of the glass over a period of months. The accumulation

Elevage de poussière (Dust Breeding). *1920.*
(Photograph by Man Ray.)

of dust is a kind of physical index for the passage of time. *Dust Breeding (Elevage de poussière)* Duchamp calls it, in the photograph of the work's surface that Man Ray took and Duchamp included in the notes for the *Large Glass*. The signatures of both men appear along the bottom of the photograph.

Man Ray intersects with Duchamp's career not only in this document for the *Large Glass* but in those other photographic occasions of Duchamp's work: in the production of the film *Anémic Cinèma*; and in the transvestite portraits of Duchamp/Rrose Sélavy. Which is interesting. Because Man Ray is the inventor of the Rayograph—that subspecies of photo which forces the issue of photography's existence as an index. Rayographs (or as they are more generically termed, photograms) are produced by placing objects on top of light-sensitive paper, exposing the ensemble to light, and then developing the result. The image created in this way is of the ghostly traces of departed objects; they look like footprints in sand, or marks that have been left in dust.

But the photogram only forces, or makes explicit, what is the case of *all* photography. Every photograph is the result of a physical imprint transferred by light reflections onto a sensitive surface. The photograph is thus a type of icon, or visual likeness, which bears an indexical relationship to its object. Its separation from true icons is felt through the absolutness of this physical genesis, one that seem to short-circuit or disallow those processes of schematization or symbolic intervention that operate within the graphic representations of most paintings. If the Symbolic finds its way into pictorial art through the human consciousness operating behind the forms of representation, forming a connection between objects and their meaning, this is not the case for photography. Its power is as an index and its meaning resides in those modes of identification which are associated with the Imaginary. In the essay "The Ontology of the Photographic Image," André Bazin describes the indexical condition of the photograph:

> Painting is, after all, an inferior way of making likenesses, an ersatz of the processes of reproduction. Only a photographic lens can give us the kind of image of the object that is capable of satisfying the deep need man has to substitute for it something more than a mere approximation . . . The photographic image is the object itself, the object freed from the conditions of time and space that govern it. No matter how fuzzy, distorted, or discolored, no matter how lacking in documentary value the image may be, it shares, by virtue of the very process of its becoming, the being of the model of which it is the reproduction; it *is* the model.[9]

Whatever else its power, the photograph could be called sub- or pre-symbolic, ceding the language of art back to the imposition of things.

9.   In André Bazin, *What Is Cinema?*, trans. Hugh Gray, Berkeley, University of California Press, 1967, p. 14.

11. In this connection the preface to the *Large Glass* makes fairly arresting reading. It begins, "Given 1. the waterfall 2. the illuminating gas, we shall determine the conditions for the instantaneous State of Rest . . . of a succession . . . of various facts . . . in order to isolate the sign of the accordance between . . . this State of Rest . . . and . . . a choice of Possibilities . . ." And there follow two other notes: "For the instantaneous state of rest = bring in the term: extra-rapid;" and "We shall determine the conditions of [the] best exposure of the extra-rapid State of Rest [of the extra-rapid exposure . . ." This language of rapid exposures which produce a state of rest, an isolated sign, is of course the language of photography. It describes the isolation of something from within the succession of temporality, a process which is implied by Duchamp's subtitle for *La mariée mise à nu . . .* which is "Delay in Glass."

If Duchamp was indeed thinking of the *Large Glass* as a kind of photograph, its processes become absolutely logical: not only the marking of the surface with instances of the index and the suspension of the images as physical substances within the field of the picture; but also, the opacity of the image in relation to its meaning. The notes for the *Large Glass* form a huge, extended caption, and like the captions under newspaper photographs, which are absolutely necessary for their intelligibility, the very existence of Duchamp's notes—their preservation and publication—bears witness to the altered relationship between sign and meaning within this work. In speaking of the rise of photography in the late 19th century, Walter Benjamin writes, "At the same time picture magazines begin to put up signposts for [the viewer], right ones or wrong ones, no matter. For the first time, captions have become obligatory. And it is clear that they have an altogether different character than the title of a painting. The directives which the captions give to those looking at pictures in illustrated magazines soon become even more explicit and more imperative in the film where the meaning of each single picture appears to be prescribed by the sequence of all preceding ones."[10] The photograph heralds a disruption in the autonomy of the sign. A meaninglessness surrounds it which can only be filled in by the addition of a text.

It is also, then, not surprising that Duchamp should have described the Readymade in just these terms. It was to be a "snapshot" to which there was attached a tremendous arbitrariness with regard to meaning, a breakdown of the relatedness of the linguistic sign:

> Specifications for "Readymades."
>   by planning for a moment
> to come (on such a day, such
> a date such a minute), "to inscribe
> a readymade."—the readymade
> can later
> be looked for. (with all kinds of delays)

10.   Walter Benjamin, "The Work of Art in the Age of Mechanical Reproduction," in *Illumina-tions*, New York, Schocken Books, 1969, p. 226.

Marcel Duchamp. The Bride Stripped Bare by Her Bachelors, Even (The Large Glass). *1915–23. (Philadelphia Museum of Art, Bequest of Katherine S. Dreier, 1953.)*

> The important thing is just
> this matter of timing, this snapshot effect, like
> a speech delivered on no matter
> what occasion but at <u>such and such an hour</u>.[11]

The readymade's parallel with the photograph is established by its process of production. It is about the physical transposition of an object from the continuum of reality into the fixed condition of the art-image by a moment of isolation, or selection. And in this process, it also recalls the function of the shifter. It is a sign which is inherently "empty," its signification a function of only this one instance, guaranteed by the existential presence of just this object. It is the meaningless meaning that is instituted through the terms of the index.

12. There is a late work by Duchamp that seems to comment on this altered relationship between sign and meaning given the imposition, within the work of art, of the index. *With My Tongue in My Cheek* (1959) is yet another self-portrait. This time it is not split along the lines of sexual identity, but rather along the semiotic axis of icon and index. On a sheet of paper Duchamp sketches his profile, depicting himself in the representational terms of the graphic icon. On top of this drawing, coincident with part of its contour, is added the area of chin and cheek, cast from his own face in plaster. Index is juxtaposed to icon and both are then captioned. "With my tongue in my cheek," is obviously a reference to the ironic mode, a verbal doubling to redirect meaning. But it can also be taken literally. To actually place one's tongue in one's cheek is to lose the capacity for speech altogether. And it is this rupture between image and speech, or more specifically, language, that Duchamp's art both contemplates and instances.

As I have been presenting it, Duchamp's work manifests a kind of trauma of signification, delivered to him by two events: the development, by the early teens, of an abstract (or abstracting) pictorial language; and the rise of photography. His art involved a flight from the former and a pecularilarly telling analysis of the latter.

13. If we are to ask what the art of the '70s has to do with all of this, we could summarize it very briefly by pointing to the pervasiveness of the photograph as a means of representation. It is not only there in the obvious case of photo-realism, but in all those forms which depend on documentation—earthworks, particularly as they have evolved in the last several years, body art, story art—and of course in video. But it is not just the heightened presence of the photograph itself that is significant. Rather it is the photograph combined with the explicit terms of the index. For, everywhere one looks in '80s art, one finds instances of this connection. In the work that Dennis Oppenheim made in 1975 called *Identity Stretch*, the

11.   See *The Bride Stripped Bare by Her Bachelors, Even.* A typographical version by Richard Hamilton, *op. cit.,* n. p.

> *Marcel Duchamp.* With My Tongue in My Cheek,
> *1959. Plaster, pencil and paper, mounted on wood.*
> $9^{13}/_{16} \times 5^{7}/_{8}$ *inches. (Coll: Robert Lebel, Paris.)*

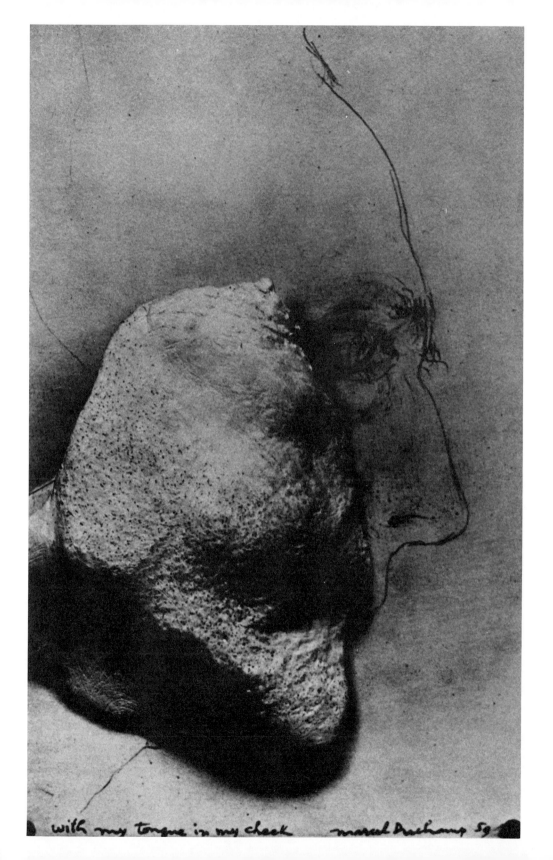

with my tongue in my cheek   marcel duchamp 59

Dennis Oppenheim. Identity Stretch. *1975.*
Photographs mounted on board. (Courtesy: The
John Gibson Gallery.)

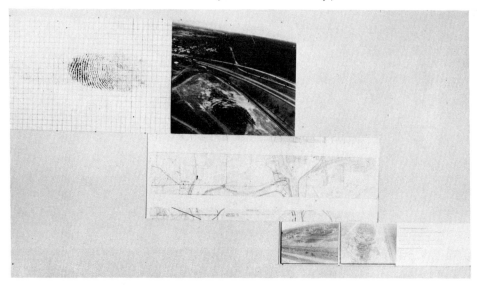

artist transfers the image (index) of his own thumbprint onto a large field outside of Buffalo by magnifying it thousands of times and fixing its traces in the ground in lines of asphalt. The meaning of this work is focused on the pure installation of presence by means of the index. And the work as it is presented in the gallery involves the documentation of this effort through an arrangement of photographs.

Or, the panels that comprise the works of Bill Beckley are also documents of presence, fixed indexically. A recent object combines photographic enlargements of fragments of the artist's body with a panel of text giving us the 'story' of his physical position at a given time and place.

Or, David Askevold's work *The Ambit: Part I* (1975) is likewise made up of photographic panels captioned by text. In his case, like Oppenheim's, we find the index pure and simple: the images are of the cast shadows of an outstretched arm falling onto a luminous plane. The text speaks of an interruption of meaning: ". . . an abstraction within the order of reference which resembles another and also is the identity within this order." The meaning of these three works involves the filling of the "empty" indexical sign with a particular presence. The implication is that there is no convention for meaning independent of or apart from that presence.

This sense of isolation from the workings of a convention which has evolved as a succession of meanings through painting and sculpture in relation to a history of style is characteristic of photo-realism. For there the indexical presence of either the photograph or the body-cast demands that the work be viewed as a deliberate short-circuiting of issues of style. Countermanding the artist's possible formal intervention in creating the work is the overwhelming physical presence of the original object, fixed in this trace of the cast.

14. The functioning of the index in the art of the present, the way that it operates to substitute the registration of sheer physical presence for the more highly articulated language of aesthetic conventions (and the kind of history which they encode), will be the subject of the second part of these notes. The instances involve a much wider field than the types of objects I have just named. They include a shifting conception of abstract art as well, one collective example of which was mounted last spring in the opening exhibition of P.S. 1.

An enormous, derelict building in Long Island City, P.S. 1 was taken over by the Institute for Art and Urban Resources and, renamed Project Studios One, became the site for showing the work of 75 artists, most of whom did "installation pieces." There was tremendous variation in the quality of these works, but almost none in their subject. Again and again this group of artists, working independently, chose the terminology of the index. Their procedures were to exacerbate an aspect of the building's physical presence, and thereby to embed within it a perishable trace of their own.

New York, 1976

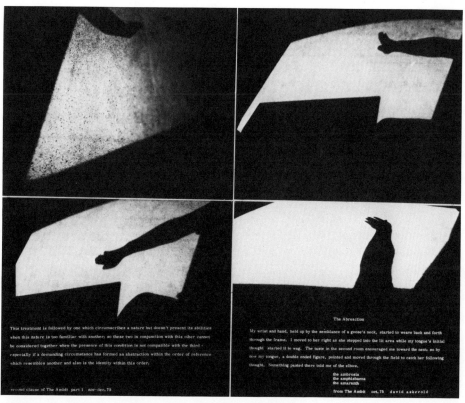

David Askevold. The Ambit. Part I. *1975. Photographs mounted on board. (Courtesy: The John Gibson Gallery.)*

Nothing could seem further apart than photography and abstract painting, the one wholly dependent upon the world for the source of its imagery, the other shunning that world and the images it might provide. Yet now, in the '70s, over large stretches of the abstract art that is being produced, the conditions of photography have an implacable hold. If we could say of several generations of painters in the late 19th and early 20th centuries that the conscious aspiration for their work was that it attain to the condition of music, we have now to deal with an utterly different claim. As paradoxical as it might seem, photography has increasingly become the operative model for abstraction.

I am not so much concerned here with the genesis of this condition within the arts, its historical process, as I am with its internal structure as one now confronts it in a variety of work. That photography should be the model for abstraction involves an extraordinary mutation, the logic of which is, I think, important to grasp.

In trying to demonstrate how this is at work I wish to begin with an example drawn not from painting or sculpture, but rather from dance. The instance concerns a performance that Deborah. Hay gave last fall in which she explained to her audience that instead of dancing, she wished to talk. For well over an hour Hay directed a quiet but insistent monologue at her spectators, the substance of which was that she was there, presenting herself to them, but not through the routines of movement, because these were routines for which she could no longer find any particular justification. The aspiration for dance to which she had come, she said, was to be in touch with the movement of every cell in her body; that, and the one her audience was witnessing: as a dancer, to have recourse to speech.

The event I am describing divides into three components. The first is a refusal to dance, or what might be characterized more generally as a flight from the terms of aesthetic convention. The second is a fantasy of total self-presence: to be in touch with the movement of every cell in one's body. The third is a verbal discourse through which the subject repeats the simple fact that she is present— thereby duplicating through speech the content of the second component. If it is interesting or important to list the features of the Hay performance, it is because there seems to be a logical relationship between them, and further, that logic seems to be operative in a great deal of the art that is being produced at present. This logic involves the reduction of the conventional sign to a trace, which then produces the need for a supplemental discourse.

Within the convention of dance, signs are produced by movement. Through the space of the dance these signs are able to be coded both with relation to one another, and in correlation to a tradition of other possible signs. But once movement is understood as something the body does not produce and is, instead, a circumstance that is registered on it (or, invisibly, within it), there is a fundamental alteration in the nature of the sign. Movement ceases to function symbolically, and takes on the character of an index. By index I mean that type of sign which arises as the physical manifestation of a cause, of which traces, imprints, and clues are examples. The movement to which Hay turns—a kind of Brownian motion of the self—has about it this quality of trace. It speaks of a literal manifestation of presence in a way that is like a weather vane's registration of the wind. But unlike the weather vane, which acts culturally to code a natural phenomenon, this cellular motion of which Hay speaks is specifically uncoded. It is out of reach of the dance convention that might provide a code. And thus, although there is a message which can be read or inferred from this trace of the body's life—a message that translates into the statement "I am here"—this message is disengaged from the codes of dance. In the context of Hay's performance it is, then, a message without a code. And because it is uncoded—or rather uncodable—it must be supplemented by a spoken text, one that repeats the message of pure presence in an articulated language.

If I am using the term "message without a code" to describe the nature of Hay's physical performance, I do so in order to make a connection between the features of that event and the inherent features of the photograph. The phrase "*message sans code*" is drawn from an essay in which Roland Barthes points to the fundamentally uncoded nature of the photographic image. "What this [photographic] message specifies," he writes, "is, in effect, that the relation of signified and signifier is quasi-tautological. Undoubtedly the photograph implies a certain displacement of the scene (cropping, reduction, flattening), but this passage is not a *transformation* (as an encoding must be). Here there is a loss of equivalency (proper to true sign systems) and the imposition of a quasi-identity. Put another way, the sign of this message is no longer drawn from an institutional reserve; it is not coded. And one is dealing here with the paradox of a message without a code."[1]

It is the order of the natural world that imprints itself on the photographic emulsion and subsequently on the photographic print. This quality of transfer or trace gives to the photograph its documentary status, its undeniable veracity. But at the same time this veracity is beyond the reach of those possible internal

1.   Roland Barthes, "Rhetorique de l'image," [my translation], *Communications*, no. 4 (1964), 42.

adjustments which are the necessary property of language. The connective tissue binding the objects contained by the photograph is that of the world itself, rather than that of a cultural system.

In the photograph's distance from what could be called syntax one finds the mute presence of an uncoded event. And it is this kind of presence that abstract artists now seek to employ.[2]

Several examples are in order. I take them all from an exhibition last year at P. S. 1,[3] an exhibition that had the effect of surveying much of the work that is being produced by the current generation of artists. Each of the cases I have in mind belongs to the genre of installation piece and each exploited the derelict condition of the building itself: its rotting floors, its peeling paint, its crumbling plaster. The work by Gordon Matta-Clark was produced by cutting away the floorboards and ceiling from around the joists of three successive stories of the building, thereby threading an open, vertical shaft through the fabric of the revealed structure. In *East/West Wall Memory Relocated*, Michelle Stuart took rubbings of sections of opposing sides of a corridor, imprinting on floor-to-ceiling sheets of paper the traces of wainscotting, cracked plaster, and blackboard frames, and then installing each sheet on the wall facing its actual origin. Or, in the work by Lucio Pozzi, a series of two-color, painted panels were dispersed throughout the building, occuring where, for institutional reasons, the walls of the school had been designated as separate areas by an abrupt change in the color of the paint. The small panels that Pozzi affixed to these walls aligned themselves with this phenomenon, bridging across the line of change, and at the same time replicating it. The color of each half of a given panel matched the color of the underlying wall; the line of change between colors reiterated the discontinuity of the original field.

In this set of works by Pozzi one experiences that quasi-tautological relationship between signifier and signified with which Barthes characterizes the photograph. The painting's colors, the internal division between those colors, are occasioned by a situation in the world which they merely register. The passage of the features of the school wall onto the plane of the panel is analogous to those of the photographic process: cropping, reduction, and self-evident flattening. The effect of the work is that its relation to its subject is that of the index, the

---

2.   The pressure to use indexical signs as a means of establishing presence begins in Abstract-Expressionism with deposits of paint expressed as imprints and traces. During the 1960s, this concern was continued although changed in its import in, for example, the work of Jasper Johns and Robert Ryman. This development forms a historical background for the phenomenon I am describing as belonging to 1970s art. However, it must be understood that there is a decisive break between earlier attitudes towards the index and those at present, a break that has to do with the role played by the photographic, rather than the pictorial, as a model.

3.   P.S.1 is a public school building in Long Island City which has been leased to the Institute for Art and Urban Resources for use as artists' studios and exhibition spaces. The exhibition in question was called "Rooms." Mounted in late May, 1976, it was the inaugural show of the building. A catalogue documenting the entire exhibition was issued in Summer 1977, and is available through the Institute.

Gordon Matta-Clark. Doors, Floors, Doors. *1976.*
Removal of floor through 1st, 2nd and 3rd floors.

p. 214:
Lucio Pozzi. P.S.1 Paint. *1976. Acrylic on wood panel.*

impression, the trace. The painting is thus a sign connected to a referent along a purely physical axis. And this indexical quality is precisely the one of photography. In theorizing about the differences among the sign-types—symbol, icon, and index—C. S. Peirce distinguishes photographs from icons even though icons (signs which establish meaning through the effect of resemblance) form a class to which we would suppose the photograph to belong. "Photographs," Peirce says, "especially instantaneous photographs, are very instructive, because we know that they are in certain respects exactly like the objects they represent. But this resemblance is due to the photographs having been produced under such circumstances that they were physically forced to correspond point by point to nature. In that aspect, then, they belong to the second class of signs [indices], those by physical connection."[4]

I am claiming, then, that Pozzi is reducing the abstract pictorial object to the status of a mould or impression or trace. And it seems rather clear that the nature of this reduction is formally distinct from other types of reduction that have operated within the history of recent abstract art. We could, for example, compare this work by Pozzi with a two-color painting by Ellsworth Kelly where, as in the case of the Pozzi panels, two planes of highly saturated color abut one another, without any internal inflection of the color within those planes, and where this unmodulated color simply runs to the edges of the work's physical support. Yet whatever the similarities in format the most obvious difference between the two is that Kelly's work is detached from its surroundings. Both visually and conceptually it is free from any specific locale. Therefore whatever occurs within the perimeters of Kelly's painting must be accounted for with reference to some kind of internal logic of the work. This is unlike the Pozzi, where color and the line of separation between colors are strictly accountable to the wall within which they are visually embedded and whose features they replicate.

In the kind of Kelly I have in mind, the demands of an internal logic are met by the use of joined panels, so that the seam between the two color fields marks an actual physical rift within the fabric of the work as a whole. The field becomes a conjunction of discrete parts, and any drawing (lines of division) that occurs within that field is coextensive with the real boundaries of each part. Forcing "drawn" edge to coincide with the real edge of an object (a given panel), Kelly accounts for the occurance of drawing by literalizing it. If the painting has two visual parts, that is because it has two real parts. The message imparted by the drawing is therefore one of discontinuity, a message that is repeated on two levels of the work: the imagistic (the split between color fields) and the actual (the split between panels). Yet what we must realize is that this message—"discontinuity"—is suspended within a particular field: that of painting, painting understood conventionally as a continuous, bounded, detachable, flat surface. So that if we wish to interpret the message of the work ("discontinuity") we do so by reading it

4. C.S. Peirce, "Logic as Semiotic: The Theory of Signs," *Philosophic Writings of Peirce*, New York, Dover Publications, 1955, p. 106.

against the ground within which it occurs. *Painting* in this sense is like a noun for which *discontinuous* is understood as a modifier, and the coherence of Kelly's work depends on one's seeing the logic of that connection. What this logic sets out is that unlike the continuum of the real world, painting is a field of articulations or divisions. It is only by disrupting its physical surface and creating discontinuous units that it can produce a system of signs, and through those signs, meaning. An analogy we could make here is to the color spectrum which language arbitrarily divides up into a set of discontinuous terms—the names of hues. In order for a language to exist, the natural order must be segmented into mutually exclusive units. And Kelly's work is about defining the pictorial convention as a process of arbitrary rupture of the field (a canvas surface) into the discontinuous units that are the necessary constituents of signs.

One could say, then, that the reduction that occurs in Kelly's painting results in a certain schematization of the pictorial codes. It is a demonstration of the internal necessity of segmentation in order for a natural continuum to be divided into the most elementary units of meaning. However we may feel about the visual results of that schematic—that it yields sensuous beauty coupled with the pleasure of intellectual economy, or that it is boringly minimal—it is one that takes the process of pictorial meaning as its subject.

Now, in the '70s, there is of course a tremendous disaffection with the kind of analytic produced by the art of the 1960s, of which Kelly's work is one of many possible instances. In place of that analytic there is recourse to the alternative set of operations exemplified by the work of Pozzi. If the surface of one of his panels is divided, that partition can only be understood as a transfer or impression of the features of a natural continuum onto the surface of the painting. The painting as a whole functions to point to the natural continuum, the way the word *this* accompanied by a pointing gesture isolates a piece of the real world and fills itself with a meaning by becoming, for that moment, the transitory label of a natural event. Painting is not taken to be a signified to which individual paintings might meaningfully refer—as in the case of Kelly. Paintings are understood, instead, as shifters, empty signs (like the word *this*) that are filled with meaning only when physically juxtaposed with an external referent, or object.

The operations one finds in Pozzi's work are the operations of the index, which seem to act systematically to transmute each of the terms of the pictorial convention. Internal division (drawing) is converted from its formal status of encoding reality to one of imprinting it. The edge of the work is redirected from its condition as closure (the establishment of a limit in response to the internal meaning of the work) and given the role of selection (gathering a visually intelligible sample of the underlying continuum). The flatness of the support is deprived of its various formal functions (as the constraint against which illusion is established and tested; as the source of conventional coherence) and is used instead as the repository of evidence. (Since this is no longer a matter of convention but merely of convenience, the support for the index could obviously take any configuration, two- or three-dimensional.) Each of these transformations operates in the direction of photography as a functional model. The photograph's status as a trace or index, its dependence on selection from the natural array by means of cropping, its indifference to the terms of its support (holography constituting a three-dimensionalization of that support), are all to be found in Pozzi's efforts at P.S. 1. And of course, not in his alone. The work by Michelle Stuart—a rubbing— is even more nakedly involved in the procedures of the trace, while the Matta-Clark cut through the building's interior becomes an instance of cropping, in order that the void created by the cut be literally filled by a natural ground.

In each of these works it is the building itself that is taken to be a message which can be presented but not coded. The ambition of the works is to capture the presence of the building, to find strategies to force it to surface into the field of the work. Yet even as that presence surfaces, it fills the work with an extraordinary sense of time-past. Though they are produced by a physical cause, the trace, the impression, the clue, are vestiges of that cause which is itself no longer present in the given sign. Like traces, the works I have been describing represent the building through the paradox of being physically present but temporally remote. This sense is made explicit in the title of the Stuart work where the artist speaks of relocation as a form of memory. In the piece by Matta-Clark the cut is able to signify the building—to point to it—only through a process of removal or cutting away. The procedure of excavation succeeds therefore in bringing the building into the consciousness of the viewer in the form of a ghost. For Pozzi, the act of taking an impression submits· to the logic of effacement. The painted wall is signified by the work as something which was there but has now been covered over.

Like the other features of these works, this one of temporal distance is a striking aspect of the photographic message. Pointing to this paradox of a presence seen as past, Barthes says of the photograph:

> The type of perception it implies is truly without precedent. Photography set up, in effect, not a perception of the *being-there* of an object (which all copies are able to provoke, but a perception of its *having-been-there*. It is a question therefore of a new category of space-time: spatial immediacy and temporal anteriority. Photography produces an illogical conjunction of the *here* and the *formerly*. It is thus at the level of the denotated message or message without code that one can plainly understand the *real unreality* of the photograph. Its unreality is that of the here, since the photograph is never experienced as an illusion; it is nothing but a *presence* (one must continually keep in mind the magical character of the photographic image). Its reality is that of a *having-been-there*, because in all photographs there is the constantly amazing evidence: *this took place in this way*. We possess, then, as a kind of

precious miracle, a reality from which we are ourselves sheltered.[5]

This condition of the having-been-there satisfies questions of verifiability at
the level of the document. Truth is understood as a matter of evidence, rather than
a function of logic. In the 1960s, abstract art, particularly painting, had aspired to
a kind of logical investigation, attempting to tie the event of the work to what
could be truly stated about the internal relations posited by the pictorial code. In
so doing, this art tied itself to the convention of painting (or sculpture) as that
continuous present which both sustained the work conceptually and was understood as its content.

In the work at P. S. 1, we are obviously dealing with a jettisonning of
convention, or more precisely the conversion of the pictorial and sculptural codes
into that of the photographic message without a code. In order to do this, the
abstract artist adapts his work to the formal character of the indexical sign. These
procedures comply with two of the components of the Hay performance described
at the beginning of this discussion. The third feature of that performance—the
addition of an articulated discourse, or text, to the otherwise mute index—was, I
claimed, a necessary outcome of the first two. This need to link text and image has
been remarked upon in the literature of semiology whenever the photograph is
mentioned. Thus Barthes, in speaking of those images which resist internal
divisibility, says, "this is probably the reason for which these systems are almost
always duplicated by articulated speech (such as the caption of a photograph)
which endows them with the discontinuous aspect which they do not have."[6]

Indeed, an overt use of captioning is nearly always to be found in that
portion of contemporary art which employs photography directly. Story art, body
art, some of conceptual art, certain types of earthworks, mount photographs as a
type of evidence and join to this assembly a written text or caption.[7] But in the
work I have been discussing—the abstract wing of this art of the index—we do not
find a written text appended to the object-trace. There are, however, other kinds of
texts for photographs besides written ones, as Walter Benjamin points out when
he speaks of the history of the relation of caption to photographic image. "The
directive which the captions give to those looking at pictures in illustrated
magazines," he writes, "soon become even more explicit and more imperative in
the film where the meaning of each single picture appears to be prescribed by the
sequence of all preceding ones."[8] In film each image appears from within a
succession that operates to internalize the caption, as narrative.

At P. S. 1 the works I have been describing all utilize succession. Pozzi's
panels occur at various points along the corridors and stairwells of the building.

5.   Barthes, "Rhetorique de l'image," p. 47.
6.   Roland Barthes, *Elements of Semiology*, trans. Annette Lavers and Colin Smith, Boston,
Beacon Press, 1967, p. 64.
7.   See Part I of this essay, *October*, 3 (Spring 1977), 82.
8.   Walter Benjamin, "The Work of Art in the Age of Mechanical Reproduction," *Illuminations*,
trans. Harry Zohn, New York, Schocken Books, 1969, p. 226.

Stuart's rubbings are relocated across the facing planes of a hallway. The Matta-Clark cut involves the viewer in a sequence of floors. The "text" that accompanies the work is, then, the unfolding of the building's space which the successive parts of the works in question articulate into a kind of cinematic narrative; and that narrative in turn becomes an explanatory supplement to the works.

In the first part of this essay I suggested that the index must be seen as something that shapes the sensibility of a large number of contemporary artists; that whether they are conscious of it or not, many of them assimilate their work (in part if not wholly) to the logic of the index. So, for example, at P. S. 1 Marcia Hafif used one of the former classrooms as an arena in which to juxtapose painting and writing. On the walls above the original blackboards Hafif executed abstract paintings of repetitive colored strokes while on the writing surfaces themselves she chalked a detailed, first-person account of sexual intercourse. Insofar as the narrative did not stand in relation to the images as an explanation, this text by Hafif was not a true caption. But its visual and formal effect was that of captioning: of bowing to the implied necessity to add a surfeit of written information to the depleted power of the painted sign.

New York, 1977

Marcia Hafif. Untitled. 1976. Paint and chalk on walls and blackboards.

Reading Jackson Pollock, Abstractly

Are there two distinct readings to be performed with regard to the work of art, one by the practicing critic, the other by the art historian? Can we locate these two as separate specializations, each with its own texts (works of the present, works of the past), tools (the exercise of sensibility, the carrying out of research), and tasks (Eliot's "the interpretation of works of art and the correction of taste"; Ranke's filling in of the historical record to recreate the past "as it really was")? And is this distinction now being threatened with collapse?

For the last ten years Jackson Pollock's work has been the subject of a battle over "subject," but it is not clear whether this warfare has broken out in the critical or the historical community, or whether it is possible, now, to separate the two. For modern art has entered the university art-history department as surely as the trained art historian has made his way into those domains understood formerly as the preserve of a uniquely critical response, and it is this presumably new breed, the historian/critic, who is correcting taste *by* filling in the historical record.

But this distinction between critic and art historian would seem to be a false distinction. Art history, as an academic discipline, shares its historical moment with the birth and development of modernist art. The perceptions out of which art history grew — perceptions that immediately widened the field of inquiry — depended in turn on the radicalizing experience of that art. Riegl's opticality, Worringer's expressionism, the career revivals of Piero della Francesca or Georges de la Tour, the attempts to construct out of "style" an impersonal visual language — the list of those major planks in the art-historical program that were dictated by a specifically modernist experience of art is extremely long. And this symbiosis between modernism and art history affected critics as well. Roger Fry did not limit his subjects to Cézanne and cubist painting; they include Western painters from Giotto to Claude Lorrain in addition to topics within primitive art.

Thus we cannot say that different "texts" automatically separate two functions, that of critic from that of historian; and it can certainly be argued that their "tools" are shared insofar as fundamental notions about the *goals* of works of art, of how and what they mean based on conceptions of signification and reference, will affect both groups equally and at once.

The debate over how to read Jackson Pollock's work, even though it has an art-historical gait (with its inevitable *longeurs* and its necessary attention to the details of the record rather, it would seem, than to those of the object), is fundamental to the critical experience of modernism. When, in the summer of 1982, the curator of twentieth-century art at the National Gallery of Art publishes a long, elaborately documented and illustrated essay entitled "The Church Project: Pollock's Passion Themes," he is asking his readers, the audience of a major critical journal, to revise everything they might have thought about the nature of abstraction. Though its pretext — "the church project" — may be thought to be a footnote in the recent art-historical record, that revision, it would seem, is a fundamental request.

> *But how does one distinguish the false (the simulators, the "so-called") from the authentic (the unadulterated and pure)? Certainly not by discovering a law of the true and false (truth is not opposed to error but to false appearances). . . .*
>
> — Michel Foucault

When E. A. Carmean initially recovered the "Pollock-Smith church project" from the oblivion into which it had sunk in the pages of the first attempt at a Pollock biography, it was to use it to construct a *true* picture to defeat a set of false ones.[1] It was obvious to Carmean that Pollock's great 1947–1950 abstractions were the most rigorously nonfigurative paintings ever produced; and thus the increasingly current, graduate-school picture of these works as veils behind which lurked complex figuration seemed to him a misrepresentation, simultaneously falsifying Pollock's process and his achievement.

Carmean's move to try to right this wrong was simple and, within a certain kind of reasoning, efficient. He used the 1951–52 black-and-white paint-

1.   E. A. Carmean, Jr., and Eliza E. Rathbone, *The Subjects of the Artist*, The National Gallery of Art, Washington, D.C., 1978. See Carmean's essay "Jackson Pollock: Classic Painting of 1950," pp. 127–153. The essay by Carmean that went on to enlarge this theme is "The Church Project: Pollock's Passion Themes," *Art in America*, LXX (Summer 1982), 110–122, the English version of the essay he contributed to the catalogue of the 1981–82 Pollock retrospective in Paris ("Les peintures noires de Jackson Pollock et le projet d'église de Tony Smith," in *Jackson Pollock*, Paris, Musée National de l'Art Moderne, 1981). Inverted commas are used around the term *Pollock-Smith church project* because Pollock's explicit collaboration in the design and concept of the church is what I feel is not proved by Carmean's argument. It is, however, a label that Carmean applies to the project. The first biography of Pollock is B. H. Friedman's *Energy Made Visible*, New York, McGraw-Hill, 1972.

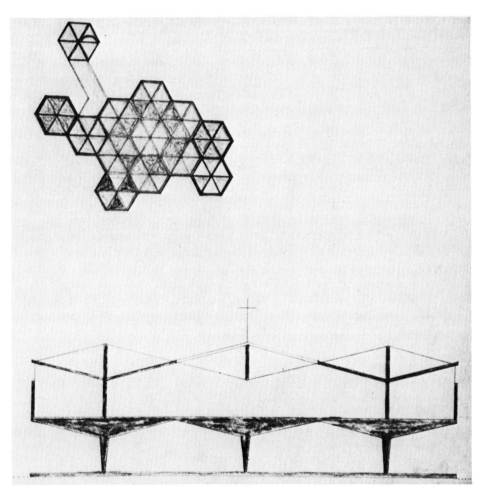

Tony Smith's plan for a Catholic church. 1950-51.
The upper portion represents the church's ceiling,
the lower, a central cross-section.

ings as a kind of negative demonstration to argue: 1) that Pollock had no need to veil his figures, because when he wanted them he simply put them in his work for all to see; and 2) that Pollock's only figurative episode, once he had reached aesthetic maturity, was confined to a brief (one-and-a-half-year) period and was determined by a specific figurative program that was outside of Pollock's psychological space, so to speak, the program thus constituting a distinct, historical cause of which the figurative episode was the effect. To this end Carmean introduced the "church project" and the cycle of black-and-white figurative works, now posited by him to be a kind of iconographic aberration, the exploration of specifically Christian imagery.

Buried in the midst of a large exhibition catalogue devoted to other artists and other cycles of work, this argument appears to have gone unnoticed.[2] Three years later, on the occasion of the 1981 Pollock retrospective at Beaubourg, Carmean revived the subject. But this time the context was different. The black-and-white paintings and their putative cause—the "church project"—were extracted from their earlier strategic place within an attempt to construct a true picture of Pollock's method in his abstract works. What was now being constructed, with all attempts at historical rigor and accuracy, was quite a different picture: that of Pollock's ambition in 1951–52 to engage with the problems of iconography. With this new conception the old argument was given a quite different form and inflection. The picture that was initially to be used to restore truth to the falsified image of Pollock's abstraction was now projected, alone, onto the scene of Pollock's process. Inflated and isolated, it assumed its own particular shape and now it, too, threatens to cast over Pollock's work the strangely distorting shadows of the "so-called," the misrepresentational, the inauthentic.

I will say right out that I believe that this reading of specific paintings from 1951–52 falsifies Pollock's working methods and, from this, miscasts the meaning of the works. In addition, I believe that Carmean's picture of the collaboration between Pollock and Smith falsifies Smith's art—not only his aspirations for architecture but also his passionate commitment to abstraction in the work of his colleagues as well as in what would soon be his own. Further, I feel that Carmean's idea of historical method—that events are to be "explained" by "causes,"—is misguided; and that it is necessary to examine this problem of method in order to understand the reasons for the misfit between the shape of

2.   William Rubin's 1979 reference to Carmean's "formal discussion" of Pollock—as opposed to the "emphasis on iconography" of other studies—indicates that Rubin did not focus at that time on Carmean's suggestions about the black-and-white pictures. See William Rubin, "Pollock as Jungian Illustrator: The Limits of Psychological Criticism," *Art in America*, LXVII (November 1979), 105. Francis O'Connor seems, similarly, to have overlooked the essay in this regard since it is not cited in his specific study of this phase of Pollock's work. See Francis V. O'Connor, *Jackson Pollock: The Black Pourings, 1951–1953*, Boston, Institute of Contemporary Art, 1980.

the argument and the shape of the event. Finally, I believe that Carmean's notion of subject as it develops through his argument contributes — even if unwillingly — to the growing confusion that surrounds twentieth-century abstract art in general, and abstract expressionism in particular. This confusion relates to what Barnett Newman meant when he said, "Most people think of subject-matter as what Meyer Schapiro has called 'object-matter.'"[3] Which is to say most people confuse a painting's theme or subject, in short, its meaning, with its pretext, its figural referent, its depicted objects. As a result of current revisionist attitudes, Newman's "most people," which in the 1950s and early '60s was understood to exempt critics and that tiny band of art historians who were the fellow-travelers of modernism, must now be enlarged. For some time now it has been a category energetically filled by scholars.[4]

My discussion of Carmean's thesis about the black-and-white paintings will move from an examination of the specific details of his argument outward, to a consideration of the larger questions of critical and historical method. But I must begin this subject at the very heart of his reconstruction, with Pollock putatively designing the windows of a church.

Black and White "Windows"

Here is Francis O'Connor on the subject of the black-and-white paintings: "These stark and highly figurative works raise a number of questions. How can the change from the multi-colored to the black pourings be explained? . . . Each of these questions seeks the causes of an event. What caused the sudden re-emergence of figuration and what causes may inform its meanings?"[5]

As though in response to these questions, Carmean offers a "cause."[6] The works are black and white, or more accurately black line traced on an open, undifferentiated ground, he argues, *because* they were envisoned as the tracery of windows: a network of line, rendered black by its relation to the luminosity of the sky, suspended in a field of glass. This architectural situation is the technical cause. The related cause is the place of the windows and their supposed function within an iconographic program that is ecclesiastical. The works are figurative *because* they were conceived for a church.

---

3.   Dorothy Seckler, "Interview with Barnett Newman," *Art in America*, LX (Summer 1962), 83. This comment is quoted by Carmean in his introduction to *The Subjects of the Artist* catalogue, p. 34. This exhibition stands as a monument to the special idea of subject professed by the abstract expressionists, one that resists specific iconographic interpretation.
4.   See my "In the Name of Picasso," this volume. This problem is specifically discussed in relation to recent Pollock scholarship in William Rubin's essay on the Jungian analysis of the artist's work, cited above.
5.   O'Connor, *The Black Pourings*, p. 1.
6.   Carmean's initial discussion of the church was in 1978, two years prior to O'Connor's questions.

Thus at a certain moment something quite programmatic *causes* Pollock to decide to do figures, and not just any figures, but crucifixions, descents, lamentations, and to do these for a specific place for which black tracery is the only appropriate mode. If I am stressing this issue of the moment and the cause and the response, it is because Carmean feels that the black-and-white figurative works can be explained in relation to a single cause — the church — and without that cause they are wholly anomalous, inexplicable, peculiar, within Pollock's oeuvre. Carmean's argument hinges on a single-issue cause, and he carefully sets the stage for his scenario.

The crucial date is June 14, 1951. Pollock goes to the screening of Hans Namuth's film of his painting *Number 29*, his only work on glass. He leaves the screening and reportedly asks Tony Smith if the method he used for the film could be applied to the windows of the church project he had discussed with Smith the previous summer. Smith says it can. And then, according to Carmean's script, Pollock embarks on a year of figurative paintings of religious themes envisoned as cartoons for windows. The following summer — August of 1952 — the church project aborts and, just as precipitously as he began, Pollock stops work on the "windows."

One major documentary detail threatens this scenario. It is a letter that Pollock wrote to Alfonso Ossorio on June 7, 1951, one week *before* he saw the film. This is the famous "I've had a period of drawing on canvas in black — with some of my earlier images coming thru" letter, in which Pollock is quite specific about the mood that surrounded this work. For he continues, "[I] think the nonobjectivists will find them disturbing — and the kids who think it simple to splash a Pollock out."[7]

The figurative quality of the black-and-white canvases (but the extent to which they *are* figurative obviously needs further discussion) was understood by Pollock as being continuous with the rest of his oeuvre and the variety of issues that informed it. Not only is there Pollock's own assertion of a connection to the "earlier images," but there is the implication that he was responding to three years of having been accused of splashing out mere decoration — "panels for wallpaper," "meaningless tangles of cordage and smears," "negligible content"[8] — a misrepresentation of his work that particularly angered Pollock, given that the "subject" had been a constant preoccupation throughout his career.[9] This

7.   *Jackson Pollock: A Catalogue Raisonné*, Francis V. O'Connor and Eugene V. Thaw, eds., New Haven, Yale University Press, 1978, vol. IV, p. 261.
8.   "Roundtable on Modern Art," *Life* (1948), cited by B. H. Friedman, p. 125; Douglas Cooper, *The Listener*, July 6, 1950, cited by Friedman, p. 155; and Howard Devree, the *New York Times*, December 3, 1950, cited by Friedman, p. 167.
9.   Pollock made the unusual move of responding to the characterization of his work when *Time*, November 20, 1950, called it "chaos." He sent a telegram that began "NO CHAOS DAMN IT." In his biography of the artist, Friedman focuses on Pollock's anger about being misread by the press. For example, he writes of 1949, "It had been a good year . . . everywhere, except in those publications where words came between him and his work" (p. 145).

concern for subject, for content, for meaning, was shared with other abstract expressionists and was reflected in the name of the school started in 1948 by Rothko, Newman, Still, Motherwell, Baziotes, and Hare: "The Subjects of the Artist." "Subject" was precisely the point of tension between these artists and the "nonobjectivists"—the programmatic, "mechanical" abstract artists whose work they in fact saw as having negligible content and failing to communicate.

Thus not only were the black-and-white paintings well under way by the time Pollock saw the Namuth film, but the figuration in them is neither alien to the rest of his work nor the result of the sudden advent of an iconographic program. Add to this the internal evidence that the paintings are not modular, do not conform in either size or format, and are therefore hard to imagine as the studies for a regularized architectural element,[10] and the windows theory becomes increasingly tenuous. What would seem to finish it off altogether is that in the model of the Smith church that was used for the (unsuccessful) presentation of the project in 1952, there is no provision for these "windows."

Although Carmean's argument depends on the efficiency of a technical cause (black lines as the tracery of windows) coincident with a thematic one (Christian imagery), there *is* a fallback position to which he can retreat should the window theory prove untenable. This is the idea that Pollock could *tout court* have envisioned black-and-white paintings for the walls of the church on the precedent of Matisse's figurative scheme for the chapel at Venice.[11] Carmean's answer to O'Connor's exasperated "what caused the sudden re-emergence of figuration and what causes may inform its meaning?" turns partly on a kind of archaeological unpacking of the figuration of several of the paintings to demonstrate a deliberate intention toward the iconographic. This theater of deliberation has Pollock copying not only the compositional format of Picasso's 1930 *Crucifixion*, but mastering its quirky iconographic scheme, which has been called "unique in the iconography of modern painting and of Christianity."[12] From this careful (perhaps we should call it scholarly?) study of a painting he has never seen in the flesh, Pollock proceeds, according to Carmean's projection, to make a set of religious pictures that deploy their iconographic elements — schematizations of St. John, the Magdalene, the weeping Virgin, the centurion — like the pawns on a chessboard of ecclesiastical space to compose the various

10.   Carmean suggests that the strip of small, abstract pourings in regularized formats might be pressed into service as studies for "windows." They could just as easily be seen as studies on anything regularized such as the project that seems to interest Pollock and which he describes in a letter (the same letter containing his comments about the earlier images coming through in the black-and-white paintings) to Ossorio: "Tony Smith suggested I make the drawings I've made into a portfolio of prints—either lithographs or silk screen—I may try a couple to see how they look."
11.   Carmean suggests this possibility. See p. 116.
12.   William Rubin, *Dada and Surrealist Art*, New York, Abrams, 1968, p. 291.

Picasso. Crucifixion. *February 7, 1930. Oil on wood, 19¾ by 25⅞ inches. Musée Picasso, Paris.*

scenes of the crucifixion, the descent, and, as is imputed to *Number 14, 1951*, the lamentation.

This is the operation we can project for a mannerist artist reworking the figurative elements of Michelangelo, or for Poussin, recombining the fragments of the canonical repertory of antiquity. We can imagine this procedure in academic artists of the nineteenth century. But can we really imagine this kind of methodical preplanning, copying, and transposition as part of Pollock's process in 1951? Not only does Carmean presuppose a working method absolutely at odds with the technique of poured line as an index of the spontaneous and the improvisatory (a working method that in Pollock's words leaves no room for the preparatory drawing, the preconceived format: "I don't work from drawings, I don't make sketches and drawings and color sketches into a final painting. Painting, I think today—the more immediate, the more direct, the greater the possibilities of making . . . a statement"[13]) but he pictures Pollock *consciously*, deliberately, doing the one thing he was adamantly against: illustration. Pollock's attacks on the very idea of the illustrational were constant. In the summer of 1951, the very moment when Carmean has him constructing a large-scale descent from the cross based on the iconographical shards of a Picasso he would have had to study in a small reproduction, Pollock was broadcast on radio saying, "The modern artist is working with space and

13.   This is from a 1950 interview with William Wright. *Catalogue Raisonné*, vol. IV, p. 251.

Jackson Pollock. Untitled. *1951. Sepia ink on*
rice paper, 24⅞ by 39⅛ inches. Collection Mrs.
Penelope S. Potter, Amagansett, New York.

time, and expressing his feelings rather than illustrating."[14] And an undated
note in Pollock's files that reads like a manifesto addressed to himself underlines
the words *"No Sketches"* and repeats the admonition "Experience of our age in
terms of painting—not an illustration of—(but *the equivalent.*)"[15]

Again, in Carmean's reasoning, the Picasso *Crucifixion* plays a crucial
causal role. Pollock's figuration is posited as specifically based on the Picasso
model, which is then used as a means of deciphering what is otherwise a complex of a highly ambiguous nature. Indeed, scholars who have looked very
closely at Pollock's work have assigned vastly different identities to the figures
that Carmean sees as religious. What seems clearly a crucified Christ to Carmean, in a given painting, was just as obviously a monkey (female) to O'Connor.[16] For Carmean's argument to persuade we must accept a particular
process that is posited for Pollock—otherwise the Picasso *Crucifixion* does not

14.   *Ibid.*, p. 250.
15.   *Ibid.*, p. 253.
16.   *The Black Pourings*, p. 13.

Jackson Pollock. Black and White Painting II.
1951. Oil on canvas, 34 by 30⅝ inches.
Collection Dr. and Mrs. Russell H. Patterson, Jr.

Jackson Pollock. Black and White Painting
III. *1951. Oil on canvas, 35 by 31 inches.*
Private collection.

Jackson Pollock. Number 14, 1951. *1951.*
Enamel on canvas, 57⅜ by 106 inches.
Collection Lee Krasner Pollock.

serve as a key.[17] This would seem to be a process that no one (except possibly the art historian, who with increasing frequency tends to construct a picture of aesthetic procedure based on self-projection) could ever contemplate.[18]

A Church in "Stages"

If the Tony Smith "church" is to function as the motive for a set of events in Pollock's career, it is necessary to establish a more than casual connection between Pollock and the project, a connection furthermore that will conform to the facts of Pollock's actual chronology. To this end Carmean constructs another scenario. The opening scene is sometime in the summer of 1950 when Smith broached the idea to Pollock, and Alfonso Ossorio is supposed to have joined the other two for talks. The closing scene is two years later when a group of Catholics, sympathetic to modernist art, was convened by Ossorio in his New York studio only to reject the project.[19] A model and a schematic drawing showing a plan and an elevation in section were used for this presentation. Carmean seems to think that the date of this drawing is "late 1950, early 1951," although he gives no basis for his thought. But the *reason* he wants to posit this early date, which is more than a year prior to the presentation of the scheme, is clear. Neither the verbal record nor the visual one provided by the preliminary drawing makes room for either the putative "windows" or for wall paintings. Thus the drawing must be posited as preceding the revelation of the Namuth film and Pollock's "decision" to execute windows. To defend his argument Carmean projects the entire design for the church as evolving in three stages.

Stage one is initiated when Smith first raises the idea of the project, which was a totally speculative one, there being neither site nor client. Pollock's ambitions for mural commissions are a matter of record. One can hear this in

17. Carmean acknowledges that other Picassos seem to leave an impress on these works, particularly *Guernica*, with its fallen soldier, a work hanging in New York that Pollock could not only see but that was also in his way as he developed. Carmean also admits that some of the formats of the black-and-white paintings recall much earlier compositions by Pollock, like *Stenographic Figure* and *Pasiphaë*. Thus to the picture of the church-project/*Crucifixion*-model as efficient cause, there is added another, more organically connected set of elements that reopen the meaning of these pictures to quite other areas of content. Thus we run into what Freud called the borrowed pot argument: "I never borrowed the pot you accuse me of having ruined, and even if I did, it already had a hole in it when you lent it to me."
18. Rubin writes, "As the international consensus on Pollock's importance confirmed itself in the '60s, he became increasingly a subject for art history. Much of the commentary on him in the last decade, the Jungian criticism especially, has come from young writers just emerging from art-history graduate schools (many of which witnessed in the '70s a marked impetus in favor of social, political and psychological—as against stylistic—studies). Whether influenced by this trend or no, the Jungians have adopted an almost exclusively literary, intellectual approach that smacks more of the library than the studio." "Pollock as Jungian Illustrator," p. 106.
19. Eloise Spaeth's recollection of the grounds for this rejection is that the project seemed too abstract to have a chance of ever getting built.

Pollock's 1949 letter to his dealer, Betty Parsons, announcing, "I want to mention that I am going to try and get some mural commissions thru an agent . . . I feel it important for me to broaden my possibilities in this line of development."[20] It is not hard to imagine Pollock embracing Smith's scheme. Pollock's interest is all the more plausible if we assume that Smith's original idea involved *only* the installation of a series of Pollock's classic, allover, mural-sized paintings, which is to say, more of what Pollock was then (1950) working on, and what he felt frustrated at not being able to place.[21] Pollock told an interviewer, "The direction that painting seems to be taking here is away from the easel, into some sort, some kind of wall—wall painting. . . . [Some of my canvases are] an impractical size—9 × 18 feet. But I enjoy working big and, whenever I have a chance, I do it whether it's practical or not."[22]

But Pollock's agreement to make a group of large abstract paintings and to contribute them to the ensemble of a future church is not the evidence necessary to support Carmean's thesis. Indeed, Smith's vision of an architecture that would work specifically with the particular luminosity and spatiality of the classic abstractions speaks *against* the kind of figurative intervention that Carmean ascribes to Pollock. Two things are necessary. Pollock must first be shown to be more deeply engrossed in working on the project than anyone has heretofore thought. Second, the plan for the project must be thought of as changing in relation to Pollock's June 14, 1951, revelatory experience of the Namuth film.

The argument for Pollock's collaboration in the working out of the initial designs for the church—"collaborative in the fullest sense"—is based on the schematic drawings of the church in which Smith pencils "squiggly lines" onto the ceiling modules. Carmean interprets these lines as projections for ceiling paintings and sees them as representing "Pollock's intended participation." "Indeed," writes Carmean, "the final articulation of the design rests so firmly upon them that the paintings must be seen as intrinsic to the overall conception, rather than as decoration added to an architectural space."

For this entire contention there is no proof whatever. Carmean has no evidence about when the squiggly lines were added to the undated drawing. They could have been penciled in at any time during the two years that separated an early phase of the project from the presentation. They could even have been penciled in as a last desperate move during the flagging presentation. There is certainly no evidence that Pollock would have wanted to use the ceiling as a surface for viewing his art, particularly a surface as ill-suited as that

---

20. *Catalogue Raisonné*, vol. IV, p. 245.
21. This is Lee Krasner's recollection of the suggestions made by Smith for Pollock's contribution.
22. *Catalogue Raisonné*, vol. IV, p. 251.

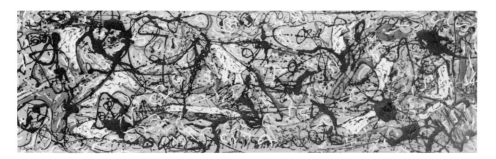

Jackson Pollock. White Cockatoo: Number
24 A. *1948. Enamel and oil on canvas. 35*
by 114 inches. Collection American Broadcasting
Companies, Inc.

one. The paintings would have been impossible to light during the daytime because the major area projected for these canvases would have flanked a large
skylight. Any painter knows that work cannot be seen in direct contiguity with
a window. The only scrap of evidence to relate Pollock to a ceiling installation
is the peculiar hanging of *White Cockatoo* in the 1954 exhibition of Pollock's work
at the Janis Gallery. But this was done on Sidney Janis's initiative—he acted
alone—because his gallery lacked the space to accommodate the large works;
both Pollock and Krasner were at first taken aback when they saw what he had
done, and then, apparently, amused.[23]

The next step after Pollock's supposed work on the design of the church is
his suggestion, and Smith's acceptance, of "windows" for the putative second
stage. Carmean admits that there is no evidence that Smith's plans were ever
modified to accommodate such elements. The only source he has for this
"stage" is the report Smith gave him in 1978 of Pollock's comments as the two
men left the film. Whatever we may feel about the accuracy of this report, it is
important to place it in the context of other discussions Tony Smith had, in his
capacity as witness to the work and life of Jackson Pollock. Between the years
1969 and 1971, nearly a dozen hours of interview with Smith were conducted
by William Rubin in an effort to flesh out the record of Pollock's career. In that
time no mention was ever made by Smith of either his church project or Pollock's supposed collaboration in it. This omission is all the more telling in that
Rubin's book *Modern Sacred Art and the Church of Assy* was known to Tony Smith
and this fact would have made Rubin a natural auditor for whatever Smith re-
membered about the project. The one reference by Smith to something that

23.   Reported to me by Sidney Janis. Lee Krasner described to me the reactions to the installation.

sounds like the church scheme is telling in its inflection of the meaning of this experience. He spoke about a project for a building to house the allover classic pictures, which would look splendid, he said, like a cathedral.[24] The central elements of this recollection are, first, that the project specified Pollock's classic pictures, and second, that "cathedral" functions as the *metaphor* for a certain experience of space.

According to Carmean's script a third stage ensues. This is just prior to the committee presentation in 1952, by which time the elaborate projections for Pollock's participation have mysteriously shrunk. "One room (?) was now to contain six paintings by Pollock," Carmean reports. "Five were to be new pictures commissioned from the artist, while the sixth would have been *Lucifer*, an earlier poured painting of 1947."

Quite understandably, Carmean follows the notion of a Pollock "room" with a note of surprise. Nowhere on Smith's plan is there any provision for a closed room. But he might also have expressed surprise over a plan that would organize, within a single room, an installation that combined the colorful allover *Lucifer* with the black-and-white paintings that Pollock was executing in 1952. Which is another way of pointing to the incongruities that emerge from Carmean's hypothetical script of the two men's collaboration, not only from the course of the narrative itself—with its curious anticlimactic ending—but also from the confusion generated by a drama in which an initial grand coordination of effort between painting and architecture finally eventuates in a kind of conceptual mismatch (between architecture and painting, as well as between painting and painting).

The preliminary scheme for a church that Tony Smith developed sometime between 1950 and 1952 does not represent the first time he had thought about sacred architecture. He had, shortly after he came East from California in 1945, designed a chapel in Provincetown for the painter Fritz Bultman.[25] This chapel was projected as a complex of hexagonal units and was to be raised on pilotis. Thus the hexagonal module and the elevation of the building were constants in Smith's mind between 1945 and 1950-1952. This is partly due to Smith's ambition for architecture, which was to achieve the perfection of a universal language of form—architecture as an opening onto the abstract experience of Mind. Lifting a building off its site had been, since Le Corbusier, an accepted way of declaring its formal independence. A universal module would be the next stage; and the hexagonal cell that Smith developed in his

24.   This is from a verbal account to me by William Rubin. The substance of his discussions with Smith will be published in his forthcoming book on Jackson Pollock.
25.   The significance of this early scheme was indicated to me by a former associate of Smith's, the architect Theodore Van Fossen. My analysis of Smith's ambitions in this ongoing church project depends on information he supplied to me, for which I am grateful.

church projects went as far as he could envision architecture — with its need for
floors and ceilings and entrances — accommodating itself to a kind of total symmetry. (Only in sculpture would the tetrahedron be able to function as a perfectly enclosed, generative form.)

The achievement of Smith's plan is in its subtle inflection of the "Universal
space" of modernist architecture's open plan. The Mies van der Rohe "universal spaces" articulate no function whatever. They are space frames within
which anything might be accommodated. Smith's church is almost such an
open plan except that the hexagonal modules permit him to build into the
system the kind of cross-axiality necessary to the expression of a liturgical program. The result is a particular blend of an organic unity based on the articulation of parts and a conceptual unity based on the totalization of a floating,
luminous space.

A floating, luminous space is, of course, what is constituted within the
fields of Pollock's allover pictures. And these works are what, to all accounts,
Smith wanted to synchronize with his design: two aesthetic experiences of the
transcendence of matter and of particularity were to be juxtaposed, coordinated. The terms of this coordination are not hard to imagine. Mies's museums,
conceived as universal spaces, designated paintings mounted on free-standing
panels. More to the point, Peter Blake had designed a "Pollock Museum" in
1949 that was precisely an application of Mies to the single instance of the
classic pictures. Smith now called for six classic Pollocks for the church, of
which one was to be *Lucifer* (a favorite of Smith's). Lee Krasner remembers that
these were to be mounted (or perhaps suspended) freestanding to form a hexa-
gon; not the "room" of Carmean's description but a kind of sacred enclosure
whose visual meaning would echo, by transposing to a different key, the religio-
aesthetic aspirations Smith had for his church.[26] There is no reason to believe
that Smith ever really modified this vision.

No Chaos, Damn It

What does it mean to take a stand against illustration? And more importantly, what does it mean to call oneself an abstract artist who nevertheless
has a subject? The claim that abstract art constructs a visual/auditory/verbal

---

26.   Meyer Schapiro sets the general stage on which the abstract expressionists can be viewed
through the experience of religious feeling: "[Painting and sculpture] offer to many an equivalent
of what is regarded as part of religious life: a sincere and humble submission to a spiritual object,
an experience which is not given automatically, but requires preparation and purity of spirit."
(See Schapiro, *Modern Art*, New York, Braziller, 1978, p. 224.) This was a common analogy at
the time. But within Tony Smith's own practice it was far more specific, as when he suggested to
Barnett Newman that he extend two abstract paintings already completed into a larger series that
would be designated as the Stations of the Cross. And, it must be stressed, this designation renders the Newmans no less abstract.

"equivalent" for experience is a claim that has been voiced since the late nineteenth century. Pollock, as we have seen, also thought in terms of the "equivalent." But he knew that for some people there was an internal contradiction between the idea of abstraction and the idea of subject. In 1950, speaking for publication in *The New Yorker*, he chose the term that would leave the least doubt about where he stood at the level of a simple either/or. "I decided to stop adding to the confusion," he said, referring to the numerical titles he was now giving his work. "Abstract painting is abstract. It confronts you."[27]

But the problem, of course, is that the either/or is a misrepresentation of what an abstract painter is up to. His greatest fear is that he may be making *mere* abstraction, abstraction uninformed by a subject, contentless abstraction, for which the term — wholly pejorative for everyone from Kandinsky and Mondrian to Pollock and Newman — is *decoration*.

Pollock's painting was a frequent target for the accusation that what he was doing was nothing but decoration — so much so that in reviewing Pollock's 1948 exhibition Clement Greenberg made the acerbic aside, "I already hear: 'wallpaper patterns,'" before going on to analyze and defend the work. And this general accusation, in its utter failure to grasp Pollock's subject, or even to see that his work *had* a subject, is reported as having been extremely upsetting to the artist.

The reason that Newman's "most people" have to reduce the pair abstraction/subject to an either/or is because most people think that the work of art is a picture and that its subject is what it is a picture of. What's in the work is what the work pictures. The dog, or landscape, or black square, is the work's referent. It is what the work is *about*. Thus a work in which nothing is pictured cannot be a work that is about something. Nor, by the same token, can there be a serious work that is about nothing.

But the twentieth century's first wave of pure abstraction was based on the goal, taken most seriously indeed, to make a work about Nothing. The uppercase *n* in Nothing is the marker of this absolute seriousness. If anything ever drove Mondrian and Malevich, it was Hegelianism and the notion that the vocation of art was defined by its special place in the progress of Spirit. The ambition finally to succeed at painting nothing is fired by the dream of being able to paint Nothing, which is to say, all Being once it has been stripped of every quality that would materialize or limit it in any way. So purified, this Being is identical with Nothing. It is onto this experience of identity that Hegel's dialectic opens. To wish to paint the operations of the dialectic is no small ambition. On every page of his writing Mondrian invokes Hegel. His dicta about "dynamic equilibrium" translate into the grand condition of his subject, another

27. *Catalogue Raisonné*, vol. IV, p. 247.

term for Becoming. There is no way into this art without grasping the full degree of abstraction of Hegel's logic.

But how would one paint Nothing? Clearly one approach is by means of that structure of oppositions in which each term of the oppositional pair is deprived to the greatest possible degree of its positive (limited, material, denotative) status. The strategy is not unlike that described by the first account of structural linguistics, in which meaning is understood as a pure function of oppositions. Meaning is not visualized as the result of the positive value of *a*, but only of *a*'s relation to *b*; and within this system, which Saussure characterized as one of "differences *without positive* tems," *a* is more accurately characterized as *not-b*.[28] In Malevich's dictum, "The square is an expression of binary thought. . . . Binary thought distinguishes between impulse and no impulse, between one and nothing,"[29] we hear an attempt to describe the kinds of significations of which abstract art is capable: significations generated from relationships of pure difference. The Nothing that emerges from this play of oppositions, this structuration of binaries, is absolutely beyond picturing.

The art-historical literature, increasingly gripped by the picture theory of art, cannot accommodate the Hegelian subject. And so Malevich is seen as making pictures of icons and Mondrian as making pictures of theosophical diagrams or esoteric emblemata or constellations.[30] Following the logic of the picture theory, if these artists were to be deprived of iconographic imagery and its denotative referents, they could only be seen as "formalists." And through this particular operation of the either/or we look down into an abyss of ignorance in which Hegel could be confused with "formalism."

The second great wave of visual abstractionists, which is to say postwar painters and most prominently the abstract expressionists, instinctively understood this Nothing, this dialectical signified. Generalizing about the terms of this understanding, Meyer Schapiro wrote, "The artist came to believe that what was essential . . . [was] that every work of art has an individual order or coherence, a quality of unity and necessity in its structure regardless of the kind of forms used," and further, "in painting the random or accidental is the beginning of an order. It is that which the artist wishes to build up into an order, but a kind of order that in the end retains the aspect of the original disorder as a manifestation of freedom."[31] He called this the work's "becoming."

28.   Ferdinand de Saussure, *Course in General Linguistics*, New York, McGraw-Hill, 1966, p. 120.
29.   Troels Andersen, *Malevich*, The Stedelijk Museum, Amsterdam, 1970, p. 26.
30.   See, for example, Robert Welsh, "The Birth of de Stijl: The Subject Matter of Abstraction," *Artforum* (April 1973); and his essay "Mondrian and Theosophy," in *Piet Mondrian*, New York, The Solomon Guggenheim Museum, 1970; also, Erik Saxon, "Mondrian's Diamond Compositions," *Artforum* (December 1979).
31.   Schapiro, *Modern Art*, pp. 215, 221.

Jackson Pollock. "Summertime": Number 9A.
*1948. Oil and enamel on canvas, 33 ¼ by
218 inches. Collection Lee Krasner Pollock.*

The great Pollocks, like the great Mondrians, operate through a structure of oppositions: line as opposed to color; contour as opposed to field; matter as opposed to the incorporeal. The subject that then emerges is the provisional unity of the identity of opposites: as line becomes color, contour becomes field, and matter becomes light. Pollock characterized this as "energy and motion made visible"; Lee Krasner spoke of it as "unframed space." Pollock's most serious critics have described it with great care and eloquence.

There is nothing "formalist" about this ambition. Its subject — the operation of an abstract logic — also contained the psychological, although a condition of the psychological that was de-specified, like a dream that is both charged with feeling and stripped of images. So, to the above characterization of his art, Pollock adds "memories arrested in space."[32] The absorption of the "image" into the dialectical structure, so that memories arrested in space assume the same level of abstraction as everything else, was constant in Pollock's work. Not only is contour *as such* (that is, the formal means of calling forth the figure) the major visual resource of Pollock's mature art; but, more to the point, there is not one single year (with the possible exception of 1950) when he is not operating specifically with the binary opposition figure/nonfigure, which means infiltrating a nonspecific figuration into the linear matrix of even the allover paintings. We have only to think of *Summertime* from 1948, or *Out of the Web* from 1949, or *Ocean Greyness* from 1953. Beyond the in-painting of certain areas, Pollock's technical inventiveness extended to the excision of shapes from the canvas grounds as well as the exploitation of collage elements torn from abstract, linear drawings.

The period of black-and-white paintings from 1951–52 does not constitute a break in this ambition. And, indeed, these works were not perceived as indicating such a break at the time they were made.[33] They are instead an intensification of the configurative power of Pollock's means: it is as though this more pregnant sense of the image's presence — no matter how shifting and in-

32.   *Catalogue Raisonné*, vol. IV, p. 253.
33.   This is true of Greenberg's discussion of them. See "Art Chronicle," *Partisan Review* (January 1952), 102.

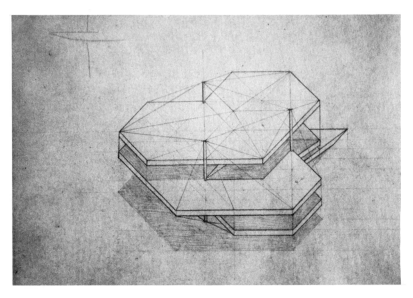

Tony Smith. Fritz Bultman chapel project.
c. 1945. Collection: Fritz Bultman, New York.

definable—underscores the condition of "subject" that had always been in the work.[34] In this sense, the paintings specifically resist the either/or view whereby abstraction had to be subjectless—decoration—and a subject had to be a picture of something objective. For Pollock, the either/or had become exasperating: "No chaos, damn it."

This either/or situation is, of course, precisely the one suggested by both Carmean and O'Connor when they posit a rupture between the classic pictures and the black-and-white canvases. For O'Connor, this rupture is undoubtedly more dramatic than it is for Carmean, who has a complex vision of the classic pictures. O'Connor's sense of the allover works, on the other hand, is nothing if not reductive. He labels them "pure decorative abstraction."[35] But the experience of rupture or break seems to call for explanation, and these two scholars are as one in identifying explanation with "cause."

34.   The sense of "imagery" in the black-and-white works sometimes allows for the identification of an anatomical fragment and, occasionally, a full figure. These partially recognizable bits then encourage what could be called the *projective space of figuration*—a constant field of suggestiveness something like a Rorschach inkblot. This analogy to the inkblot and the projective test was raised by William Rubin in conversation. It seems to me helpful in sorting out the relation of imagery to subject.
35.   *Black Pourings*, p. 2.

Art and Act: On Causes in History

Looking for an answer to his questions about cause, Francis O'Connor also looks for a methodological model. He chooses a text by "the eminent Yale historian" Peter Gay, a book called *Art and Act: On Causes in History—Manet, Gropius, Mondrian*. This study, which locates the cause of Mondrian's work in sexual repression, is a questionable model, not simply for the poverty of its reading of modern art but also because it projects "cause" as an entirely unproblematic issue for historians.

The discipline of art history emerged at a time when serious debate was being conducted over the propriety of incorporating the idea of causality into the study of human action. Wilhelm Dilthey, in the 1880s, launched an attack on positivist method applied to the cultural sciences—psychology, anthropology, political economy, law, history, aesthetics, and philology. He argued that the notion of causality as it operates within the physical sciences was inapplicable to the cultural sciences, and functioned as a totally inappropriate explanatory model. "Psychic and psychophysical facts," he wrote, "form the basis of the theory not only of the individual, but also of the systems of culture, as well as of the external organization of society, and the same underlie the historical view and analysis in each of its stages. From there the epistemological investigation concerning the manner, the 'how' it is given to us, and the evidence that belongs to it, alone can really establish the methodology of the cultural sciences."[36] In 1885 and 1886, Wölfflin studied in Berlin with Dilthey. This association taught him, among other things, that history should not be discussed in the language of *cause* but rather in that of *functions*, as in the algebraic description of variables and the relations that obtain between terms.

Positivist art history is now on the rise. Sometimes a careful defense of method is prepared, as when Gombrich uses Karl Popper's *The Poverty of Historicism* (an attack on Dilthey) to argue for the applicability of scientific method to the domain of aesthetic change. But mostly matters of methodology are not defended, and art history proceeds as if there were nothing at all going on in the domain of historiography, no questions being raised, no serious examinations of the role of cause.

This is not the place to open what could be an extended discussion of this issue. But it is necessary to glimpse, no matter how briefly, the attack on cause now being assembled by large groups of historians, described here by Michel Foucault:

---

36.   This translation from Dilthey's *Einleitung in die Geisteswissenschaften*, 1883, is by Joan Hart, from her unpublished Ph.D. dissertation, "Heinrich Wölfflin," University of California, Berkeley, 1981. My discussion of Dilthey's contribution to Wölfflin's formation depends on hers. See her essay, "Reinterpreting Wölfflin: Neo-Kantianism and Hermenuetics," *Art Journal*, XLII (Winter 1982).

In its traditional form, history proper was concerned to define relations (of simple causality, of circular determination, of antagonism,
of expression) between facts or dated events: the series being known,
it was simply a question of defining the position of each element in
relation to the other elements in the series. [But] the problem now is
to constitute series: to define the elements proper to each series, to
fix its boundaries, to reveal its own specific type of relations, to formulate its laws, thus constituting the series of series, or "tables."
. . . Thus, in the place of the continuous chronology of reason, which
was invariably traced back to some inaccessible origin, there have
appeared scales that are sometimes very brief, distinct from one another, irreducible to a single law, scales that bear a type of history
peculiar to each one, and which cannot be reduced to the general
model of a consciousness that acquires, progresses, and remembers.[37]

Cause is a very special kind of motor that drives an argument in fixed
directions. Once we define historical problems in terms of cause, there will
always be fragments lying about on the scrap heap of history, fragments that
we can try to bring into association: there will always, for example, be church
projects for which we can call into being hypothetical windows.

New York, 1982

---

37.   Michel Foucault, *The Archaeology of Knowledge*, trans. A.M. Sheridan Smith, New York,
Harper Books, 1976, pp. 7–8.

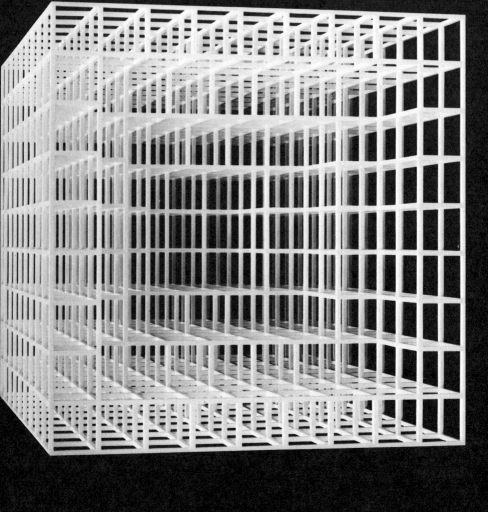

LeWitt in Progress

The process of "algebrization," the over-automatization of an object, permits the greatest economy of perceptive effort. Either objects are assigned only one proper feature—a number, for example—or else they function as though by formula and do not even appear in cognition.

Victor Shklovsky
"Art as Technique"

Consider the following three documents: The first is an article entitled "Sol LeWitt—The Look of Thought," by the critic Donald Kuspit. The second is a book-length essay called *Progress in Art* by the artist and writer Suzi Gablik. The third is the critic Lucy Lippard's contribution to the catalogue for the LeWitt retrospective at the Museum of Modern Art.

Taken together these essays put forward a set of claims, addressed initially to the work of a specific artist, but extended to the larger context of abstract art in general, or at least to the abstract art of LeWitt's generation. What these claims amount to is a declaration of the mission and achievement of this abstraction. It is, they collectively assert, to serve as triumphant illustration of the powers of human reason. And, we might ask, what else could Conceptual Art be?

Kuspit signals this grand theme with the title of his essay. "The Look of Thought" is what stares back at us from the modular structures, the openwork lattices, the serial progressions of LeWitt's sculpture. Thought, in Kuspit's terms, is deductive, inferential, axiomatic. It is a process of finding within the manifold of experience a central, organizing principle; it is the activity of a transcendental ego.

"In LeWitt," Kuspit writes, "there is no optical induction; there is only deduction by rules, which have an axiomatic validity however much the work created by their execution has a tentative, inconsequential look." And, he continues, "rationalistic, deterministic abstract art links up with a larger Western tradition, apparent in both classical antiquity and the Renaissance, *viz.*, the

Sol LeWitt. Floor Piece #4. 1976. Painted wood, 43 1/4 by 43 1/2 by 43 1/4 inches.

pursuit of intelligibility by mathematical means. This tradition is profoundly humanistic in import, for it involves the deification of the human mind by reason of its mathematical prowess."[1]

The specific work in which Kuspit sees this deification of the human mind in operation is called *Variations of Incomplete Open Cubes* (1974). It is a modular structure composed of 122 units, each a member of a finite series, the series ordered in terms of a numerical progression. Throughout the series the "cube" as such is given only inferentially, initially by providing the least possible information (three edges set perpendicular to one another), and then progressively supplying more of the missing edges, ending with the greatest possible information (eleven edges). Each of the modules in the series is eight inches on a side; each is painted white; and the 122 skeletal structures are assembled on a vast platform.

"The viewer," Kuspit informs us, "completed the incomplete cubes by mentally supplying the missing edges, and experienced the tension between the literally unfinished and the mentally finished cubes—between what Kant would call the phenomenal cube and the idea of the cube."[2]

For almost no writer who deals with LeWitt is there any question that these geometric emblems are the illustration of Mind, the demonstration of rationalism itself. "At times," one critic writes, "the most elaborate of these constructions resemble translations of complete philosophical systems into a purely formal language. If anyone could perceive the structural beauty of, say, Descartes's or Kant's treatises and then go on to recreate them as exclusively visual metaphor, it is surely LeWitt."[3]

There may of course be readers of this kind of criticism who balk at statements of this sort. They may find it strange that in the last quarter of the twentieth century there should have arisen an art dedicated to a triumphant Cartesianism, that when almost everything else in our cultural experience has instructed us about the necessity of abandonning the fantasy of the transcendental subject, LeWitt should be capable of reassuring us about its powers.

> For if I see myself putting to sea, and the long hours without landfall, I do not see the return, the tossing on the breakers, and I do not hear the frail keel grating on the shore. I took advantage of being at the seaside to lay in a store of sucking-stones. They were pebbles but I call them stones. Yes, on this occasion I laid in a considerable store. I distributed them equally among my four pockets, and sucked them turn and turn about.[4]

But the power of human reason has captured the imagination of a number of contemporary writers on art, for whom abstraction is necessarily the outcome of

1.   Donald Kuspit, "Sol LeWitt: The Look of Thought," *Art in America*, LXIII (September-October 1975), 48.
2.   *Ibid.*, p. 43.
3.   Robert Rosenblum, in *Sol LeWitt*, New York, The Museum of Modern Art, p. 14.
4.   Samuel Beckett, *Molloy*, New York, Grove Press, 1965, p. 69. All subsequent extracted passages appear on pp. 69–72.

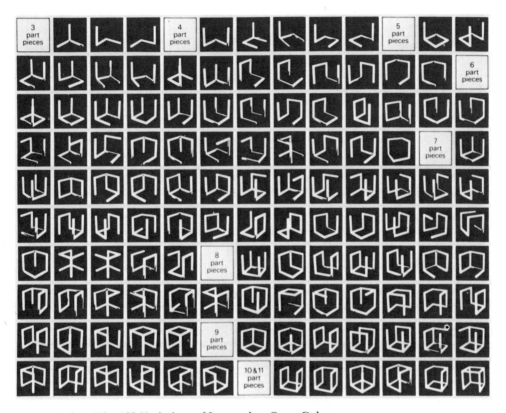

Sol LeWitt. 122 Variations of Incomplete Open Cubes.
1974.

the triumphant progress of rationality. It is instructive, therefore, to think about the claims that are made for LeWitt in the context of a broader argument about the nature of abstraction. Suzi Galik's *Progress in Art*, for example, views the entire range of the world's visual culture as a problem in cognitive development. And abstract art, set within this problematic, appears as the necessary fruits of some kind of world intellectual growth.

Put very briefly, her argument is that the history of art divides into three distinct periods, the first consisting of all visual representation prior to the discovery of systematic perspective, the second, beginning with the Renaissance, defined by the mastery of perspective, and the third, that of modernism, heralded by the onset of abstraction. As one might gather from the title of her book, the arthor's contention is that these divisions mark off stages in a radical progression, each stage outmoding and superseding the one that came before it. The model for this idea of "progress in art" is that of human cognitive development, beginning with the most childlike modes of thought and moving forward towards the greater complexity of operational, formal reasoning. Projecting this developmental model of the individual, taken from the work of Piaget, onto the entire corpus of world art, Gablik speaks of the history of styles as a matter of "advance"—a process of "evolution" towards stages of increasingly higher intellectual organization. "The history of art exemplifies fundamental patterned principles of mental growth," she writes.[5] Thus the Renaissance superseded all previous forms of representation because of the axiomatic, deductive nature of perspective, so that the space of the phenomenal world could be understood as unified by a system of coordinates independent of "raw" perception. But the modern period (beginning with Cubism) cognitively outdistances the Renaissance by withdrawing this power of coordination from the real world entirely. In so doing it demonstrates the independence of all deductive or logical systems from the process of observation. In Gablik's view the achievement of abstract art is its freedom from the demands of perceptual reality and its amibition to demonstrate what Piaget has termed the "formal-operational stage" of human thinking.

> This raised a problem which I first solved in the following way. I had say sixteen stones, four in each of my four pockets these being the two pockets of my trousers and the two pockets of my greatcoat. Taking a stone from the right pocket of my greatcoat, and putting it in my mouth, I replaced it in the right pocket of my greatcoat by a stone from the right pocket of my trousers, which I replaced by a stone from the left pocket of my trousers, which I replaced by a stone from the left pocket of my greatcoat, which I replaced by the stone which was in my mouth, as soon as I had finished sucking it.

It is not surprising that LeWitt's defenders would find much to admire in the thesis of *Progress in Art*. For an argument that draws a direct parallel between

5.   Suzi Gablik, *Progress in Art*, New York, Rizzoli, p. 147.

Piaget's "genetic epistemology" and the course of several millenia of aesthetic endeavor necessarily places artists of LeWitt's generation at the "formal-operational stage" of development, as manipulators of a propositional logic far "in advance" of anything that has come before it. Indeed, Lucy Lippard, in her essay for the Museum of Modern Art catalogue on LeWitt, claims that Gablik's description of this type of thinking applies most securely to the work of this artist. "It is only LeWitt's 'reflective abstraction,'" Lippard maintains, "that fully fits into these theories, only his work that can be said to articulate 'the moment in artistic thinking when a structure opens to questioning and reorganizes itself according to a new meaning *which is nevertheless the meaning of the same structure*, but taken to a new level of complexity.'"[6]

> Thus there were still four stones in each of my four pockets, but not quite the same stones. And when the desire to suck took hold of me again, I drew again on the right pocket of my greatcoat, certain of not taking the same stone as the last time. And while I sucked it I rearranged the other stones in the way I have just described. And so on.

In speaking of Lippard and Kuspit as defenders of LeWitt's work I do not mean to imply that anyone who disputes their view of it is automatically a detractor. Rather I am focusing on a particular type of defense. It is one that undoubtedly finds its rhetorical force and psychological energy in reaction to the hostility that is generally directed at work like LeWitt's. This hostility is rather muted inside the self-immured space of the art world, where LeWitt is considered a contemporary master, but outside those walls it is extremely pronounced. LeWitt's white lattices, serially disposed or not, are viewed by the audience of a wider culture as baffling and meaningless. For after all, what could they possible represent? To which the answer comes, as outlined above: they are representations of Mind. Freed at last from making pictures of things in the world, the artist is depicting the cognitive moment as such.

> But this solution did not satisfy me fully. For it did not escape me that, by an extraordinary hazard, the four stones circulating thus might always be the same four. In which case, far from sucking the sixteen stones turn and turn about, I was really only sucking four, always the same, turn and turn about.

For these writers the cognitive moment has a particular form, assumes a particular shape. From the references to Descartes and the allusions to Euclidean diagrams, it is obvious that the form it takes is a kind of centering of thought—the discovery of a root principle, an axiom by which all the variables of a given system might be accounted for. It is the moment of grasping the idea or theorem that both generates the system and also explains it. Seen as being interior to the system, and constituting the very ground of its unity, the center is also visualized as being

6.   Lucy Lippard, in *Sol LeWitt*, New York, The Museum of Modern Art, p. 27.

above or outside it. Hence Kuspit's wish to link the idea of pure intelligibility, which he sees as the goal of LeWitt's art, with the notion of transcendence.

> For no matter how I caused the stone to circulate, I always ran the same risk. It was obvious that by increasing the number of my pockets I was bound to increase my chances of enjoying my stones in the way I planned, that is to say one after the other until their number was exhausted. Had I had eight pockets, for example, instead of the four I did have, then even the most diabolical hazard could not have prevented me from sucking at least eight of my sixteen stones, turn and turn about. The truth is I should have needed sixteen pockets in order to be quite easy in my mind.

But in stating the conditions by which abstract art might be freed from the obligation to picture the world, this kind of critical argument merely substitutes a

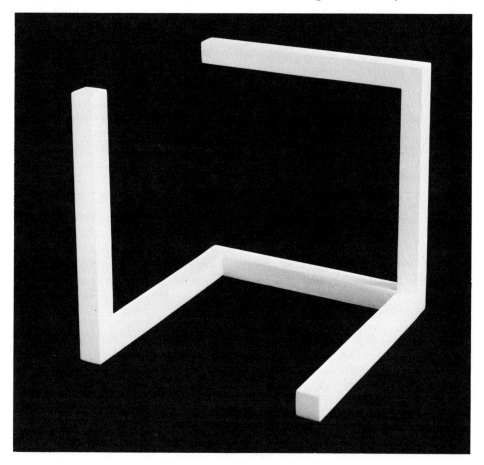

new obligation. Abstract art is no longer tested by the faithfulness by which it transcribes appearances; it is now to be tested by its transparency to a different model. Visual reality no longer has a privileged status with relation to the work of art, no longer forms the text which the art is to illustrate. Now it is logic that constitutes the "text"; and the space onto which the art is now to open, the model it is to "picture" and by which it is to be tested is Mind.

LeWitt's art would, of course, fail this test. His math is far too simple; his solutions are far too inelegant; the formal conditions of his work are far too scattered and obsessional to produce anything like the diagram of human reason these writers seem to call for.

> And for a long time I could see no other conclusion than this, that short of having sixteen pockets, each with its stone, I could never reach the goal I had set myself, short of an extraordinary hazard. And if at a pitch I could double the number of my pockets, were it only by dividing each

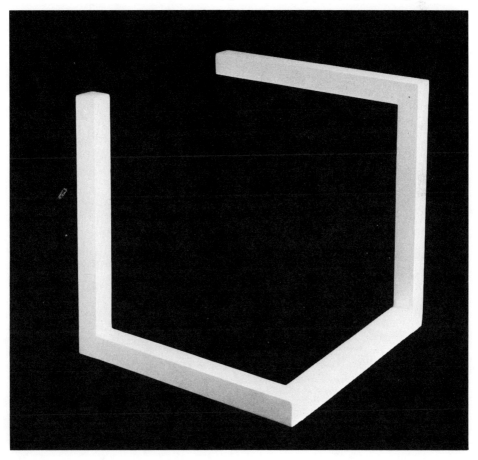

pocket in two, with the help of a few safety-pins let us say, to quadruple them seemed to be more than I could manage. And I did not feel inclined to take all that trouble for a half-measure. For I was beginning to lose all sense of measure, after all this wrestling and wrangling, and to say, All or nothing.

Like most of LeWitt's work, *Variations of Incomplete Open Cubes* provides one with an experience that is obsessional in kind. On the vast platform, too splayed to be taken in at a glance, the 122 neat little fragmented frames, all meticulously painted white, sit in regimented but meaningless lines, the demonstration of a kind of mad obstinacy. Quite unlike the diagrams in Euclid, where the axiomatic relationships are stated but once and the variety of possible applications left to the reader; or unlike the algebraic expression of the expansion

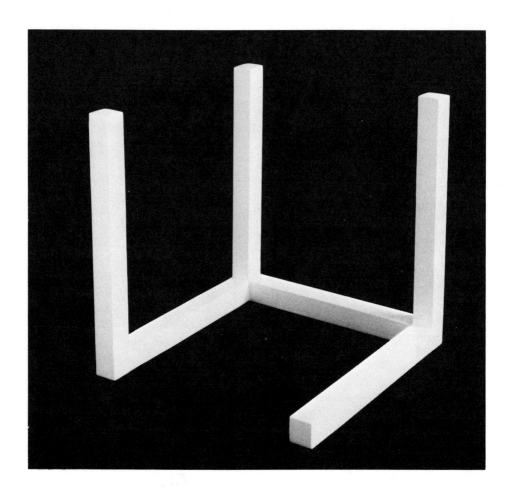

of a given series, where the formulaic is used precisely to foreclose the working out of every term in the series, LeWitt's work insistently applies its generative principle in each of its possible cases. The experience of the work goes exactly counter to "the look of thought," particularly if thought is understood as classical expressions of logic. For such expressions, whether diagramatic or symbolic, are precisely about the capacity to abbreviate, to adumbrate, to condense, to be able to imply an expansion with only the first two or three terms, to cover vast arithmetic spaces with a few ellipsis points, to use, in short, the notion of *etcetera*. The babble of a LeWitt serial expansion has nothing of the economy of the mathematician's language. It has the loquaciousness of the speech of children or of the very old, in that its refusal to summarize, to use the single example that would imply the whole, is like those feverish accounts of events composed of a string of almost identical details, connected by "and."

And while I gazed thus at my stones, revolving interminable martin-
gales all equally defective, and crushing handfulls of sand, so that the
sand ran through my fingers and fell back on the strand, yes, while thus
I lulled my mind and part of my body, one day suddenly it dawned on
the former, dimly, that I might perhaps achieve my purpose without
increasing the number of my pockets, or reducing the number of my
stones, but simply by sacrificing the principle of trim.

But it is not entirely like those examples. For garrulousness, babble, the
spasmodic hiccup of repetitive detail, have about them a quality of randomness,
disorganization, a lack of system. And LeWitt's outpouring of example, his piling
up of instance, is riddled with system, shot through with order. There is, in
Variations of Incomplete Open Cubes, as they say, a method in this madness. For
what we find is the "system" of compulsion, of the obsessional's unwavering
ritual, with its precision, its neatness, its finicky exactitude, covering over an abyss
of irrationality. It is in that sense design without reason, design spinning out of
control. The obsessional's solutions to problems strike us as mad, not because the
solutions are wrong, but because in the setting of the problem itself there is a
strange short-circuit in the lines of necessity.

Now I am willing to believe, indeed I firmly believe, that other
solutions to this problem might have been found, and indeed may still
be found, no less sound, but much more elegant, than the one I shall
now describe, if I can. And I believe too that had I been a little more
insistent, a little more resistant, I could have found them myself. But I
was tired, but I was tired, and I contented myself ingloriously with the
first solution that was a solution, to this problem.

LeWitt once explained, "If I do a wall drawing, I have to have the plan
written on the wall or label because it aids the understanding of the idea. If I just
had lines on the wall, no one would know that there are ten thousand lines within
a certain space, so I have two kinds of form—the lines, and the explanation of the
lines. Then there is the idea, which is always unstated."[7] The lines are raw
phenomena for which the label is not an explanation in the sense of a reason or an
interpretation, but an explanation in the sense of a documentary narrative or
commentary, like a guide's telling his listener how high this particular redwood
is, or how many years it took the Colorado River to cut the Grand Canyon. The
label is the document of persistence, of invention dancing over the pit of non-
necessity. And then, as LeWitt was fond of saying, "there is the idea, which is
always unstated."

Sometimes, however, LeWitt did state the "idea." For instance in 1969 he was
to have an exhibition in Nova Scotia, and for this occasion he mailed the

7.   Lippard, p. 24.

directions for the work, along with the kind of articulation that never appears on the wall-label: "A work that uses the idea of error, a work that uses the idea of infinity; a work that is subversive, a work that is not original. . . ."[8] These "ideas" exist on an entirely different order than that of the mathematical, the deductive, the axiomatic. If one uses the "idea of error" to generate a work, one has done something quite different from illustrating an order that is ideated or Ideal, the order LeWitt's critics keep insisting on associating with his art.

> But not to go over the heartbreaking stages through which I passed before I came to it, here it is, in all its hideousness. All (all!) that was necessary was to put for example, to begin with, six stones in the right pocket of my greatcoat, or supply-pocket, five in the right pocket of my trousers, and five in the left pocket of my trousers, that makes the lot, twice five ten plus six sixteen, and none, for none remained, in the left pocket of my greatcoat, which for the time being remained empty, empty of stones that is, for its usual contents remained, as well as occasional objects. For where do you think I had my vegetable knife, my silver, my horn and the other things that I have not yet named, perhaps shall never name.

LeWitt did indeed write about ideas and how he wished to relate them to his work, when he declared that "the idea becomes a Machine that makes the art."[9] He also seemed to be addressing himself to an order superior to the merely visual when he used the word "conceptual" to characterize his work in two manifesto-like pronouncements he published in the late 1960s. And once the term was put in play, "conceptual art" was like a ball that the art-world immediately ran with, driving deep into the territory of Idealism. No Pythagorean dream was too exalted for this art not to be able to reflect it as visual metaphor, as diagramatic manifestations of the Real.

But LeWitt's "ideas" are not generally to be found in that high place. The kind of idea he inevitably uses is subversive, addressing itself to the purposelessness of purpose, to the spinning gears of a machine disconnected from reason. Robert Smithson spoke of this when he wrote, "LeWitt is concerned with ennervating 'concepts' of paradox. Everything LeWitt thinks, writes, or has made is inconsistent and contradictory. The 'original idea' of his art is lost in a mess of drawings, figurings, and other ideas. Nothing is where it seems to be. His concepts are prisons devoid of reason."[10] LeWitt spoke of it also when he wrote, "Irrational thoughts should be followed absolutely and logically."[11] The consequence of obeying this direction, and LeWitt's art does obey it, is to arrive at the opposite of

8.   *Ibid.*
9.   Sol LeWitt, "Paragraphs on Conceptual Art," *Artforum*, V (June 1967), 80.
10.   Robert Smithson, "A Museum of Language in the Vicinity of Art," *Art International*, March 1968, 21.
11.   Sol LeWitt, "Sentences on Conceptual Art," *Art-Language*, no. 1 (May 1969), 11.

Idealism. It is to achieve an absurd Nominalism—as we saw in *Variations of Incomplete Open Cubes.*

> Good. Now I can begin to suck. Watch me closely. I take a stone from the right pocket of my greatcoat, suck it, stop sucking it. put it in the left pocket of my greatcoat, the empty one (of stones). I take a second stone from the right pocket of my greatcoat, suck it, put it in the left pocket of my greatcoat. And so on until the right pocket of my greatcoat is empty (apart from its usual and casual contents) and the six stones I have just sucked, one after the other, are all in the left pocket of my greatcoat.

The aesthetic manipulations of an absurdist nominalism are hardly new with LeWitt. They appear everywhere throughout the production of Minimalism, beginning in the very early '60s, and are of course to be found in the literature most venerated by that group of sculptors and painters: the literature of the *nouveau roman* and of Samuel Beckett. To speak of what LeWitt shares expressively with his generation is not to diminish his art; rather it is to help locate the real territory of its meaning.

It is an absurdist Nominalism, for instance, that flattens the narrator's voice in *Jealousy,* as we are told of a grove of bannana trees through the painstaking, persistent, sadistic description of its individual rows. The effect is of course to drive attention away from the grove of trees and back to the voice and its obsession to count.

> Pausing then, and concentrating, so as not to make a balls of it, I transfer to the right pocket of my greatcoat, in which there are no stones left, the five stones in the right pocket of my trousers, which I replace by the five stones in the left pocket of my trousers, which I replace by the six stones in the left pocket of my greatcoat. At this stage then the left pocket of my greatcoat is again empty of stones, while the right pocket of my greatcoat is again supplied, and in the right way, that is to say with other stones than those I have just sucked. These other stones I then begin to suck, one after the other, and to transfer as I go along to the left pocket of my greatcoat, being absolutely certain, as far as one can be in an affair of this kind, that I am not sucking the same stones as a moment before, but others.

And the passage from *Molloy* about the sucking stones is one of many possible instances from Beckett in which the gears of rationcination proceed to spin in an extraordinary performance of "thinking," where it is clear that the object of this "thought" is entirely contained within the brilliance of the routine. It is like music-hall performers doing a spectacular turn, switching hats from one head to the other at lightning speed. No one thinks of the hat as an idea; it is

Sol LeWitt. Come and Go. *Drawing for play by Samuel Beckett,* Harper's Bazaar, *April 1969. Pen and ink, 18 by 22 1/4 inches.*

simply a pretext for a display of skill—as is the "problem" of the stones. It is the ironical presence of the false "problem" that gives to this outburst of skill its special emotional tenor, its sense of its own absolute detachment from a world of purpose and necessity, its sense of being suspended before the immense spectacle of the irrational.

For LeWitt's generation a false and pious rationality was seen uniformly as the enemy of art. Judd spoke of his own kind of order as being "just one thing after another." Morris and Smithson spoke of the joy of destruction. For this generation the mode of expression became the deadpan, the fixed stare, the uninflected repetitious speech. Or rather, the correlatives for these modes were invented in the object-world of sculpture. It was an extraordinary decade in which objects proliferated in a seemingly endless and obsessional chain, each one answering the other—a chain in which everything linked to everything else, but nothing was referential.

To get inside the systems of this work, whether LeWitt's or Judd's or Morris's, is precisely to enter a world without a center, a world of substitutions and transpositions nowhere legitimated by the revelations of a transcendental subject. This is the strength of this work, its seriousness, and its claim to modernity. To give accounts of this kind of art that misconstrue its content, that entirely misplace the ground of its operations, is to invent a false justification of the work which traduces and betrays it. Aporia is a far more legitimate model for LeWitt's art than Mind, if only because aporia is a *dilemma* rather than a *thing*.

New York, 1977

Laying-out Shift.

Richard Serra, a Translation

*But the system of experience is not arrayed
before me as if I were God, it is lived by me
from a certain point of view; I am not the
spectator, I am involved, and it is my in-
volvement in a point of view which makes
possible both the finiteness of my perception
and its opening out upon the complete world
as a horizon of every perception.*

— Merleau-Ponty[1]

How is one to begin, in France, to speak of the work of Richard Serra?
How to explain the beauty of the work's relentless aggressiveness, its acceptance of the technologically *brut*, to an audience whose ideas of beauty have
been formed in other schools and are, quite simply, invested elsewhere? How
to speak of the contents of the work's abstractness without seeming, in the experience of the reader, to lapse into nonsense, above all for a reader whose culture has been consistently closed to the very possibility of an abstract art that
could transcend decoration?

In relation to art, we live in a time of cultural schizophrenia. Both the art
market and the art press are international phenomena, resulting in a world-
wide homogenization of what is exhibited, collected, known. From this we are
led to think that the constant circulation of contemporary art from country to
country is the expression of an international culture, the warrant of shared
aesthetic criteria, shared conceptions of the goals of art, shared visions.

Nothing could be less true. Despite the leveling effect of mass culture, it is
precisely in that mute, still space that separates the viewer from the work of art,
a space traversed only by his gaze, that we find an acute resistance to the in-

1.   Maurice Merleau-Ponty, *Phenomenology of Perception*, trans. Colin Smith, London, Rout-
ledge and Kegan Paul, 1962, p. 304.

ternationalization of culture. For that gaze is the extension of the viewer's aloneness as he confronts the work, a solitude that throws into sharpest relief the nature of his aesthetic demands: what he expects a work of art to satisfy; what arouses his interest and fixes his attention; what his attitudes are about the relation between art and seriousness, art and taste, art and pleasure. These attitudes are culturally rooted, and those roots grow differently as they burrow into different soils. The space traversed by the viewer's understanding is differently determined in different countries, though the art press would tell us otherwise.

This leads me to the most tactless question of all: how, without giving offense to Serra (for whom Giacometti's work has neither any real interest nor any relevance to his own) or without completely baffling the French reader (for whom nothing could be more distant than these two domains of sculpture — one figurative, expressive, richly connotative, the other abstract, uninflected, associatively raw), how to suggest that it is precisely by means of the mutual repulsion and antagonism between the work of Giacometti and that of Serra, precisely through the operations of what could be called a model of negative relations, that Serra's work might become available in France? In constructing this particular *dispositif* of repulsion — Giacometti/Serra — one can see as clearly as possible the aesthetic operations (Serra's) that produce what could be called the abstract subject.

And yet, if this *dispositif* is capable of promoting a certain clarity of vision, that is because it operates not only on the principle of mutual repulsion but also on the grounds of a single text that mediates between these two radically distinct worlds of sculptural practice.

The text in question is Merleau-Ponty's *Phenomenology of Perception*, which is commonly understood to provide a kind of narrative against which to experience the formal decisions taken in Giacometti's postwar work. Those elongated, bladelike figures, shuddering from within a plastic elaboration that leaves them defined by a permanent visual vagueness, are often read as the sculptural parallel of phenomenology's recharacterization of perception as a function of intentionality, as the simultaneous cause and result of the viewer's *prise sur le monde*. In the light of this reading no objects are given to us neutrally, as it were, to be modified by the distance from which we see them or the angle of view we are forced to take. The distance and the viewpoint are not added to the object, but inhere in the object's meaning, like the sounds that infuse our language with an always-already given ground of sense, separating it at the start from mere noise or babble. "Is not a man *smaller* at two hundred yards than at five yards away?" Merleau-Ponty asks his reader. "He becomes so if I isolate him from the perceived context and measure his apparent size. Otherwise he is neither smaller nor indeed equal in size: he is anterior to equality and inequality; he is *the same man seen from farther way.*"² Perceptual "data" are thus recharacterized as the meanings that things present to a given point of view. "Convergence and apparent size are neither signs nor causes of depth: they are present in the experience of depth in the way that a *motive*, even when it is not articulate and separately posited, is present in a decision."³ Or further, "They do not act miraculously as 'causes' in producing the appearance of organization in depth, they tacitly motivate it in so far as they already contain it in their significance, and in so far as they are both already a certain way of looking at distance."⁴

It was this notion of "a certain way of looking at distance" that affected the enthusiastic viewers of Giacometti's work, leading them to say, "He invented a new field of creation. He introduced the representation of distance into the three-thousand-year-old history of sculpture."⁵ And this representation of distance carried by Giacometti's figures was associated with phenomenology because it was seen as the representation of the mutual relationship between the object and the spectator, the viewer and the viewed. It was understood as a representation of "seeing at a distance" that no examination of the work close-to would dissipate and that no magnification would disperse. For the object carried as its meaning the mark of the viewer's separation from it; the sculpture represented a human body forever caught in the aureole of the beholder's look, bearing forever the trace of what it means to be seen *by* another *from* the place from which he views. The indistinctness, the elongation, the frontality of Giacometti's figures were all understood to be these marks of the beholder's distant gaze. This reading, enunciated with great force by Sartre in 1948 as "La Recherche de l'Absolu," entered the literature on art to become a critical commonplace through the 1950s in France.⁶

In the United States, however, the existentialist reading of the aesthetic field (whether that entailed the interpretation of Giacometti or of the local phenomenon of action painting) was curiously shorn of its relation to a phenomenology of perception. For Merleau-Ponty was not translated into English in the 1950s, and Sartre's man-in-a-situation was commonly understood to be moral, not perceptual man. The *Phenomenology of Perception* thus entered the consciousness of American artists only after a lag of twenty years: precisely the period during which American art underwent a radical conversion and passionate commitment to the power and meaning of abstract art.

2.   *Ibid.*, p. 261.
3.   *Ibid.*, p. 258.
4.   *Ibid.*, p. 259.
5.   Reinhold Hohl, *Alberto Giacometti*, Lausanne, 1971, p. 107.
6.   Jean-Paul Sartre, "La recerce de l'absolu," *Les Temps Modernes*, III (1948), 1153–1163. Reprinted in *Situations III*, Paris, Gallimard, 1949, pp. 289–305.

Thus when the minimalist generation first took up Merleau-Ponty's book in the early 1960s, they did so against the background of Pollock and Still, Newman and Rothko. They therefore had a very different understanding of what could be meant by Merleau-Ponty's notion of a "preobjective experience" than did artists of the 1940s working in France. Or again, they received in a different way the notion that "Once the experience of spatiality is related to our implantation in the world, there will always be a primary spatiality for each modality of this implantation. When, for example, the world of clear and articulate objects is abolished, our perceptual being, cut off from its world, evolves a spatiality without things. This is what happens in the night. . . . Night has no outlines; it is itself in contact with me."[7] The *Phenomenology of Perception* became, in the hands of the Americans, a text that was consistently interpreted in the light of their own ambitions toward meaning within an art that was abstract.

It is in this context that we, in turn, might read what Serra wrote about the conception of *Shift*, an immense sculpture, constructed over a two-year period (1970–1972), that spans a distance of nearly 300 meters within a field in rural Canada:

Surrounded on three sides by trees and swamp, the site is a farming field consisting of two hills separated by a dog-leg valley. In the summer of 1970, Joan (Jonas) and I spent five days walking the place. We discovered that two people walking the distance of the field opposite one another, attempting to keep each other in view despite the curvature of the land, would mutually determine a topological definition of the space. The boundaries of the work became the maximum distance two people could occupy and still keep each other in view. The horizon of the work was established by the possibilities of maintaining this mutual viewpoint. From the extreme boundaries of the work, a total configuration is always understood. As eye-levels were aligned — across the expanse of the field — elevations were located. The expanse of the valley, unlike the two hills, was flat.

What I wanted was a dialectic between one's perception of the place in totality and one's relation to the field as walked. The result is a way of measuring oneself against the indeterminacy of the land.

. . . Insofar as the stepped elevations [the six "walls" that are the built elements of the work] function as horizons cutting into and extending towards the real horizon, they suggest themselves as orthogonals within the terms of a perspective system of measurement.

7.   Merleau-Ponty, p. 283.

Richard Serra. Shift. *1970–72. Six concrete sections, 5 feet high by 8 inches thick, total length of the sections, 815 feet. King City, Canada.*

Shift *(detail)*.

Shift *(detail)*.

The machinery of renaissance space depends on measurements remaining fixed and immutable. These steps relate to a continually shifting horizon, and as measurements, they are totally transitive: elevating, lowering, extending, foreshortening, contracting, compressing, and turning. The line as a visual element, per step, becomes a transitive verb.[8]

From its inception as a trace of the mutal sighting of two people walking opposite sides of a hilly ground but struggling always to keep each other in view; to its conception as a network of perspectives that would establish an internal "horizon" for the work (as opposed to the real horizon), which in turn would constantly define one's vision of the object in terms of one's relation to it; to its idea of the transitivity of this relationship ("elevating," "extending," "compressing," "turning") such that the work marks the activity of the viewer's relationship to his world; all of this flows—with breathtaking naturalness— from the *Phenomenology of Perception.*

This is not to say that *Shift* has Merleau-Ponty's text as anything like a specific "source" or direct influence. Rather, almost ten years of general absorption of these ideas developed an American context in which sculpture lived in a play of perspectives, as in the minimalist work of Donald Judd or Robert Morris, where abstract geometries are constantly submitted to the definition of a sited vision. And in this context a work formed by the mutually established "horizons" of two people at a distance made a certain kind of intuitive sense.

Of course, within the aesthetic domain of *Shift* this notion of "horizon" could not be further from the sculptural ideas of Giacometti's standing figures marked by the perceptual signs of the distance from which they are "seen." For where Giacometti lodges the depiction of distance in the object world, and specifically in the representation of the human figure, Serra wishes to operate on the "preobjective experience." And it is his conviction that the only way to approach that primordial, preobjective world is through a use of form that, though palpable and material—directly engaging the viewer's body—is rigorously nonfigurative, which is to say, abstract.

One sees this conception of the abstract at work in *Shift*. As one moves over the grounds of the work, the tops of the walls are in gradual but constant transformation. From being the lines along which one sights as one stands above them and looks down, thereby establishing one's connection to the distance, the walls change as one "descends" the work to become an enclosure that binds one within the earth. Felt as barrier rather than as perspective, they then heighten the experience of the physical place of one's body. Without depicting

8.   Richard Serra, "Shift," *Arts Magazine* (April 1973). Reprinted in *Richard Serra: Interviews, etc.; 1970-1980*, Yonkers, New York, The Hudson River Museum, 1980.

anything — this nearby human figure, that distant tree — the walls' linear/physical network articulates both a situation and a lived perspective. And it does this in the abstractest way possible: by the rotation in and out of depth of a plane.

The opening sections of the *Phenomenology of Perception* sketch something of the preobjectival world when they speak of the internal horizon of an object as that network of views from everywhere within which it is caught: "When I look at the lamp on my table, I attribute to it not only the qualities visible from where I am, but also those which the chimney, the walls, the table can 'see'; the back of my lamp is nothing but the face which it 'shows' to the chimney. I can therefore see an object in so far as objects form a system or a world, and in so far as each one treats the others round it as spectators of its hidden aspects which guarantee the permanence of those aspects by their presence."[9]

This passage occurs at the beginning of the section titled The Body, and it is the interconnectedness of "back" and "front" within a system of the *meanings* of these relationships, given preobjectively by the space of the body, that Merleau-Ponty constructs as a primordial model. The body as the preobjective ground of all experience of the relatedness of objects is the first "world" explored by the *Phenomenology of Perception.*

The rotating plane of *Shift*, now internal, now external horizon, is thus a syntaxical marker — an equivalent within the abstract language of sculpture for the connection between the body's "horizon" and that of the real world. Although it is a more or less geometrical element, this plane could not be further, in terms of meaning, from the transparent planes of constructivist sculpture, or the hovering, frontal planes of much nonobjective painting. The planes of constructivist sculpture are concerted to create the illusion that they occupy what could be called a diagrammatic space. These sculptures are often made of a transparent material — glass, celluloid, open networks of string — and this material transparency is the signal for a kind of transparency sought for at the level of meaning: the transparency or lucidity of the explanatory model that lays bare the essence of things, exposing their real structures to view. This lucidity is intended wholly to suffuse the constructivist sculpture, rendering it "transparent" to perception from any given point of view so that it is as though seen from everywhere at once in a moment of complete self-revelation. It was with this model of the diagrammatic and its explanatory power that the constructivists devised their own "abstract subject" as a gift to the scientific community and its burgeoning technology.

The plane in *Shift*, no matter how geometrical or rigid or flat, is — from the point of view of meaning — utterly distinct from the constructivist plane. For the constructivist plane seeks to overcome the "appearances" of things and to

9.   Merleau-Ponty, p. 68.

Richard Serra. Different and Different Again.
1973. Steel.

redefine the object itself as the *géometral* of all possible perspectives, which is to say, the object seen from nowhere, or as Merleau-Ponty describes it, the object as seen by God: "For God, who is everywhere, breadth is immediately equivalent to depth. Intellectualism and empiricism do not give us any account of the human experience of the world; they tell us what God might think about it."[10]

The plane in *Shift* rejects this notion of transparency, not because it is literally opaque (made of concrete, half buried in the earth, at one with the density of the land) but because it participates in a system that acknowledges that "to look at the object is to plunge oneself into it . . . because objects form a system in which one cannot show itself without concealing others. More precisely, the inner horizon of an object cannot become an object without the surrounding objects' becoming a horizon, and so vision is an act with two facets."[11] Acknowledging that vision is this "act with two facets," the plane in *Shift* renders both the density of the body and that of the world, as well as the mutual, motile engagement that is at the heart of perception. The viewer of Serra's work, unlike the spectator of constructivist sculpture, is never represented (in the sculpture) as stationary. The viewer is always described as in motion even if that motion is only the constant micromuscular adjustments that are the corporealized condition of bifocal vision. This bridging between the body's horizon and that of the world, this abstract transitivity — "fore-shortening," "contracting," "compressing," "turning" — must be seen as the subject matter of *Shift*.

The mutual transitivity of seer and seen, their activity as they exchange positions through visual space to affect one another — this chiasmatic trajectory is Serra's subject in much of his work. It is an abstract subject, most often given "support" by correspondingly "abstract" forms, like the diagonally oriented five-meter-long bars and the two steel blocks that they visually "displace" in *Different and Different Again* (1973, installed at the Guggenehim Museum), or the enormous steel plates (8' × 24') of *Circuit* that extend from the four corners of a room to leave a one-meter gap in the work's "center" within which the viewer's body is invited to turn. But it is a subject that loses none of its abstractness when its support is a real object, as is the case in the beautiful film from 1976, *Railroad Turnbridge.*

In this film the camera is placed at one end of a revolving bridge, sighting down its entire length so that the view beyond this tunnel-like construction is entirely a function of the distant aperture at the bridge's end. The "view" and the "viewer" are thus mutually implicated at the level of "form" — the aperture of the camera and the opening at the far end of the bridge that frames the distant landscape mirror each other in terms of shape — and at the level of the *dispositif*

10.   *Ibid.*, p. 255.
11.   *Ibid.*, p. 67.

Richard Serra. Railroad Turnbridge. *1976. Film, 19 minutes.*

Railroad Turnbridge.

Railroad Turnbridge.

of vision; the majestically slow turning of the sun-struck bridge operates simultaneously on the position of the seer and on that limited part of the world available to be seen. As Serra says about this work, "Not only does it use the device of the tunneling of the bridge to frame the landscape, but then it returns on itself and frames itself. In that, there is an illusion created that questions what is moving and what is holding still. Is the camera moving and the bridge holding still or vice versa? That is contained within the framing structure of the material of the bridge itself, right down to its internal functioning element — the gear."[12]

The substantiality of the bridge, its real-world function and its iconological profile (the way, for instance, its trusswork calls to mind the historical phenomenon of nineteenth-century cast-iron construction), do not disappear in *Railroad Turnbridge* any more than does the landscape at the end of the tunnel that is the putative goal of the camera's vision. But all of these, in their objective character, are eclipsed by the film's abstract subject, by that thing that fills the frame and that is not so much a thing as a relationship, a transitivity. A space made visible in and of itself by the fact that it is in motion, a space swollen by a brilliant luminosity that serves as a metaphor for vision, yet a space traversed by the mutual implication of back and front, thus creating a visual figure for the preobjective space of the body, this spatial trajectory is what one sees in Serra's film. The physical turnbridge is the support of this experience, not its subject. *Railroad Turnbridge* follows *Shift* by four years and although its "pretext," the bridge, is a real, not an abstract element, as a work it corresponds to what Serra said the year it was made about what being a sculptor meant to him: "It means to follow the direction of the work I opened up early on for myself and try to make the most abstract moves within that."[13]

But another aspect of the abstract subject emerges from an examination of both *Railroad Turnbridge* and *Shift*, one that is further illuminated by the *dispositif* Giacometti/Serra with their mutual but not overlapping relationship to a phenomenology of perception. The abstract subject, for Serra, can only be a function of time. Any subject that is fixed in time, isolated and unchanging, becomes for him an image, and an image is by definition not abstract. It is always an image of something, always a depiction. Thus beyond the fact that Giacometti's world is "peopled" so that distance is bound to a distant face, a distant body, this distance has been rendered a sculptural image. It is there in the object, stamped onto its surface through the indelible fracture of the modeling, through the abruptness with which the sides of the face recede before our eyes,

12.   Annette Michelson, Richard Serra, Clara Weyerfraf, "The Films of Richard Serra: An Interview," *October*, no. 10 (Fall 1979). Reprinted in *Richard Serra: Interviews*.
13.   Richard Serra, "Sight Point '72–75/Delineator '74–'76," *Art in America* (May/June 1976). Reprinted in *Richard Serra: Interviews*.

so that whether physically far or near, we are always presented with this image of "distance."

For Serra the abstract subject only yields itself up within a kind of experiential ground through which space and time are felt to be functions of one another. For it is within the very moment of a shift in vision that what is seen is experienced as not bounded by the condition of being fixed, as is an image. In this insistence on an abstraction that unifies space and time into a continuum, so that the bridge of Serra's film is imaginable as a medium only because, like the gears of the camera itself, it is turning, one continues to feel a phenomenological preoccupation: "This quasi-synthesis is elucidated if we understand it as temporal. When I say that I see an object at a distance, I mean that I already hold it, or that I still hold it, it is in the future or in the past as well as being in space. . . . But co-existence, which in fact defines space, is not alien to time, but is the fact of two phenomena belonging to the same temporal wave."[14] And once again Merleau-Ponty links the space of this continuum to something pre-objective and abstract: "There is, therefore, another subject beneath me, for whom a world exists before I am here, and who marks out my place in it. This captive or natural spirit is my body, not that momentary body which is the instrument of my personal choices and which fastens upon this or that world, but the system of anonymous 'functions' which draw every particular focus into a general project."[15]

This sense that the abstract subject can only be approached within the condition of time separates most definitively the two halves of the paradigm Giacometti/Serra. If the *Phenomenology of Perception* furnishes one kind of critical gloss on this aesthetic premonition, other texts provide other types of access.[16] One of these is the famous passage from *A la recherche du temps perdu,* where Proust links his desire to write with a need to penetrate the surfaces of things to find the ground of the pleasure he derives from them, and he produces as the first example of his "writing" the fragment in which the bell towers of Martinville appear to him from within a particular confluence of space and time:

> . . . we had left Martinville some little time, and the village, after accompanying us for a few seconds, had already disappeared, when lingering alone on the horizon to watch our flight, its steeples and that of Vieuxvicq waved once again, in token of farewell, their sun-bathed pinnacles. Sometimes one would withdraw, so that the other two might watch us for a moment still; then the road changed direction, they veered in the light like three golden pivots, and vanished

14.   Merleau-Ponty, p. 265.
15.   *Ibid.*, p. 254.
16.   See Yve-Alain Bois, "Promenade pittoresque autour de *Clara-Clara,*" *Richard Serra,* Musée National d'Art Moderne, Centre Georges Pompidou, Paris, 1983.

from my gaze. But, a little later, when we were already close to
Combray, the sun having set meanwhile, I caught sight of them for
the last time, far away, and seeming no more now than three flowers
painted upon the sky above and low line of fields.[17]

For the young Proust it is the changing relationship that makes perceptible the link between his winding road and the choreography of the appearances
and disappearances of the three towers. This change occurs in time and it is
that which lies behind the aesthetic object, as its subject.

Paris, 1983 *

17.   Marcel Proust, *Swann's Way*, trans. C. K. Scott Moncrieff, New York, Vintage Books,
1970, p. 139.

*   Written for the catalogue of the Richard Serra exhibition at the Musée National d'Art
Moderne, Centre Georges Pompidou, Paris (October–December 1983), this essay was conceived
as an introduction of Serra's work to an audience that could not be expected to have encountered
it in depth before, this being Serra's first one-man show in France.

No sooner had minimal sculpture appeared on the horizon of the aesthetic experience of the 1960s, than criticism began to construct a paternity for this work, a set of constructivist fathers who could legitimize and thereby authenticate the strangeness of these objects. Plastic? inert geometries? factory production?—none of this was *really* strange, as the ghosts of Gabo and Tatlin and Lissitzky could be called in to testify. Never mind that the content of the one had nothing to do with, was in fact the exact opposite of, the content of the other. Never mind that Gabo's celluloid was the sign of lucidity and intellection, while Judd's plastic-tinged-with-dayglo spoke the hip patois of California. It did not matter that constructivist forms were intended as visual proof of the immutable logic and coherence of universal geometries, while their seeming counterparts in minimalism were demonstrably contingent—denoting a universe held together not by Mind but by guy wires, or glue, or the accidents of gravity. The rage to historicize simply swept these differences aside.

Richard Serra. 5:30. 1969.

Sculpture in the Expanded Field

Toward the center of the field there is a slight mound, a swelling in the earth, which is the only warning given for the presence of the work. Closer to it, the large square face of the pit can be seen, as can the ends of the ladder that is needed to descend into the excavation. The work itself is thus entirely below grade: half atrium, half tunnel, the boundary between outside and in, a delicate structure of wooden posts and beams. The work, *Perimeters/Pavilions/Decoys*, 1978, by Mary Miss, is of course a sculpture or, more precisely, an earthwork.

Over the last ten years rather surprising things have come to be called sculpture: narrow corridors with TV monitors at the ends; large photographs documenting country hikes; mirrors placed at strange angles in ordinary rooms; temporary lines cut into the floor of the desert. Nothing, it would seem, could possibly give to such a motley of effort the right to lay claim to whatever one might mean by the category of sculpture. Unless, that is, the category can be made to become almost infinitely malleable.

The critical operations that have accompanied postwar American art have largely worked in the service of this manipulation. In the hands of this criticism categories like sculpture and painting have been kneaded and stretched and twisted in an extraordinary demonstration of elasticity, a display of the way a cultural term can be extended to include just about anything. And though this pulling and stretching of a term such as sculpture is overtly performed in the name of vanguard aesthetics—the ideology of the new—its covert message is that of historicism. The new is made comfortable by being made familiar, since it is seen as having gradually evolved from the forms of the past. Historicism works on the new and different to diminish newness and mitigate difference. It makes a place for change in our experience by evoking the model of evolution, so that the man who now is can be accepted as being different from the child he once was, by simultaneously being seen—through the unseeable action of the telos—as the same. And we are comforted by this perception of sameness, this strategy for reducing anything foreign in either time or space, to what we already know and are.

Mary Miss. Perimeters/Pavillions/Decoys. *1978.*
(Nassau County, Long Island, New York.)

Of course, with the passing of time these sweeping operations got a little harder to perform. As the 1960s began to lengthen into the 1970s and "sculpture" began to be piles of thread waste on the floor, or sawed redwood timbers rolled into the gallery, or tons of earth excavated from the desert, or stockades of logs surrounded by firepits, the word *sculpture* became harder to pronounce—but not really that much harder. The historian/critic simply performed a more extended sleight-of-hand and began to construct his genealogies out of the data of millenia rather than decades. Stonehenge, the Nazca lines, the Toltec ballcourts, Indian burial mounds—anything at all could be hauled into court to bear witness to this work's connection to history and thereby to legitimize its status as sculpture. Of course Stonehenge and the Toltec ballcourts were just exactly *not* sculpture, and so their role as historicist precedent becomes somewhat suspect in this particular demonstration. But never mind. The trick can still be done by calling upon a variety of primitivizing work from the earlier part of the century—Brancusi's *Endless Column* will do—to mediate between extreme past and present.

But in doing all of this, the very term we had thought we were saving—*sculpture*—has begun to be somewhat obscured. We had thought to use a universal category to authenticate a group of particulars, but the category has now been forced to cover such a heterogeneity that it is, itself, in danger of collapsing. And so we stare at the pit in the earth and think we both do and don't know what sculpture is.

Yet I would submit that we know very well what sculpture is. And one of the things we know is that it is a historically bounded category and not a universal one. As is true of any other convention, sculpture has its own internal logic, its own set of rules, which, though they can be applied to a variety of situations, are not themselves open to very much change. The logic of sculpture, it would seem, is inseparable from the logic of the monument. By virtue of this logic a sculpture is a commemorative representation. It sits in a particular place and speaks in a symbolical tongue about the meaning or use of that place. The equestrian statue of Marcus Aurelius is such a monument, set in the center of the Campidoglio to represent by its symbolical presence the relationship between ancient, Imperial Rome and the seat of government of modern, Renaissance Rome. Bernini's statue of the *Conversion of Constantine,* placed at the foot of the Vatican stairway connecting the Basilica of St. Peter to the heart of the papacy is another such monument, a marker at a particular place for a specific meaning/event. Because they thus function in relation to the logic of representation and marking, sculptures are normally figurative and vertical, their pedestals an important part of the structure since they mediate between actual site and representational sign. There is nothing very mysterious about this logic; understood and inhabited, it was the source of a tremendous production of sculpture during centuries of Western art.

But the convention is not immutable and there came a time when the logic began to fail. Late in the nineteenth century we witnessed the fading of the logic of the monument. It happened rather gradually. But two cases come to mind, both bearing the marks of their own transitional status. Rodin's *Gates of Hell* and his statue of *Balzac* were both conceived as monuments. The first were commissioned in 1880 as the doors to a projected museum of decorative arts; the second was commissioned in 1891 as a memorial to literary genius to be set up at a specific site in Paris. The failure of these two works as monuments is signaled not only by the fact that multiple versions can be found in a variety of museums in various countries, while no version exists on the original sites—both commissions having eventually collapsed. Their failure is also encoded onto the very surfaces of these works: the doors having been gouged away and anti-structurally encrusted to the point where they bear their inoperative condition on their face; the *Balzac* executed with such a degree of subjectivity that not even Rodin believed (as letters by him attest) that the work would ever be accepted.

With these two sculptural projects, I would say, one crosses the threshold of the logic of the monument, entering the space of what could be called its negative condition—a kind of sitelessness, or homelessness, an absolute loss of place. Which is to say one enters modernism, since it is the modernist period of sculptural production that operates in relation to this loss of site, producing the monument as abstraction, the monument as pure marker or base, functionally placeless and largely self-referential.

It is these two characteristics of modernist sculpture that declare its status, and therefore its meaning and function, as essentially nomadic. Through its fetishization of the base, the sculpture reaches downward to absorb the pedestal into itself and away from actual place; and through the representation of its own materials or the process of its construction, the sculpture depicts its own autonomy. Brancusi's art is an extraordinary instance of the way this happens. The base becomes, in a work like the *Cock*, the morphological generator of the figurative part of the object; in the *Caryatids* and *Endless Column*, the sculpture is all base; while in *Adam and Eve*, the sculpture is in a reciprocal relation to its base. The base is thus defined as essentially transportable, the marker of the work's homelessness integrated into the very fiber of the sculpture. And Brancusi's interest in expressing parts of the body as fragments that tend toward radical abstractness also testifies to a loss of site, in this case the site of the rest of the body, the skeletal support that would give to one of the bronze or marble heads a home.

In being the negative condition of the monument, modernist sculpture had a kind of idealist space to explore, a domain cut off from the project of temporal and spatial representation, a vein that was rich and new and could for a while be profitably mined. But it was a limited vein and, having been opened in the early part of the century, it began by about 1950 to be exhausted. It began, that is, to be experienced more and more as pure negativity. At this point modernist sculpture appeared as a kind of black hole in the space of consciousness, something whose positive content was increasingly difficult to define, something that was possible to locate only in terms of what it was not. "Sculpture is what you bump into when

Auguste Rodin. Balzac. *1897.*

Constantin Brancusi. Beginning of the World.
1924.

Robert Morris. Green Gallery Installation. 1964.
Untitled (Mirrored Boxes). 1965.

you back up to see a painting," Barnett Newman said in the fifties. But it would probably be more accurate to say of the work that one found in the early sixties that sculpture had entered a categorical no-man's-land: it was what was on or in front of a building that was not the building, or what was in the landscape that was not the landscape.

The purest examples that come to mind from the early 1960s are both by Robert Morris. One is the work exhibited in 1964 in the Green Gallery—quasi-architectural integers whose status as sculpture reduces almost completely to the simple determination that it is what is in the room that is not really the room; the other is the outdoor exhibition of the mirrored boxes—forms which are distinct from the setting only because, though visually continuous with grass and trees, they are not in fact part of the landscape.

In this sense sculpture had entered the full condition of its inverse logic and had become pure negativity: the combination of exclusions. Sculpture, it could be said, had ceased being a positivity, and was now the category that resulted from the addition of the *not-landscape* to the *not-architecture*. Diagrammatically expressed, the limit of modernist sculpture, the addition of the neither/nor, looks like this:

not-landscape   not-architecture

sculpture

Now, if sculpture itself had become a kind of ontological absence, the combination of exclusions, the sum of the neither/nor, that does not mean that the terms themselves from which it was built—the *not-landscape* and the *not-*

architecture—did not have a certain interest. This is because these terms express a strict opposition between the built and the not-built, the cultural and the natural, between which the production of sculptural art appeared to be suspended. And what began to happen in the career of one sculptor after another, beginning at the end of the 1960s, is that attention began to focus on the outer limits of those terms of exclusion. For, if those terms are the expression of a logical opposition stated as a pair of negatives, they can be transformed by a simple inversion into the same polar opposites but expressed positively. That is, the *not-architecture* is, according to the logic of a certain kind of expansion, just another way of expressing the term *landscape*, and the *not-landscape* is, simply, *architecture*. The expansion to which I am referring is called a Klein group when employed mathematically and has various other designations, among them the Piaget group, when used by structuralists involved in mapping operations within the human sciences.* By means of this logical expansion a set of binaries is transformed into a quaternary field which both mirrors the original opposition and at the same time opens it. It becomes a logically expanded field which looks like this:

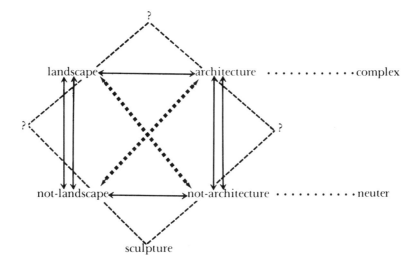

*   The dimensions of this structure may be analyzed as follows: 1) there are two relationships of pure contradiction which are termed *axes* (and further differentiated into the *complex axis* and the *neuter axis*) and are designated by the solid arrows (see diagram); 2) there are two relationships of contradiction, expressed as involution, which are called *schemas* and are designated by the double arrows; and 3) there are two relationships of implication which are called *deixes* and are designated by the broken arrows.
    For a discussion of the Klein group, see Marc Barbut, "On the Meaning of the Word 'Structure' in Mathematics," in Michael Lane, ed., *Introduction to Structuralism*, New York, Basic Books, 1970; for an application of the Piaget group, see A.-J. Greimas and F. Rastier, "The Interaction of Semiotic Constraints," *Yale French Studies*, no. 41 (1968), 86–105.

Another way of saying this is that even though *sculpture* may be reduced to what is in the Klein group the neuter term of the *not-landscape* plus the *not-architecture*, there is no reason not to imagine an opposite term—one that would be both *landscape* and *architecture*—which within this schema is called the *complex*. But to think the complex is to admit into the realm of art two terms that had formerly been prohibited from it: *landscape* and *architecture*—terms that could function to define the sculptural (as they had begun to do in modernism) only in their negative or neuter condition. Because it was ideologically prohibited, the complex had remained excluded from what might be called the closure of post-Renaissance art. Our culture had not before been able to think the complex, although other cultures have thought this term with great ease. Labyrinths and mazes are *both* landscape and architecture; Japanese gardens are *both* land-landscape and architecture; the ritual playing fields and processionals of ancient civilizations were all in this sense the unquestioned occupants of the complex. Which is *not* to say that they were an early, or a degenerate, or a variant form of sculpture. They were part of a universe or cultural space in which sculpture was simply another part—not somehow, as our historicist minds would have it, the same. Their purpose and pleasure is exactly that they are opposite and different.

The expanded field is thus generated by problematizing the set of oppositions between which the modernist category *sculpture* is suspended. And once this has happened, once one is able to think one's way into this expansion, there are—logically—three other categories that one can envision, all of them a condition of the field itself, and none of them assimilable to *sculpture*. Because as we can see, *sculpture* is no longer the privileged middle term between two things that it isn't. *Sculpture* is rather only one term on the periphery of a field in which there are other, differently structured possibilities. And one has thereby gained the "permission" to think these other forms. So our diagram is filled in as follows:

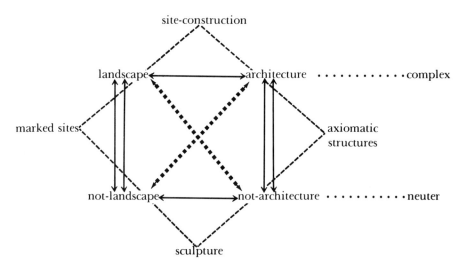

Robert Smithson. Spiral Jetty. *1969–70. (Photo Gianfranco Gorgoni.)*

Robert Morris. Observatory. *1970.*

Alice Aycock. Maze. *1972.*

Carl Andre. Cuts. *1967.*

It seems fairly clear that this permission (or pressure) to think the expanded field was felt by a number of artists at about the same time, roughly between the years 1968 and 1970. For, one after another Robert Morris, Robert Smithson, Michael Heizer, Richard Serra, Walter De Maria, Robert Irwin, Sol LeWitt, Bruce Nauman . . . had entered a situation the logical conditions of which can no longer be described as modernist. In order to name this historical rupture and the structural transformation of the cultural field that characterizes it, one must have recourse to another term. The one already in use in other areas of criticism is postmodernism. There seems no reason not to use it.

But whatever term one uses, the evidence is already in. By 1970, with the *Partially Buried Woodshed* at Kent State University, in Ohio, Robert Smithson had begun to occupy the complex axis, which for ease of reference I am calling *site construction*. In 1971 with the observatory he built in wood and sod in Holland, Robert Morris had joined him. Since that time, many other artists—Robert Irwin, Alice Aycock, John Mason, Michael Heizer, Mary Miss, Charles Simonds—have operated within this new set of possibilities.

Similarly, the possible combination of *landscape* and *not-landscape* began to be explored in the late 1960s. The term *marked sites* is used to identify work like Smithson's *Spiral Jetty* (1970) and Heizer's *Double Negative* (1969), as it also describes some of the work in the seventies by Serra, Morris, Carl Andre, Dennis Oppenheim, Nancy Holt, George Trakis, and many others. But in addition to actual physical manipulations of sites, this term also refers to other forms of marking. These might operate through the application of impermanent marks— Heizer's *Depressions*, Oppenheim's *Time Lines*, or De Maria's *Mile Long Drawing*, for example—or through the use of photography. Smithson's *Mirror Displacements in the Yucatan* were probably the first widely known instances of this, but since then the work of Richard Long and Hamish Fulton has focused on the photographic experience of marking. Christo's *Running Fence* might be said to be an impermanent, photographic, and political instance of marking a site.

The first artists to explore the possibilities of *architecture* plus *not-architecture* were Robert Irwin, Sol LeWitt, Bruce Nauman, Richard Serra, and Christo. In every case of these *axiomatic structures*, there is some kind of intervention into the real space of architecture, sometimes through partial reconstruction, sometimes through drawing, or as in the recent works of Morris, through the use of mirrors. As was true of the category of the *marked site*, photography can be used for this purpose; I am thinking here of the video corridors by Nauman. But whatever the medium employed, the possibility explored in this category is a process of mapping the axiomatic features of the architectural experience—the abstract conditions of openness and closure—onto the reality of a given space.

The expanded field which characterizes this domain of postmodernism possesses two features that are already implicit in the above description. One of these concerns the practice of individual artists; the other has to do with the question of medium. At both these points the bounded conditions of modernism have suffered a logically determined rupture.

With regard to individual practice, it is easy to see that many of the artists in question have found themselves occupying, successively, different places within the expanded field. And though the experience of the field suggests that this continual relocation of one's energies is entirely logical, an art criticism still in the thrall of a modernist ethos has been largely suspicious of such movement, calling it eclectic. This suspicion of a career that moves continually and erratically beyond the domain of sculpture obviously derives from the modernist demand for the purity and separateness of the various mediums (and thus the necessary special-ization of a practitioner within a given medium). But what appears as eclectic from one point of view can be seen as rigorously logical from another. For, within the situation of postmodernism, practice is not defined in relation to a given medium—sculpture—but rather in relation to the logical operations on a set of cultural terms, for which any medium—photography, books, lines on walls, mirrors, or sculpture itself—might be used.

Thus the field provides both for an expanded but finite set of related positions for a given artist to occupy and explore, and for an organization of work that is not

Robert Smithson. First and Seventh Mirror Displacements, Yucatan. *1969.*

dictated by the conditions of a particular medium. From the structure laid out above, it is obvious that the logic of the space of postmodernist practice is no longer organized around the definition of a given medium on the grounds of material, or, for that matter, the perception of material. It is organized instead through the universe of terms that are felt to be in opposition within a cultural situation. (The postmodernist space of painting would obviously involve a similar expansion around a different set of terms from the pair *archi-tecture/ landscape*—a set that would probably turn on the opposition *unique-ness/reproducibility*.) It follows, then, that within any one of the positions generated by the given logical space, many different mediums might be employed. It follows as well that any single artist might occupy, successively, any one of the positions. And it also seems the case that within the limited position of sculpture itself the organization and content of much of the strongest work will reflect the condition of the logical space. I am thinking here of the sculpture of Joel Shapiro, which, though it positions itself in the neuter term, is involved in the setting of images of architecture within relatively vast fields (landscapes) of space. (These considerations apply, obviously, to other work as well—Charles Simonds, for example, or Ann and Patrick Poirier.)

Richard Long. Untitled. 1969. (Krefeld, Germany.)

I have been insisting that the expanded field of postmodernism occurs at a specific moment in the recent history of art. It is a historical event with a determinant structure. It seems to me extremely important to map that structure and that is what I have begun to do here. But clearly, since this is a matter of history, it is also important to explore a deeper set of questions which pertain to something more than mapping and involve instead the problem of explanation. These address the root cause—the conditions of possibility—that brought about the shift into postmodernism, as they also address the cultural determinants of the opposition through which a given field is structured. This is obviously a different approach to thinking about the history of form from that of historicist criticism's constructions of elaborate genealogical trees. It presupposes the acceptance of definitive ruptures and the possibility of looking at historical process from the point of view of logical structure.

New York, 1978

Joel Shapiro. Untitled (Cast Iron and Plaster Houses).
1975.

Poststructuralism and the Paraliterary

Last fall Partisan Review *conducted a two-day symposium under the general title "The State of Criticism." Although various sessions were designed to treat a variety of topics, most presentations were dominated by one continuing theme: structuralist and poststructuralist critical theory and the threat that it somehow poses for literature. My own role in these proceedings was limited to that of discussant; I was to comment on the main paper, written by Morris Dickstein and delivered as the substance of a session dedicated to the influence of recent critical theory on the vehicles of mass culture. As will become obvious, Dickstein's paper was yet another statement of the general sense that literary criticism (understood as an academic discipline) had fallen hostage to an invading force, that this force was undermining critical practice (understood as close reading) and, through that corrosive effect, was eating away at our concept of literature itself.*

My comments had, then, a very particular point of origin. But the views against which those comments were directed are extremely widespread within the literary establishment—both inside and outside the academy—where a sense of the pernicious nature of poststructuralism has led to more recent projects devoted to "How to Rescue Literature."[1] *Thus, despite the specific occasion that gave rise to my discussion of the "paraliterary," I believe this is of much wider conceptual interest. I therefore reproduce in full my remarks.*

The title of this morning's session—"The Effects of Critical Theories on Practical Criticism, Cultural Journalism, and Reviewing"—suggests that what is at issue is the dissemination, or integration, of certain theoretical perspectives into an apparatus of critical practice that reaches well beyond the graduate departments of English or Comp. Lit. at Harvard, Yale, Cornell, and Johns Hopkins. The subject appears to be the effect of theory on what Mr. Dickstein describes as "the mediating force between an increasingly difficult literature and an increas-

---

1.   Two particularly vociferous attacks on poststructuralism have appeared recently in *The New York Review of Books*: Roger Shattuck, "How to Rescue Literature," *NYR*, XXVI, 6 (April 17, 1980), 29-35; and Denis Donoghue "Deconstructing Deconstruction," *NYR*, XXVII, 10 (June 12, 1980), 37-41.

ingly diverse audience," a mediating force represented in this country by a long list of magazines and journals, headed, undoubtedly, by *The New York Review of Books*. Now this is a subject on which Mr. Dickstein's paper—obsessed by what he sees as the deepening technocratization of graduate studies—does not touch. If by this omission he means to imply that he thinks that advanced critical theory has had *no* effect whatsoever on that wider critical apparatus, then he and I are in complete agreement.

But the question would seem to be—Mr. Dickstein's laments aside—*why* has there been no such effect? In order to broach that subject I would like to recall briefly two lectures I attended by two of the technocrats in Mr. Dickstein's account: Jacques Derrida and Roland Barthes. Derrida's lecture was the presentation of part of an essay called "Restitutions," which, in examining the claims Heidegger makes in "The Origin of the Work of Art," focuses on a painting by Van Gogh commonly thought to be the depiction of a pair of shoes. In that lecture, Derrida placed special emphasis on the role of a voice that continually interrupted the flow of his own more formal discourse as it spun out the terms of philosophical debate. Enacted in a slight falsetto, this voice was, Derrida explained, that of a woman who repeatedly breaks into the measured order of the exposition with questions that are slightly hysterical, very exasperated, and above all *short*. "What pair?" she keeps insisting, "Who said they were a *pair* of shoes?" Now this voice, cast as a woman's, is of course Derrida's own, and it functions to telegraph in a charged and somewhat disguised way the central argument which for other reasons must proceed at a more professorial pace. But aside from its rather terroristic reductiveness, this voice functions to open and theatricalize the space of Derrida's writing, alerting us to the dramatic interplay of levels and styles and speakers that had formerly been the prerogative of literature but not of critical or philosophical discourse.

This arrogation of certain terms and ruses of literature leads me to the lecture by Roland Barthes entitled *"Longtemps je me suis couché de bonne heure"* in which, by analogizing his own career to that of Proust, Barthes more explicitly pointed to an intention to blur the distinction between literature and criticism. Indeed, much of Barthes's recent work—I am thinking of *The Pleasure of the Text*, *A Lover's Discourse*, and *Roland Barthes by Roland Barthes*—simply cannot be called criticism, but it cannot, for that matter, be called not-criticism either. Rather, criticism finds itself caught in a dramatic web of many voices, citations, asides, divigations. And what is created, as in the case of much of Derrida, is a kind of paraliterature. Since Barthes's and Derrida's projects are extremely different, it is perhaps only in this matter of inaugurating a paraliterary genre that their work can be juxtaposed.

The paraliterary space is the space of debate, quotation, partisanship, betrayal, reconciliation; but it is not the space of unity, coherence, or resolution that we think of as constituting the work of literature. For both Barthes and Derrida have a deep enmity towards that notion of the literary work. What is left is drama without the Play, voices without the Author, criticism without the Argument. It is no wonder that this country's critical establishment—outside the university, that is—remains unaffected by this work, simply cannot use it. Because the paraliterary cannot be a model for the systematic unpacking of the meanings of a work of art that criticism's task is thought to be.

The creation of the paraliterary in the more recent work of these men is, of course, the result of theory—their own theories in operation, so to speak. These theories run exactly counter to the notion that there is a work, x, behind which there stands a group of meanings, a, b, or c, which the hermeneutic task of the critic unpacks, reveals, by breaking through, peeling back the literal surface of the work. By claiming that there is not, *behind* the literal surface, a set of meanings to which it points or models to which it refers, a set of originary terms onto which it opens and from which it derives its own authenticity, this theory is not prolonging the life of formalism and saying what Mr. Dickstein claims "we all know"—that writing is about writing. For in that formula a different object is substituted for the term "about"; instead of a work's being "about" the July Monarchy or death and money, it is "about" its own strategies of construction, its own linguistic operations, its own revelation of convention, its own surface. In this formulation it is the Author or Literature rather than the World or Truth that is the source of the text's authenticity.

Mr. Dickstein's view of this theory is that it is a jazzed-up, technocratized version of formalism, that its message is that writing is about writing, and that in a work like *S/Z*, "Barthes's purpose is to preserve and extract the multiplicity of the text's meanings." Here we arrive not only at the point where there is no agreement whatsoever between us, but also at the second reason why this theory has left the wider critical establishment of this country in such virginal condition. For where that establishment has not been largely ignorant of the work of Barthes or Derrida or Lacan, it has misconceived or misconstrued it. To use the example that Mr. Dickstein has provided, *S/Z* is precisely not the preservation and extraction of "the multiplicity of the text's meanings." Nor is it what the jacket copywriter for the American edition claims: the semantic dissection of a Balzac novella, "in order to uncover layers of unsuspected meanings and connotations." For both these notions—"extraction" and "dissection"—presuppose an activity that is not Barthes's own, just as they arise from a view of the literary object that Barthes wishes not so much to attack as to dispel. For *extract* and *dissect* assume a certain relation between denotation and connotation as they function within the literary text; they assume, that is, the primacy of the denotative, the literal utterance, beyond which lies the rich vein of connotation or association or meaning. Common sense conspires to tell us that this should be so. But Barthes—for whom common sense is the enemy, due to its unshakable habit of fashioning everything on the model of nature—demonstrates the opposite: that denotation is the effect of connotation, the last block to be put in place. *S/Z* is a demonstration of the way that systems of connotation, stereotype, cliché, gnomic utterance—in short, the always already-known, already-experienced, already-given-within-a-culture—concatenate to produce a text. Further, he claims that it is not only this connotational system that writes the text, but that it is, literally, what we read when we read the literary work. Nothing is buried that must be "extracted"; it is all part of the surface of the text.

Thus, in introducing the three women who surround the narrator of *Sarrasine*, Balzac describes Marianina as "a girl of sixteen whose beauty embodied the fabled imaginings of the Eastern poets! Like the sultan's daughter, in the story of the Magic Lamp, she should have been kept veiled." To this description Barthes responds, "This is a vast commonplace of literature: the Woman copies the Book. In other words, every body is a citation: of the 'already-written.' The origin of desire is the statue, the painting, the book." Then Marianina's mother is introduced with the question, "Have you ever encountered one of those women whose striking beauty defies the inroads of age?" To which Barthes's response is: "Mme de Lanty's body is drawn [with the words *one of those women*] from another Book: the Book of Life." Again, after the opening description of Mme de Rochefide as a woman "delicately formed, with one of those faces as fresh as that of a child," Barthes pounces again on the term "one of those faces": "The body is a duplicate of the Book: the young woman originates in the Book of Life, the plural refers to a total of stored-up and recorded experiences." The text's invocation of those books, those vast storehouses of cliché, creates what Barthes refers to as the "stereographic space of writing," as well as the illusion that there is a denotational object—Marianina, or Mme de Lanty—that precedes the connotational system signaled by "one of those faces." But if writing sets up the pretense that denotation is the first meaning, for Barthes denotation is "no more than the last of the connotations (the one which seems both to establish and to close the reading)." Identifying these connotational systems as codes, Barthes writes, "To depict is to unroll the carpet of the codes, to refer not from a language to a referent, but from one code to another. Thus, realism consists not in copying the real but in copying a (depicted) copy of the real. . . . This is why realism cannot be designated a 'copier' but rather a 'pasticheur' (through secondary mimesis, it copies what is already a copy)."

The painstaking, almost hallucinatory slowness with which Barthes proceeds through the text of *Sarrasine* provides an extraordinary demonstration of this chattering of voices which is that of the codes at work. If Barthes has a purpose, it is to isolate these codes by applying a kind of spotlight to each instance of them, to expose them "as so many fragments of something that has always been already read, seen, done, experienced." It is also to make them heard as voices "whose origin," he says, "is lost in the vast perspective of the already-written" and whose interweaving acts to "de-originate the utterance." It is as impossible to reconcile this project with formalism as it is to revive within it the heartbeat of humanism. To take the demonstration of the de-originated utterance seriously would obviously put a large segment of the critical establishment out of business;

it is thus no wonder that poststructuralist theory should have had so little effect in that quarter.

There is however another place where this work has met with a rather different reception: in graduate schools where students, whatever their other concerns might be, are interested in reading. These students, having experienced the collapse of modernist literature, have turned to the literary products of postmodernism, among the most powerful examples of which are the paraliterary works of Barthes and Derrida. If one of the tenets of modernist literature had been the creation of a work that would force reflection on the conditions of its own construction, that would insist on reading as a much more consciously *critical* act, then it is not surprising that the medium of a *post*modernist literature should be the critical text wrought into a paraliterary form. And what is clear is that Barthes and Derrida are the *writers*, not the critics, that students now read.

New York, 1981

Some of these essays, or versions of these essays, have appeared previously:

Part I

"Grids." *October,* no. 9 (Summer 1979).

"In the Name of Picasso." *October,* no. 16 (Spring 1981).

"No More Play." *Primitivism in 20th Century Art: The Affinity of the Tribal and the Modern,* New York, The Museum of Modern Art, 1984.

"The Photographic Conditions of Surrealism." *October,* no. 19 (Winter 1981).

"This New Art: To Draw in Space." *Julio Gonzalez Sculpture & Drawings,* New York, Pace Gallery, 1981.

"Photography's Discursive Spaces." *Art Journal* XLII (Winter 1982).

"The Originality of the Avant-Garde." *October,* no. 18 (Fall 1981).

"Sincerely Yours." *October,* no. 20 (Spring 1982).

Part II

"Notes on the Index." *October,* nos. 3 and 4 (Spring and Fall, 1977).

"Reading Jackson Pollock, Abstractly." *Art in America* LXX (Summer 1982).

"LeWitt in Progress." *October,* no. 6 (Fall 1978).

"Richard Serra, A Translation." *Richard Serra,* Paris, Musée National d'Art Moderne, Centre Georges Pompidou, 1982.

"Sculpture in the Expanded Field," *October,* no. 8 (Spring 1979).

"Poststructuralism and the Paraliterary." *October,* no. 13 (Summer 1980).

Photography Credits

© by ADGAP, Paris 1984: Alberto Giacometti: *Invisible Object*, p. 41; *The Couple*, p. 46; *Spoon Woman*, p. 50; *Suspended Ball*, p. 57; *Circuit*, p. 59; *Point to the Eye*, p. 60; *Flower in Danger*, p. 66; *Cage*, p. 69; *Project for a Passageway*, p. 71; *Disagreeable Object*, p. 77; *Disagreeable Object to Be Disposed Of*, p. 78; *On ne joue plus*, p. 81. Man Ray: *Minotaur*, p. 80; *Monument to de Sade*, p. 89; *Untitled*, p. 96; *Man*, p. 102; *Lilies*, p. 107; *Rrose Sélavy*, p. 201; *Elevage de poussière*, p. 202.

Collection Eugene Bergman, Chicago: Joseph Cornell, *Nouveaux Contes de Fées*, p. 20.

Collection Madame Henriette Gomès, Paris: Alberto Giacometti, *Circuit*, p. 59.

Collection Robert Lebel, Paris: Marcel Duchamp, *With My Tongue in My Cheek*, p. 207.

Collection Mrs. Julien Levy, Bridgewater, Connecticut: Alberto Giacometti, *On ne joue plus*, p. 81.

Collection Lee Krasner Pollock, New York: Jackson Pollock, *Number 14*, 1951, p. 231; and *Summertime*, p. 239.

Collection Juliet Man Ray, Paris: Man Ray, *Minotaur*, p. 80.

Collection Paul R. Walter, New York: Samuel Bourne, *Road in Kasmir*, p. 136.

Gianfranco Gorgoni; photographer: Robert Smithson, *Spiral Jetty*, p. 285.

Kunsthaus, Zürich (The Alberto Giacometti Foundation): Alberto Giacometti, *The Couple*, p. 46; *Flower in Danger*, p. 66; and *Project for a Passageway*, p. 71.

Kunsthistorisches Museum, Vienna: Caspar David Friedrich, *View from the Painter's Studio*, p. 16.

Kunstmuseum, Basel (The Alberto Giacometti Foundation): Alberto Giacometti, *Suspended Ball*, p. 57.

Kunstmuseum, Bern: Pablo Picasso, *Violin*, p. 35.

James Pipkin; photographer: National Gallery installation of *Rodin Rediscovered*, p. 174; National Gallery installation of *The Search for Alexander*, "The Tombs of Derveni," p. 192.

John Weber Gallery, New York: Alice Aycock, *Maze*, p. 286; Carl Andre, *Cuts*, p. 286; Sol LeWitt, *Floor Piece No. 4*, p. 244; Robert Smithson, *Mirror Displacements*, p. 288.

Leo Castelli Gallery, New York: Richard Serra, *Shift,* pp. 265, 266, and *Railroad Turnbridge,* p. 271; Robert Morris, *Observatory,* p. 285.

Max Protetch Gallery, New York: Mary Miss, *Perimeter/Pavillions/Decoys,* p. 276.

Moderna Museet, Stockholm: Alberto Giacometti, *Cage,* p. 69.

Musée des Arts Africains et Océaniens, Paris: New Ireland Mallanggan, p. 71.

Musée de l'Homme, Paris: New Caledonia, child's coffin, p. 73; New Caledonia, skull-crackers, p. 75; Dan spoon, p. 51; Wobe spoon, p. 51.

Musée National d'Art Moderne, Centre Georges Pompidou, Paris: Constantin Brancusi, *The Beginning of the World,* p. 281; Alberto Giacometti, *Point to the Eye,* p. 60, and *Head,* p. 60; Julio Gonzalez, *Woman Combing Her Hair,* p. 122; Pablo Picasso, *Violin,* p. 35.

Museum of Modern Art, New York: Eugène Atget, *Sceaux,* p. 149, and Verrières, *coin pittoresque,* p. 148; Pablo Picasso, *Seated Bather,* p. 24; Odillon Redon, *The Day,* p. 17; August Salzmann, *Jerusalem, The Temple Wall, West Side,* p. 137.

The Philadelphia Museum of Art, The A. E. Gallatin Collection: Pablo Picasso, *Compote Dish with Fruit, Violin and Glass,* p. 36; Bequest of Katherine S. Drier: Marcel Duchamp, *The Bride Stripped Bare by Her Bachelors, Even,* p. 204.

The Solomon Guggenheim Museum; New York: Alberto Giacometti, *Spoon Woman,* p. 50; Piet Mondrian, *Composition 1A,* p. 18, and *Composition 2,* p. 19.

Yale University Art Gallery, New Haven, Bequest of Katherine S. Drier: Marcel Duchamp, *Tu m',* pp. 198–9.

Index